D0769254

COMPARATIVE LITERATURE

Method & Perspective

REVISED EDITION

Edited by

Newton P. Stallknecht *and* Horst Frenz

Southern Illinois University Press *Carbondale & Edwardsville*

Feffer & Simons, Inc. *London & Amsterdam*

COLLEGE OF THE SEQUOIAS
LIBRARY

COPYRIGHT © 1961, 1971
by Southern Illinois University Press
All rights reserved
"Literature and Psychology" © 1961 by Leon Edel
reprinted with the permission of the author
Printed in the United States of America
Designed by Andor Braun
International Standard Book Number 0-8093-0046-X
Library of Congress Catalog Card Number 71-83780

CONTENTS

Preface vii

Notes on Contributors xiii

1 Comparative Literature 1
Its Definition and Function
HENRY H. H. REMAK

2 On Defining Terms 58
EDWARD D. SEEBER

3 Literary Indebtedness and Comparative Literary Studies 84
J. T. SHAW

4 The Art of Translation 98
HORST FRENZ

5 Literature and Psychology 122
LEON EDEL

6 Ideas and Literature 145
NEWTON P. STALLKNECHT

7 Literature and the Arts 183
MARY GAITHER

8 Literature for the Unlettered 201
STITH THOMPSON

9 Two Types of Classical Tragedy 218
The Senecan Revolution
NORMAN T. PRATT

10 The Study of Literary Genres 248
ULRICH WEISSTEIN

11 West European Romanticism 275
Definition and Scope
HENRY H. H. REMAK

12 Literatures of Asia 312
ARTHUR E. KUNST

Notes 329

Index 356

PREFACE

ALTHOUGH the essays in this volume may be considered independent contributions, it should be noted that they have been motivated by an interest, common to all the contributors, in the problems and methods the student of comparative literature may encounter. In each essay, the author has undertaken to indicate certain objectives and to characterize certain procedures which he considers essential in approaching his particular problem; and in so doing, he has tried to illustrate theoretical statements by including examples drawn from his own reading and research. As a result these essays may be of considerable assistance in helping the student, whatever his special interests, to find his way in this broad area of study.

Comparative literature is, relatively speaking, a young discipline in this country and accordingly its practitioners are still keenly interested in fixing its objectives and defining its scope. Professor Remak turns his attention to these two aspects and gives us a reasoned interpretation of his own, set against other definitions which are included as background. He has appended to his argument an annotated list of historical and critical studies, bibliographies, and similar reference works, which a student of comparative literature will find indispensable.

Professor Seeber supplements the opening essay by considering in detail certain problems of terminology which all students of comparative literature must face if they hope to speak a language intelligible to one another and to the public. He warns the students that many terms employed in the discussion of literature have changed their meaning from period to period and from area to area and must always be weighed against the background of historical interpretation.

The study of the influence of one writer upon another has long occupied a prominent place in literary research. However, it has seemed to many critics in recent years that such studies have been carried to extremes and that there has been too much speculation about the debt which almost every famous author is said to owe to certain of his predecessors, immediate and remote. The problem here has been to develop a technique for the responsible study of literary influence and literary indebtedness. Professor Shaw undertakes briefly to characterize such a technique and to illustrate its operation with reference to his own study of Anglo-Russian literary relations. As a result, it is possible to make a case in defense of this type of research which, when properly executed, contributes significantly to our understanding and appreciation of certain writers.

While the student of comparative literature should be acquainted with a number of foreign languages, he will still be deeply concerned with the problem of translation. He must, in certain cases, himself depend on the use of translations and he will recognize that translations of important literary works from one language to another constitute a major avenue of literary influence. In recent years, increasing attention has been paid to the many problems faced by the translator. Professor Frenz has discussed these problems emphasizing his belief that translating should be considered an art in itself.

Professor Edel argues that "literature and psychology have come to recognize in our century that they stand upon common ground," and explores the various ways in which this generalization may be supported. The interpretation of human consciousness and behavior springing from the works of Freud and Jung is shown to be relevant to the study of contemporary literature—Continental, British, and American. Mr. Edel defends the proposition that "psychoanalysis has contributed important aids to three facets of literary study: (1) to criticism itself, (2) to the study of the creative process in literature, (3) to the writing of biography."

Professor Stallknecht considers the study of literature in its relation to the history of ideas. He is interested in the way in which philosophical ideas are appropriated or absorbed by creative writers and in the manner in which certain ideas undergo transformation as they pass from one period to another. Mr. Stallknecht's orientation is derived from the writings of the English philosopher R. G. Collingwood and the German critic Erich Auerbach rather than from the work of A. O. Lovejoy. The latter's notion of a "unit-idea" is considered critically.

Literature, like any cultural activity, does not and cannot exist in a vacuum, and we must consider, for example, the relationship between literature and the other arts, especially music and painting. This is as rewarding a study as that of the relationship between the literatures of different periods and different countries. Professor Gaither defends this point of view with a number of illustrations which indicate certain significant connections between literature and the fine arts. In the course of her discussion, Miss Gaither comments on a number of critics who, in the tradition of Lessing's Laocoön, consider the several arts in comparison with each other.

What we call "literature" is descended from preliterary forms of expression, when the spoken word constituted virtually the only mode of communication. Professor Thompson considers the persistence of these preliterary forms in modern times and their relation to literature proper. His study ranges from comments on the composition of such epics as the Iliad and Odyssey to the development and wide diffusion of folktales in ancient and modern times. The student of comparative literature cannot ignore the relationship of literature to the vast body of "unlettered" myths, epics, and tales studied by the folklorist.

From the time of Aristotle to the present decade, students of the drama have found the interpretation of tragedy one of the most fascinating problems both in the history and the philosophy of literature. The historian, the critic, the moralist, and the student of religion alike recognize in tragedy an area of discussion where their special interests interpenetrate. In considering the development of European tragedy, an important distinction must be drawn between the classical drama of the Greeks and the Roman or Stoic drama of Seneca. Professor Pratt has turned his attention to this contrast, and his essay illustrates these two treatments of the tragic situation. Such a study is important not only for an understanding of the development of tragedy in antiquity but also for adequate interpretation of English and European drama of the sixteenth and seventeenth centuries.

In recent years there has arisen a new interest in the study of literary genre and in the definition and classification of the special genre concepts. This subject is a central one for the student of literature and offers more than merely a formal exercise. Its indispensability would become at once apparent should one attempt to discuss literature without any reference to such categories as the epic, the novel, tragedy, or lyric poetry. Professor Weisstein presents some of the major problems in the study of genres and points out the way in which certain genre concepts have developed in the course of their history. [This essay is a modified English version of a chapter from the author's Einführung in die Vergleichende Literaturwissenschaft (Stuttgart: Kohlhammer Verlag, 1968). The translation has been prepared by Laurence Kitching.]

In a second contribution to this volume, Professor Remak invites us to consider the problem involved in isolating and defining a broad literary movement such as that of European Romanticism. His résumé makes apparent the great complexity in which such discussions become involved. The resulting difficulties are multiplied by the fact that the term Romanticism, like all similar terms, receives different interpretation in different countries. Mr. Remak summarizes the many connotations that this term has acquired and, by doing so, he helps us avoid much confusion and misunderstanding.

One of the most challenging opportunities for the practice of comparative literature lies in the joint consideration and contrast of the several Oriental and Western traditions. At the present time such study often involves a tentative application of Western concepts of interpretation to the works of Asian authors. Professor Kunst raises a number of questions that face the student who approaches the literature of Asia from this point of view. His essay suggests various possibilities for criticism and research in the field of literary and cultural relations.

In a volume such as this there is almost no limit to the topics that might be selected, and one may hardly hope to offer an exhaustive or strictly systematic consideration of so wide a field. There must therefore be something arbitrary about the selection of the subjects here treated. Nonetheless, these essays may be said to characterize, though not fully to describe, the field of investigation to which they are directed. They are intended to serve primarily as an introduction or invitation to further discussion. As such the authors hope that this volume in its revised form will again prove to be of some interest to all those who are concerned, either in theory or practice, with the problems and methods of comparative literature.

Newton P. Stallknecht

Horst Frenz

January 1971

NOTES ON CONTRIBUTORS

LEON EDEL, biographer of Henry James, is author of *The Modern Psychological Novel* and many studies in literary psychology. He received the Pulitzer Prize and National Book Award in 1963 for his James biography. He is Henry James Professor of English and American Letters at New York University, a member of the National Institute of Arts and Letters, and a fellow of the American Academy of Arts and Sciences.

HORST FRENZ is Distinguished Professor of English and Comparative Literature and Chairman of the Comparative Literature Program at Indiana University, and has been Visiting Professor at Wisconsin, New York University, and several German universities. He has published *Die Entwicklung des Sozialen Dramas in England, Whitman and Rolleston,* and *Eugene O'Neill,* and translated Gerhart Hauptmann's plays into English for the Rinehart Editions. He is editor-in-chief of the *Yearbook of Comparative and General Literature* and has edited *American Playwrights on Drama* and, most recently, *Nobel Lectures: Literature, 1901–1967*.

MARY GAITHER, Professor of English at Indiana University, formerly Associate Editor, *Yearbook of Comparative and General Literature,* and a consultant on foreign literature for the *New Standard Encyclopaedia,* has written on children's literature and American drama. She has just completed a history of the Hogarth Press, founded by Leonard and Virginia Woolf.

ARTHUR E. KUNST, Associate Professor at the University of Wisconsin, has served as Chairman of the Department of Comparative Literature at that institution. He is the author of *Laf-*

cadio Hearn and several studies on problems of translation. He was Visiting Professor of American and Comparative Literature at Kyushu University in Japan during 1967–68.

NORMAN T. PRATT, Chairman of the Department of Classical Studies at Indiana University, is the author of *Dramatic Suspense in Seneca and in His Greek Precursors,* and has studied various aspects of Stoicism in Senecan tragedy and its tradition. He has been visiting professor at Columbia University, the University of Colorado, and the American School of Classical Studies in Athens.

HENRY H. H. REMAK, Professor of German and Comparative Literature at Indiana University, has published extensively on the principles and history of comparative literature as a discipline, European Romanticism and Realism, and Franco-German literary relations. With Professor Seeber he has edited the works of Charles-Michel Campion.

EDWARD D. SEEBER is Professor Emeritus of French at Indiana University and a corresponding member of the Académie des Sciences, Lettres et Beaux-Arts of Marseille. His numerous publications in the area of eighteenth-century French and comparative literature include a study of French antislavery opinion, annotated translations of two early French travelers to the United States, and an edition of rare Huguenot manuscripts.

JOSEPH T. SHAW, Professor of Slavic Languages at the University of Wisconsin and editor of the *Slavic and East European Journal,* has translated and edited a three-volume edition of Pushkin's letters and has written on Byron's relations with Russian literature.

NEWTON P. STALLKNECHT, Director of the School of Letters at Indiana, has studied the relationship of philosophy and literature both from a historical and a critical point of view. He is author of *Strange Seas of Thought: Studies in William Wordsworth's Philosophy of Man and Nature* and has also written on Wallace Stevens, George Eliot, and George Santayana. He is past president and counselor of the Metaphysical Society of America and has contributed frequently to literary and philosophical journals.

STITH THOMPSON, Distinguished Service Professor of English and Folklore, Emeritus, at Indiana University and past president of the American Folklore Society, has edited the *Motif-Index of Folklore* and is the author of *The Folktale.* Professor Thompson has long been recognized in this country and abroad as an outstanding authority in folkloristic studies.

ULRICH WEISSTEIN, Professor of German and Comparative Literature at Indiana University, has published *Einführung in die Vergleichende Literaturwissenschaft* (Stuttgart, 1968) as well as booklength monographs on Heinrich Mann (Tübingen, 1962) and Max Frisch (New York, 1967). He has edited the anthology *The Essence of Opera* (New York, 1964) and translated Wolfgang Kayser's book on the grotesque in art and literature (Bloomington, Ind., 1963).

1

COMPARATIVE LITERATURE

Its Definition and Function

HENRY H. H. REMAK

COMPARATIVE LITERATURE is the study of literature beyond the confines of one particular country, and the study of the relationships between literature on the one hand and other areas of knowledge and belief, such as the arts (e.g., painting, sculpture, architecture, music), philosophy, history, the social sciences (e.g., politics, economics, sociology), the sciences, religion, etc., on the other. In brief, it is the comparison of one literature with another or others, and the comparison of literature with other spheres of human expression.

This definition[1] is probably acceptable to many (certainly not all) students of comparative literature in this country, but would be subject to considerable argument among an important segment of comparatists which we shall, for brevity's sake, call the "French school."[2] For the purpose of clarifying these differences of opinion, some rather basic, others more of emphasis, it may be wise to take up the first part of our definition before dealing with the second.

While the American and the French "schools" will both subscribe to this portion of our definition, viz. comparative literature as the study of literature beyond national boundaries, there are important variations of relative stress in its practical application. The French are inclined to favor questions which can be solved on the basis of factual evidence (often involving personal documents). They tend to exclude literary criticism from the domain of comparative literature. They look askance at studies which "merely" compare, which "merely" point out analogies and contrasts. Carré and Guyard even warn against influence studies as being too hazy, too uncertain, and would have us concentrate on questions of reception, intermediaries, foreign travel, and attitudes toward a given country in the literature of another country during a certain period. Unlike Van Tieghem, these two scholars are also chary of vast syntheses of European literature as courting superficiality, dangerous simplifications, and slippery metaphysics.

The positivistic roots of these reservations are clearly discernible. While understandable, the French desire for "sécurité" is (or was) detrimental to the unfolding of innovative topics and methods. Pichois-Rousseau have recognized this and made appropriate adjustments. To be sure, the problem of influences is a very delicate one and requires of its devotee more encyclopedic knowledge and more finesse than has been exhibited in some past endeavors of this kind. In a good many influence studies, the location of sources has been given too much attention, rather than such questions as: what was *retained* and what was *rejected*, and *why*, and *how* was the material absorbed and integrated, and with *what success?* If conducted in this fashion, influence studies contribute not only to our knowledge of literary history but to our understanding of the creative process and of the literary work of art.

To the extent that the preoccupation with locating and proving an influence may overshadow more crucial questions of artistic interpretation and evaluation, influence studies may contribute less to the elucidation of the essence of a literary work than studies comparing authors, works, styles, tendencies, and literatures in which no influence can or is intended to be shown. Purely comparative subjects constitute an inexhaustible reservoir which is increasingly being tapped by scholars whose predecessors seemed to have forgotten that the name of our discipline is "comparative literature," not "influential literature." Herder and Diderot, Novalis and Chateaubriand, Musset and Heine, Balzac and Dickens, *Moby Dick* and *Faust*, Hawthorne's *Roger Malvin's Burial* and Droste-Hülshoff's *Judenbuche*, Hardy and Hauptmann, Azorín and Anatole France, Baroja and Stendhal, Hamsun and Giono, Thomas Mann and Gide are eminently comparable regardless of whether or how much the one influenced the other.[3]

Carré's and Guyard's disinclination toward large-scale syntheses in comparative literature strikes us likewise as excessively cautious. Here again, Pichois-Rousseau have expanded French vision. We *must* have syntheses unless the study of literature wants to condemn itself to eternal fragmentation and isolation. If we have any ambitions of participating in the intellectual and emotional life of the world, we must, now and then, pull together the insights and results achieved by research in literature and make available meaningful conclusions to other disciplines, to the nation, and to the world at large. The dangers of hurried generalizations, real as they are, are too often advanced as a shield covering up the all too human temptation of playing it safe. "We must wait till all the data are in." But all the data will never be in, and we know it. Even if a single generation succeeded in assembling all the data on a given author or topic, the same "facts" will and should always be subject to different interpretations by different generations. Scholarship must take reasonable precautions, but it should not be paralyzed by illusory perfectionism.[4]

Fortunately, the French have been far less timid and doctrinaire in actual practice than in theory.[5] To French and French-trained scholars, comparative literature owes a large, probably the largest share of important comparative scholarship. Texte's *Rousseau and the Origins of Literary Cosmopolitanism*, Baldensperger's *Goethe in France* and *The Circulation of Ideas in the French Emigration*, Carré's *Goethe in England*, Hazard's admirable panorama of the Enlightenment throughout Europe are only a few among French syntheses distinguished by a dexterous and sensitive handling of comparisons and influences, by a subtle awareness of literary values and of the fine shadings of the uniquely individual as well as an uncanny ability to direct a myriad of observations into lucid patterns of overall developments. The French introductions to comparative literature by Van Tieghem, Guyard, Etiemble, Jeune, and Pichois-Rousseau are themselves syntheses of substantial usefulness. American scholars, in their turn, must guard against dismissing lightly certain topics (studies of reception, attitudes, intermediaries, travelers, *Belesenheit*) merely because the French seem to have favored them to the exclusion or neglect of other comparative subjects.[6]

In examining the second part of our definition, viz. the relationship between literature and other fields, we come up against a difference not of emphasis but of basic distinction between the "American" and "French" schools. Van Tieghem, Guyard, Etiemble and Jeune do not discuss or even list the relationship between literature and other areas (art, music, philosophy, politics, etc.). Pichois-Rousseau give it little more than two pages. During the many years that the *Revue de littérature comparée* was directed by Baldensperger and Hazard, its quarterly bibliographies did not recognize this category of topics at all. This policy has remained unchanged under succeeding editors. In contrast, American curricula and publications in comparative literature (including bibliographies) generally take in this realm, though they sometimes insist that the artists included belong to different nationalities.

The French are certainly interested in such topics as the comparative arts, but they do not think of them as being within the jurisdiction of comparative literature.[7] There are historical reasons for this attitude. Despite the rigidities of academic compartmentalization, comparative literature has been able, for more than half a century, to occupy a distinct and distinguished niche in French universities precisely because it combined a wider coverage *of* literature with a prudent restriction *to* literature. The student and teacher of literature who venture beyond national frontiers already assume an extra burden. The French seem to fear that taking on, in addition, the systematic study of the relationship between literature and any other area of human endeavor invites the accusation of charlatanism and would, at any rate, be detrimental to the acceptance of comparative literature as a respectable and respected academic domain.[8]

A related, more fundamental objection should also be taken into consideration: the lack of logical coherence between comparative literature as the study of literature beyond national boundaries and comparative literature as the study of the ramifications of literature beyond its own boundaries.[9] Furthermore, while the geographical connotations of the term comparative literature are fairly concrete, the generic ramifications implied in the American concept raise serious problems of demarcation which American scholars have not been willing to face squarely.

It is difficult to find firm criteria for selection when one scans the mass of titles in Baldensperger-Friederich's *Bibliography of Comparative Literature*, especially in those portions of book 1 covering "Generalities," "Thematology" and "Literary Genres," and in the chapter on "Literary Currents" in book 3. We are speaking here only of entries which are, neither by title nor (upon examination) by contents comparative in the geographical sense (except incidentally), whose inclusion in the *Bibliography* must therefore have been determined by reasons of subject matter extension, or by a hazy notion of "general literature." Under the headings of "Individual Motifs" and "Collective Motifs," for example, we find a large number of investigations of love, marriage, women, fathers-and-sons, children, war, professions, etc. *within* a national literature. Can the incorporation of these items in a bibliography of *comparative* literature be justified on the premise that we are dealing here with two realms—literature and "motifs"? But motifs are part and parcel *of* literature; they are intrinsic, not extraneous. Under the headings of "Literary Genres" and "Literary Currents," we find studies on the American novel, the German *Bildungsroman*, the Spanish Generation of '98, etc., etc. But accounts of literary genres, movements, and generations in a certain country, even if they are of a general nature, are not comparative per se. The notions of genres, movements, "schools," generations, etc., are implicit in our idea of literature and literary history; they are inside, not outside of literature. We submit that, with a modicum of rationalizing, almost anything and everything in literary scholarship and criticism could lay claim to being "comparative literature" if the ultra-elastic criteria of the *Bibliography* are accepted. Comparative literature as a quasi all-inclusive term would be close to meaningless.[10]

Granting that there is a twilight zone where a case can be made pro and con the "comparativeness" of a given topic, we shall have to be more discriminating in the future about admitting a topic in this category to comparative literature. We must make sure that comparisons between literature and a field other than literature be accepted as "comparative literature" only if they are *systematic* and if a definitely *separable, coherent discipline* outside of literature is studied as such. We cannot classify scholarly endeavors as "comparative literature" merely because they discuss inherent aspects of life and art that must inevitably be reflected in all literature, for what else can literature be about? A paper on the historical sources of a Shakespearean drama would (unless it concentrates on another country) be "comparative literature" only if historiography and literature were the main poles of the investigation, if historical facts or accounts and their literary adaptations were systematically compared and evaluated, and conclusions arrived at which would bear on the two domains as such. A treatment of the role of money in Balzac's *Père Goriot* would be comparative only if it were principally (not just incidentally) concerned with the literary osmosis of a coherent financial system or set of ideas. An inquiry into the ethical or religious ideas of Hawthorne or Melville could be considered comparative only if it dealt with an organized religious movement (e.g., Calvinism) or set of beliefs. The tracing of a character in a novel by Henry James would be within the scope of comparative literature only if it developed a methodical view of this character in the light of the psychological theories of Freud (or Adler, Jung, etc.).

With this caveat in mind, our preference goes nevertheless to the more inclusive "American" concept of comparative literature. We must, to be sure, strive to achieve and maintain a minimum set of criteria marking off our chosen field; but we must not be so concerned with its theoretical unity as to forget the perhaps more important *functional* aspect of comparative literature. We conceive of comparative literature less as an independent subject which must at all costs set up its own inflexible laws, than as a badly needed auxiliary discipline, a link between smaller segments of parochial literature, a bridge between organically related but physically separated areas of human creativeness. Whatever the disagreements on the theoretical aspects of comparative literature be, there is agreement on its task: to give scholars, teachers, students, and last but not least readers a better, more comprehensive understanding of literature as a whole rather than of a departmental fragment or several isolated departmental fragments of literature. It can do so best by not only relating several literatures to each other but by relating literature to other fields of human knowledge and activity, especially artistic and ideological fields; that is, by extending the investigation of literature both geographically and generically.

Several areas and terms are contiguous to or seem to overlap with comparative literature: national literature, world literature, and general literature. A clarification of their meanings is indispensable for the delimitation of comparative-literature terms.

There is no fundamental difference between methods of research in national literature and comparative literature, between, for example, a comparison of Racine with Corneille and of Racine with Goethe. There are, however, subjects encountered in comparative-literature research which go beyond national-literature scholarship: the contact or collision between different cultures, in general, and the problems connected with translation, in particular. Other topics inherent in the study of national literature occur in somewhat different patterns and tend to occupy a place of greater importance in comparative-literature research: vogue, success, reception, and influence of literature; travel and intermediaries.

Even geographically speaking, an air-tight distinction between national literature and comparative literature is sometimes difficult. What are we to do with authors writing in the same language but belonging to different nations? We should probably not hesitate at all to assign a comparison between George Bernard Shaw and H. L. Mencken, or between Sean O'Casey and Tennessee Williams, to comparative literature, but when we go back to English and American literature of the colonial period, the case, as Wellek has suggested, becomes much less clear-cut. Maeterlinck and Verhaeren were Belgians writing in French; would a study of their intimate connections with French Symbolism be classed as comparative literature? What about Irish authors writing in English or Finnish nationals composing in Swedish? Similar difficulties arise in investigations of the Nicaraguan Rubén Darío's place in Spanish literature, or of the eminent positions of the Swiss Gottfried Keller and Conrad Ferdinand Meyer, the Austrians Adalbert Stifter and Hugo von Hofmannsthal in German literature (not to speak of the still more complicated cases of Rilke and Kafka). To what extent should legal naturalization be taken into account? There is surely a difference, in the consequences for their literary work, between the British citizenship of T. S. Eliot and the American citizenship of Thomas Mann.

Inversely, there are authors belonging to the same nation but writing in different languages or dialects. Welsh literature in relation to English, Low German literature in relation to German, Flemish literature in relation to French (in Belgium), Sicilian literature in relation to Italian, Ukrainian literature in relation to

Great Russian, Basque and Catalan literature in relation to Spanish or French, raise questions that must be answered from case to case. In general, we may state the rule that a scholar asserting that a transitional topic of this nature is comparative must assume the burden of poitive proof that he is dealing with significant differences in language, nationality, or tradition.

Most comparatists, while admitting complications and overlapping, will agree that these difficulties are neither frequent nor serious enough to invalidate the distinction between literature studied within and across national boundaries.

Between comparative literature and world literature,[11] there exist differences of degree as well as more fundamental differences. The former comprise elements of space, time, quality, and intensity. Comparative literature (geographically speaking) involves, like world literature, an element of space, but frequently, though not necessarily, a more restricted one. Comparative literature often deals with the relationship of only two countries, or two authors of different nationality, or one author and another country (e.g., Franco-German literary relations, Poe-Baudelaire, Italy in the works of Goethe). The more pretentious term "world literature" implies recognition throughout the world, ordinarily the Western world, an identification which Etiemble has attacked with gusto.

"World literature" also suggests an element of time. As a rule, the acquisition of world renown takes time, and "world literature" usually deals with literature consecrated as great by the test of time. Contemporary literature is, therefore, somewhat less frequently covered by the term "world literature," whereas comparative literature, at least in theory, may compare anything that is comparable no matter how old or how recent the work(s) may be. It must be readily admitted, however, that in practice many, perhaps most, comparative literature studies do deal with literary figures of the past who have achieved worldwide fame. Much of what we have been and shall be doing is, in effect, comparative world-literature.

World literature deals therefore predominantly with time- and world-honored literary productions of enduring quality (e.g., the *Divine Comedy; Don Quijote; Paradise Lost; Candide; Werther*), or, less markedly, with authors of our own day who have enjoyed very intense applause abroad (e.g., Faulkner, Camus, Thomas Mann), which, in many cases, may prove transitory (Galsworthy, Margaret Mitchell, Moravia, Remarque). Comparative literature is not bound to the same extent by criteria of quality and/or intensity. Illuminating comparative studies have been, and many more could be done on second-rate authors, often more representative of the time-bound features of their age than the great writers. Such investigations would include authors once thought great or known to have been very successful (e.g., Lillo, Gessner, Kotzebue, Dumas father and son, Scribe, Sudermann, Pinero), or even minor authors who never made headway abroad, but whose production might illustrate pan-European trends of literary taste (in Germany alone, such writers as Friedrich de la Motte-Fouqué, Zacharias Werner, Friedrich Spielhagen, Max Kretzer).

In addition, certain first-rate writers not yet acclaimed by world literature are eminently fitted for comparative-literature studies. The latter may actually contribute to their acceptance as figures of world literature. Among the men of letters and of related thought of the past, recently "discovered," resurrected, or fundamentally reappraised by the Western world are Donne, Diderot, Blake, Hölderlin, Büchner, Gérard de Nerval, Melville, Kierkegaard, and Hesse. Others, equally worthy of international attention, are still waiting for commensurate recognition outside their own countries: Espronceda, Larra, Galdós, Azorín, Baroja (Spain); Herder, Hebbel, Keller, Fontane, Trakl, Hofmannsthal (Germany, Austria, and Switzerland); Petöfi (Hungary); Creanga, Eminescu, Sadoveanu (Rumania); Jens Peter Jacobsen, Johannes V. Jensen, and Isak Dinesen (Denmark); Fröding (Sweden), Obstfelder (Norway); Willa Cather, F. Scott Fitzgerald—the list is endless. Baltic, Slavic (except Russian) and literatures outside the occidental tradition have hardly been touched; they are bound to contain many surprising literary nuggets.

Elements of space, time, quality, and intensity provide differences of degree between world literature and comparative literature. But there are more fundamental distinctions. In the first place, the "American" concept of comparative literature embraces inquiries into the relationship between literature and other orbits; world literature does not. In the second place, even the more restricted, "French" definition of comparative literature (where the material to be studied is entirely literary, as it is in world literature) specifies a method; world literature does not. Comparative literature requires that a work, author, trend, or theme be actually compared with a work, author, trend, or theme of another country or sphere; but a collection of essays on, let us say, Turgenev, Hawthorne, Thackeray, and Maupassant, under one cover, might very well be called *Figures of World Literature* without containing any or perhaps only incidental comparisons. Webster defines "comparative" as "studied systematically by comparison of phenomena . . . as, *comparative* literature."

Many courses devoted to the analysis of literary masterpieces from various countries, mostly read in translation, are now being offered in American colleges, and many anthologies designed for such courses have been published. These courses and textbooks should be, and usually are designated by the term "world literature" rather than "comparative literature," since the works read are by and large studied as individual masterpieces, not (at least fairly) systematically compared. It would be up to the instructor or editor to make such a course or book truly comparative, provided the choice of texts lends itself to comparative treatment.

A comparative literature study does not have to be comparative on every page nor even in every chapter, but the overall intent, emphasis, and execution must be comparative.[12] The assaying of intent, emphasis, and execution requires both objective and subjective judgment. No rigid rules can and should, therefore, be set down beyond these criteria.[13]

The term "general literature" has been used for courses and publications concerned with foreign literature in English translation, or, more loosely yet, for offerings that do not fit into departmental pigeonholes and appear to be of interest to students outside one national literature. Sometimes it refers to literary trends, problems, and theories of "general" interest, or to aesthetics. Collections of texts and of critical studies or comments dealing with several literatures have been assigned to this category (e.g., many anthologies and such historical and critical works as Laird[ed.], *The World through Literature,* Shipley[ed.], *Dictionary of World Literature* and *Encyclopedia of Literature.* See Bibliography). It must be remembered that, like the term "world literature," general literature fails to prescribe a comparative method of approach. While "general literature" courses and publications may afford an excellent basis for comparative studies, they are not necessarily comparative in themselves.

The very haziness of the term "general literature"

seems to have worked to its advantage in this country. A much more precise definition of "general literature" by the French scholar Paul Van Tieghem (Sorbonne), though not widely accepted beyond France, deserves nevertheless our attention.[14] To him, national literature, comparative literature, and general literature represent three consecutive levels. National literature treats questions confined to one national literature; comparative literature normally deals with problems involving two different literatures; general literature is devoted to developments in a larger number of countries making up organic units, such as Western Europe, Eastern Europe, Europe, North America, Europe and North America, Spain and South America, the Orient, etc. Expressed visually, national literature would be the study of literature within walls, comparative literature across walls, and general literature above walls.[15] In a comparative-literature study, national literatures would remain primary factors, serving as anchors of investigation; in a general-literature study, national literatures would simply provide examples for international trends. According to Van Tieghem, a study of the place of Rousseau's *Nouvelle Héloïse* in literature would be part of national literature; a paper on the influence of Richardson on Rousseau's *Nouvelle Héloïse* would belong to comparative literature; a survey of the European sentimental novel would be general literature. Van Tieghem himself has written a number of works illustrating his ideas of general literature: *Latin Literature of the Renaissance, Literary History of Europe and America since the Renaissance, Pre-Romanticism, European Romanticism,* and the *Discovery of Shakespeare on the Continent.* Other syntheses of this kind include Curtius' *European Literature and the Latin Middle Ages,* Farinelli's *Romanticism in the Latin World,* Friederich and Malone's *Outline of Comparative*

Literature, and Hazard's masterful twin works, *The European Mind, 1680–1715* and *European Thought in the XVIIIth Century.*

Van Tieghem's definitions raise at least one question. Is it not arbitrary and mechanical to relegate the term comparative literature, as he has done, to comparative investigations limited to two countries, while studies involving more than two countries are reserved for general literature? Why should a comparison between Richardson and Rousseau be classified as comparative literature, whereas a comparison between Richardson, Rousseau, and Goethe (as undertaken years ago by Erich Schmidt) would be assigned to general literature? Is not the term "comparative literature" sufficient to cover syntheses encompassing any number of countries (as it does in Friederich and Malone's *Outline of Comparative Literature*)?

In setting up his distinctive categories, Van Tieghem was probably thinking less of logically coherent units than of a necessary division of labor. The number of creative, historical, and critical works to be absorbed by a scholar before he can hope to portray adequately even a limited period or aspect of *one* literature has become so enormous that we cannot expect the same scholar to take on one or more additional literatures. In turn, for reasons of inclination, aptitude, and longevity, scholars specializing in comparative literature will, Van Tieghem fears, probably be unable to assemble and integrate the researches of more than two national literatures. A third group of scholars is therefore needed to pull together the findings of national literature and comparative literature and merge them into general literature.

The dangers of such an arrangement, aside from its very hypothetical workability, given the cherished individualism of the scholarly profession, are readily apparent. Comparative-literature and general-literature scholars would have to be content with organizing the findings of others (in itself a Herculean task), an assignment bound to expose them to loss of contact with the literary text, and carrying the seeds of mechanization, superficialization, and dehumanization of literature. Van Tieghem's own books certainly have not escaped this peril altogether. On the other hand, Hazard, in his two syntheses, has magnificently succeeded in presenting the spirit of an age (pre-enlightenment and rationalism) without depriving the bones of the flesh.

We are inclined to think that a rigid division of labors between national-literature, comparative-literature, and general-literature scholars is neither feasible nor desirable.[16] National-literature scholars should realize and act on their obligation to widen their perspectives, and should be encouraged to undertake, now and then, excursions into other literatures or spheres related to literature. Comparative-literature scholars should return, from time to time, to the more circumscribed areas of a national literature to make sure that at least one foot is firmly planted on the ground. This is precisely what the best scholars in the comparative field, both here and abroad, have consistently done.

None of the terms discussed are completely clear-cut. Overlapping exists among all. The definitions of and distinctions between national literature and comparative literature are, however, sufficiently clear to be useful. While we subscribe to the more inclusive "American" concept of comparative literature, we urge that topics claimed to belong to this field be subjected to closer scrutiny, on the basis of stricter criteria, than heretofore. World literature, in the sense of literature of such outstanding merit or success as to have gained international attention, is a serviceable term, but must not be laxly used as a sort of alternative for comparative literature or general literature. It is to be hoped that the term general literature will be avoided, whenever possible. It means, at least at present, too many different things to too many people. In its place, we should use synonyms for the intended connotation: comparative literature, or world literature, or literature in translation, or Western literature, or literary theory, or the structure of literature, or just literature, whichever the case may be.

It seems smug to suggest in January 1971 that ten years of aggressive worldwide discussion of the methods applicable to comparative literature do not call for modification of the attitudes indicated in the foregoing essay. I have profited much from the continuing debate which I have tried to record, describe, and evaluate in the substantially enlarged *bibliographie raisonnée* which follows. Had I worked all these data into the fabric of the preceding considerations, there might well have been defense, attack, or concessions in the light or heat of polemics and findings of the last years, there might well have occurred a shifting of accents. It seemed cleaner to me and likely to lead to fewer misunderstandings if I left the old Adam in his imperfect state of 1961 (except for minor updating and corrections) and added my views of today rather than attempt an unhappy marriage of yesterday and today. And yet I would have undertaken a thorough rejuvenation of the preceding essay if I believed that I was wrong in my essential appraisal of the fabric and the situation of comparative literature then, or if I thought the situation itself had changed drastically. I do not so believe or think.

Without engaging in needlessly long polemics, let me as concisely as I can put down my rational credo on the definition and function of comparative literature as it stands today.

Theory and Practice. There have been repeated complaints that we talk too much about how to or how not to compare the literature but do not compare it enough. Less theory, more practice. These grievances have been matched by others possibly as numerous to the effect that a field with an assignment, a methodology so confused and controversial as ours is in trouble. The richness of the definition and methodology debate in comparative literature of late shows no sign of abatement; it betrays a genuine and lasting concern.

The trite truth is that we need theory and practice simultaneously. As long as we lay claim to professionalism we must worry about theory, definition, structure, and function. But theory must constantly be monitored and modified by practice, and vice versa.

Criticism and History. There seems to be a good deal more agreement than there was ten years ago—in the West and in the East—that history and criticism can and should be combined to fulfill the promise of comparative literature. The East still is more historically and ideologically oriented than the West, and European continental (including French) usage in comparative literature still leans more toward history than American practice. European comparative literature still adheres more closely to the respective national literature than its American counterpart. But the gap has narrowed perceptibly. It might be expected to narrow even more, for better or worse, as the ideological crisis engulfing Western universities shows up in comparative-literature teaching and research. As a matter of fact, the adjustment of scientific research, whether in comparative literature or in other areas, to the social goals of humanity, without impairing the fundamental integrity of scholarship, may well be one of the burning issues of the 1970's.

French and American "Schools." I consider these present and potential developments more interesting than the much-discussed differences between French and American theory and practice in comparative literature. Nevertheless, I do not know whether to be grieved or amused by intimations that my 1961 essay has helped to consolidate a (so it is held) fictitious and regrettable national dichotomy between France and America in our common endeavor. It is curious that such criticism has, with one mild exception, come only from the United States, not from Europe, least of all from our French colleagues who, after all, should be the best informed on their part of this score. To record a fact does not mean that the recorder is responsible for or happy about it. As stated in my 1961 essay (including its footnotes) and my *Yearbook* 1960 article, "Comparative Literature at the Crossroads," which complement each other (and, I hope, will be read together), there has most certainly been a very influential French tradition in comparative-literature studies, and also a marked departure from this tradition in the United States. To maintain that this is an illusion because not *all* Frenchmen or Americans are in agreement with these tendencies (a fact to which I called attention in both essays) or because scholars of other nations also do the one or the other is to ignore reality. This reality includes the indubitable leadership of France and the United States in comparative-literature teaching and research. It includes the centralized character of French university education, especially the dominant role of the Sorbonne. It includes the emergence and stability of what most European and some American scholars have not hesitated to call the French school of comparative literature, though I chose, whenever possible, to place "school" in quotation marks. It includes the more heterogeneous character of American higher education which makes the term "school" less appropriate, albeit it is surely justified to speak of prevailing though far from exclusive American trends different from those current in France. Neither of these arose in France or America, of all places, by sheer accident.

In both essays, I endeavored to do justice to these differences and pointed out that practice was more adventurous and differentiated than theory. I suggested avenues of scholarly reconciliation and combination. I am pleased to record that the subsequent evolution has indeed gone in the hoped-for direction, although it has not erased fairly substantial differences.

Pluralism of Methods. Comparative literature, as does the study of all literature, must in principle admit of all methods of approach. It is up to the individual scholar to show that the approach chosen for a particular literary object or subject is appropriate. If it yields results persuasive to scholars of intelligence and integrity other than its author it may be held to have been relevant. The temptation is great to lay down approximate guidelines, such as recommending the sociological vantage point for fiction but not for lyrics, or the phonological vantage point for lyrics but not for fiction. It may be possible to make some roughly accurate predictions along these lines, but literary scholarship is full of surprises and a sociological interpretation of a Rilke poem or a phonological analysis of *Tonio Kröger* are not necessarily absurd undertakings. Certain approaches are more plausible given the object than others. One cannot go much farther.

Methodology and the Integrity of Comparative Literature. Comparative literature does not have, or need to have, a methodology exclusive to itself. The basic laws of gathering, sifting, and interpreting evidence governing literary research apply here as elsewhere. But this does not mean that comparative literature has to submerge in the forbiddingly extensive sea of "literature" *tout court,* as Wellek has demanded insistently. His position is unrealistic. Any demarcation has an element of artificiality about it, but this makes demarcations and divisions of labor no less inevitable nor necessarily arbitrary. Furthermore, comparative literature does have special problems which require special competences and special combinations of methods. As I have stated previously, the study of translations *is* exclusive to comparative literature and demands a sophisticated methodology. The collision between or interpenetration of different cultures and traditions demands a linguistic and cultural preparation and diversification not required of "ordinary" literary scholars and normally not possessed by them. Horizontal competences may replace, in part, vertical competences. The perspective, the flair, the temptations of the comparatist are not identical with those of the non-comparatist, though there is, of course, much overlapping. Should the investigation of the comparative arts and other interdisciplinary proclivities continue to gain favor among our aficionados, further refinement of methodology will be even more imperative.

The "comparative" in Comparative Literature. There is general agreement that the term "comparative literature," while not really accurate for what we are doing, has nevertheless acquired squatter's rights. There is much less consensus—though more than in 1961—that the "comparative" in comparative literature should be viewed as more than an historical accident, that, in fact, a systematic revitalizing of the "comparative" might be the most natural and effective way of bringing literary criticism and evaluation into comparative literature through the comparison, by analogy or contrast, of (not necessarily causally) related works, works *comparable* because of elective affinities in theme, problem, genre, style, simultaneousness, *Zeitgeist*, stage of cultural evolution, etc.

Comparative Arts and Interdisciplinary Studies. The strengthening of the concept and the increased use of comparison in comparative literature remains also one of the strongest arguments in favor of including the comparative arts and the comparison of literature (by analogy or contrast) with other areas of human cognition in the field we call "comparative literature." It is this extension of the concept "comparative literature" into "nonliterature" which has elicited some of the most stringent criticism my 1961 essay has encountered, despite my own caveat in formulating it. At the same time, the evidence since 1961 demonstrates that more and more theoreticians and practitioners of comparative literature are moving in that direction. This trend is likely to accelerate because of the expansionist, adventurous, antiorthodox intellectual trend of our times which chafes at restrictions. In particular, the current preoccupation with social, political, economic, religious, theatrical, etc., questions may well intensify the American trend toward an interdisciplinary concept of comparative literature and arouse a European movement in that direction. I find in this interdisciplinary current, however, plenty of intrinsic, structural, artistic justification to hope for a wider testing of interdisciplinary comparisons with literature in theory and in practice.

Universality and Individuality. Stress on the "comparative" while practicing comparative literature is apt to bring out the uniqueness of the works of literary art involved; as applied to the comparison of trends in two or more national literatures, differences and nuances rather than parallelisms. For the cognition of artistic or national uniqueness which we all cherish, this is fine, but for the ordering of literary history on supranational terms it sometimes proves perilous, encouraging an easy nominalism. The farther the approach veers in the direction of "general literature" or just "literature," the less the danger of becoming inhibited by personal or national individuality, but the greater the danger of getting away from individual and national reality. René Wellek, who has perhaps worked more consistently and more effectively than anyone else to break down the barriers blocking the consideration of literature as a universal totality, has shown in his practice that both points of view are necessary to make a complete picture: his arguments for Romanticism seen as a European movement are as convincing as his differentiation between "German and English Romanticism: A Confrontation" (1964).

Collaborative Projects. For the last two decades and more, comparative-literature scholars have weighed the pro's and con's of collaborative writing of supranational literary history. Fears have been expressed that the individuality of humanistic scholarship might be endangered in such undertakings and that consistency of treatment of a given topic would not be possible. In addition, there are practical difficulties in any attempt to organize scholars. Nevertheless, it is amply clear that we shall have, with the rarest of exceptions (such as Wellek), supranational histories and surveys only by resorting to teamwork. The quantity of primary and secondary sources is so overwhelming that no individual can manage this kind of subject any longer. Hence we must welcome and support such projects as "A Comparative History of European Literature" sponsored by the International Comparative Literature Association. The joint participation in this enterprise by scholars from East and West, North and South is bound to carry additional benefits of productive exchanges of view and rapprochements among scholars dedicated to the same tasks but separated for a variety of reasons.

SELECTIVE BIBLIOGRAPHY

Every effort has been made to compile the most useful, selective yet representative, annotated bibliography on the fundamentals of comparative literature so far available in English. Each item listed has been read and carefully analyzed for its contribution to the central questions discussed in the essay.

It is clear that the subjective factor in a selective bibliography cannot be gainsaid; it is hereby cheerfully acknowledged. To be persuasive a selective bibliography should also include a list of rejected items and a statement of the reasons for their exclusion. If, e.g., Fernand Baldensperger's "Litérature comparée: le mot et la chose" (*Revue de littérature comparée,* [1921],5–29) is not listed, it is partly because of its remote date, partly because it is primarily historical, partly because it does not come sufficiently to grips with the essentials of definition and function of our discipline. For all too obvious reasons, it is not practicable to explain every rejection, but we can be expected to state our general criteria.

We have aimed at providing a *working* bibliography—that is to say, a manageable list of relevant items that would be within relatively comfortable reach of American teachers and scholars. Publications in English,

French, and German have therefore been given preference, a procedure all the more justified since most (though certainly not all) important contributions to comparative literature have been in these languages. Further preference has been given to *recent* publications, since neither the essay nor the bibliography are historically oriented. Hence the vast majority of items dates from the 1950's and 1960's, a much smaller number from the late 1940's, and only a handful from an earlier period. Particular care has been taken to have various viewpoints represented.

Surveys of comparative-literature studies and facilities here and abroad were included only if the contribution in question is particularly and intentionally illuminating with regard to definition and method. Section 2 (Studies on Basic Aspects of Comparative Literature) is clearly the most complete within the limits set above, for it was felt that a maximum of guidance was needed in this highly disconcerting yet fundamental area. In the other sections, we list only an indispensable minimum of works. Scholarship dealing exclusively with the vast fields of literature and the arts, literature and science, literature and politics, etc., could, for reasons of space, not be included except for a few samples; we refer the reader to the appropriate sections of Baldensperger-Friederich's *Bibliography* and its supplements in the Yearbooks. Anthologies of World Literature have also been excluded, and the few entries on "world literature" have been admitted only because they happen to bear directly on the essence of comparative literature. In general, the items listed under the various categories must be viewed as representative samples that will easily lead to additional sources for those desiring a more complete documentation.

Within the individual sections or subsections, items have been listed in chronological order of appearance except for related works by the same author. This separates, to be sure, certain entries that seem closely related, but a grouping by "subproblems" or schools of thought would have raised difficult questions of classification and carried the subjective character of the bibliography too far. The chronological arrangement within sections, besides being clear and unequivocal, has the further advantage of reflecting the genetic and simultaneous aspects of the "great debate" and the shifts in the general evolution of opinion.

1 *Surveys of Comparative Literature as a Discipline*

PETERSEN, JULIUS. "Nationale oder vergleichende Literaturgeschichte?" *Deutsche Vierteljahresschrift für Literaturwissenschaft und Geistesgeschichte*, 6 (1928), 36–61. Still a basic, well-annotated investigation into the meaning, limitations, and potentialities of comparative literature in its relationship to national, general, world, and universal literature. Conclusions: 1] Since the characteristics of a national literature can be brought out only in comparison with other literatures, every history of national literature must be comparative. A discipline that does nothing but compare has, however, no *raison d'être*. 2] Comparative-literature studies on themes, motives, and problems belong to morphology, criticism, and aesthetics, hence to general literature, but may indirectly be of use to national literature. 3] An international literary history of certain periods must limit itself to culturally related nations (*Kulturgemeinschaften*). A history of the universal development of world literature is not feasible. 4] Analogies in the evolution of certain national literatures—outside causal connections of cultural community—represent a worthwhile field of study, as yet largely uncultivated. It requires the cooperation of several disciplines.

STRICH, FRITZ. "Weltliteratur und vergleichende Literaturgeschichte," in Emil Ermatinger, ed., *Philosophie der Literaturwissenschaft*. Berlin, 1930, pp. 422–41. Fundamental, still valid considerations on the meaning of world and comparative literature, to which several paragraphs of our preceding essay owe much. Short bibliography.

Guérard, Albert. "What Is World Literature?" in his *Preface to World Literature.* New York, 1940, pp. 3–16. A clear, (too?) simple and interestingly written introduction to the field which distinguishes between world literature ("works enjoyed in common, ideally by all mankind, practically by our own Western group of civilizations"), comparative literature ("the study of relations, in the literary field, between different national or linguistic groups") and general literature ("the study of problems common to all literatures").

Poggioli, Renato. "Comparative Literature," in Joseph Shipley, ed., *Dictionary of World Literature.* New York, 1943, pp. 114–17. Concise but pithy semihistorical, semidescriptive survey of the field.

Warren, Austin, and Wellek, René. *Theory of Literature.* New York, 1948. 3rd ed., 1963. Forceful chapter on "General, Comparative and National Literature" raises crucial questions of definition without necessarily attempting to resolve them. Valuable notes and bibliography. Revisions of this chapter in various editions limited to updating bibliography.

Van Tieghem, Paul. *La Littérature comparée.* 4th ed., rev. Paris, 1951. History, theory, problems, methods, and results of comparative and general literature. Has selective, useful bibliography of books (only a few articles) almost exclusively limited to publications written in French. First edition in 1931.

Guyard, Marius-Francois. *La Littérature comparée.* Paris, 1951. 5th ed., 1969. Concise introduction along the lines of Van Tieghem. Preface by Jean-Marie Carré omitted in 5th ed., but basic adherence to his views remains. Tables, rudimentary bibliography dropped, index of names added.

Carré, Jean-Marie. "La Littérature comparée depuis un demi-siècle," *Annales du Centre Universitaire Méditerranéen,* 3 (1951), 69–77. Although published in a remote location, important as authoritative statement of the tenets of the French school of comparative literature (see also preceding item, Guyard). Conceives comparative literature as distinct from literary comparison or general literature, is wary of influence studies, encourages work in history of literary voyages and history of literary interpretation of one country by another, and stresses "l'homme."

PORTA, ANTONIO, *La Letteratura comparata nella storia e nella critica.* Milan, 1951. Eloquent and discriminating lectures on comparative literature and literary history, comparative literature and criticism, the literary unity of Europe, the teaching of comparative literature, and the present state of comparative literature studies. Tendency toward rhetoric and generalities. Some rather shocking mistakes in names and titles. Bibliography.

WEHRLI, MAX. *Allgemeine Literaturwissenschaft.* Bern, 1951. Highly competent survey of various critical and historical approaches to literature current since the 1930's. Emphasis on German literature, but important foreign publications are considered. Chapter on world and comparative literature. Index of topics and names. Copious footnotes.

VOISINE, JACQUES. "Les Etudes de littérature comparée," *Revue de L'Enseignement supérieur,* no. 3 (1957), pp. 61–67. Convenient elementary summary of situation of comparative literature in general and French comparatism in particular.

LAIRD, CHARLTON. "Comparative Literature," in *Contemporary Literary Scholarship.* Ed. Lewis Leary. New York, 1958, pp. 339–68. A somewhat loose-jointed and, in details, not wholly reliable but very serviceable introduction to the status quo in the field. Selective annotated bibliography.

BROWN, CALVIN S. "Comparative Literature," *The Georgia Review,* 13 (Summer 1959), 167–89. Sound, spirited, and readable introduction to the field of Comparative Literature, the best brief one available to date for the nonspecialist. No bibliography.

CIORANESCU, ALEJANDRO. *Principios de literatura comparada.* La Laguna (Canary Islands), 1964. Helpful, well-informed, sensible, somewhat too restricted (historically oriented) introduction to history, definition and problems in the field. Good balance between generalities and examples, most of which come from the seventeenth, eighteenth, and nineteenth centuries. Rudimentary, chronologically arranged bibliography. No index.

THORPE, JAMES, ed. *Relations of Literary Study*. New York, 1967. Indispensable, amply annotated but readable and concise introduction to some interdisciplinary aspects of comparative literature. Contains Introduction (Thorpe), Literature and History (Colie), Literature and Myth (Frye), Literature and Biography (Edel), Literature and Psychology (Crews), Literature and Sociology (Lowenthal), Literature and Religion (Miller), Literature and Music (Bronson).

WELLEK, RENÉ. "Begriff und Idee der Vergleichenden Literaturwissenschaft," *Arcadia*, 2 (1967), 230–47. Readable history of the word and concept "Comparative Literature" in different languages, critique of definitions, and evolution of comparative literature as a discipline.

PICHOIS, CLAUDE, and ROUSSEAU, ANDRÉ-MARIE. *La Littérature comparée*. Paris, 1967. Replaces Van Tieghem and Guyard as surest French guide through comparative literature, and one of very best written in any language. Fair, intelligent, admirably open and equitable, highly concentrated, yet lively, remarkable equilibrium between analysis and synthesis, practice and theory. Many exceedingly (excessively?) concise references to secondary literature, bibliography. No index. Covers definition and history of comparative literature, international literary exchanges, general literary history, history of ideas, thematology, morphology, esthetics of translation.

WRENN, CHARLES L. *The Idea of Comparative Literature* (Presidential Address of the Modern Humanities Research Association). Leeds, 1968. Conservative, aesthetically oriented, rambling promenade favoring medieval and Renaissance topics. Particular attention to translations.

WELLEK, RENÉ. "The Name and Nature of Comparative Literature," in *Comparatists at Work*. Ed. Stephen G. Nichols, Jr., and Richard B. Vowles. Waltham, 1968, pp. 3–27. Slightly condensed as well as somewhat expanded English version of Wellek, "Begriff und Idee der Vergleichenden Literaturwissenschaft," *Arcadia,* 2 (1967), 230–47 (see above).

JEUNE, SIMON. *Littérature générale et littérature comparée. Essai d'orientation.* Paris, 1968. Sensible, elementary, voluntarily simplistic introduction to the fields of general and comparative literature between which the author, following Van Tieghem, distinguishes while conceding different usages of terms and overlapping. Traditional, pragmatic French approach but not averse to innovation (e.g., comparative "explication de textes"). Footnotes but no systematic bibliography or index.

BRANDT CORSTIUS, JAN. *Introduction to the Comparative Study of Literature.* New York, 1968. Practical preparation of college students for the study of comparative literature. Chooses certain problems illustrative of Western literary history, particularly the relationship of literary tradition to literary originality. Selective working bibliographies with some descriptive comments. Index of titles, authors, and persons.

WEISSTEIN, ULRICH. *Einführung in die Vergleichende Literaturwissenschaft.* Stuttgart, 1968. First, excellent book-length introduction to comparative literature in German. Collection and analysis, in a spirit of judicious fairness, of masses of disparate materials referring to every aspect of the field: definition, history, influence, imitation, reception, influence, periodization, genres, thematology, literature and other arts. Numerous notes, extensive bibliography, index of persons.

GIFFORD, HENRY. *Comparative Literature. Concepts of Literature.* London, 1969. Its title notwithstanding, this is mainly a series of eclectic essays on general literature ("The Education of a Modern Poet," "National Accent and Tradition," "The Mind of Europe," "Notes on Translation," "American Literature—the Special Case," plus curricular recommendations). Rather casual bibliography. No index.

ALDRIDGE, A. OWEN, ed. *Comparative Literature: Matter and Method.* Urbana, 1969. Collection of essays from *Comparative Literature Studies,* with brief general introduction ("The Purpose and Perspectives of Comparative Literature," 1–6) and very succinct section introductions, meant to give practical illustrations of various aspects of the field (Criticism and Theory, Movements, Themes, Forms, Relations). Sensible, clear prefaces and generally high quality articles. Limitation to essays published in one (fairly recent) periodical and disparateness of contributions restricts methodological instructiveness. General bibliography (333–34) very rudimentary.

THORLBY, ANTHONY. "Comparative Literature," in *Yearbook of Comparative and General Literature,* 18 (1969), 75–81. Eminently sound, fair, lucid, excellently written survey of the field in the British context. Slightly amended version of an essay which first appeared in *The Times Literary Supplement,* July 25, 1968.

DIMA, ALEXANDRU. *Principii de literatura comparata.* Bucharest, 1969. Basic treatise on field and methods of comparative literature by eminent Romanian comparatist. Position midway between historical and critical trends. Excludes comparative arts from domain of comparative literature. Stresses, in addition to traditional source and influence studies, investigation of literary parallels and the pinpointing of national particularities through comparison. Traces national cycles of receptivity and creativeness in international literary relations. Surveys progress of comparative literature as a discipline in Romania and elsewhere. See also Dima, *Conceptul de Literatura Universala si Comparata,* Bucharest, 1967; Dima and Mihai Novicov, ed., *Studii de Literatura Comparata,* Bucharest, 1968 (papers presented at the first national congress of comparative literature, Bucharest, June 25–29, 1967); Dima, "Realizari si perspective ale comparatismului roman," *Revista de Istorie si Teorie Literara,* 18 (1969), no. 4, 575–80; Victor Iancu, "Dezvoltarea literaturii comparato in Romania dupa 23 August 1944," *Orizont,* 20 (August 1969), no. 8, 10–17.

2 *Studies on Basic Aspects of the Definition and Function of Comparative Literature*

Hankiss, Jean. "Littérature universelle?" *Helicon,* 1 (1938), 156–71. Analyzes the problem inherent in writing horizontal international literary history as compared to vertical national history, and indicates that the former is less organic than the latter.

Wais, Kurt. "Vergleichende Literaturbetrachtung," in *Forschungsprobleme der Vergleichenden Literaturgeschichte,* 1. Ed. Kurt Wais. Tübingen, 1951, 7–11. Difficulty of facing both one's own and foreign literature "objectively." Qualitative differences among national literatures. Need for selectivity and aesthetic judgment in tracing portrait of European literature, for differentiation between reception and influence.

Teesing, H. P. H. "Die Bedeutung der vergleichenden Literaturgeschichte für die literarhistorische Periodisierung," in *Forschungsprobleme der Vergleichenden Literaturgeschichte,* 1. Ed. Kurt Wais. Tübingen, 1951, 13–20. Stresses differences between corresponding periods (e.g., Romanticism) in various literatures. Cautiously postulates certain regular sequences in evolution of national literatures. Immanent evolution of national literatures is primary, foreign influences secondary.

Auerbach, Erich. "Philologie der Weltliteratur," in *Weltliteratur.* Festgabe für Fritz Strich. Bern, 1952, pp. 39–50. Beautifully written, balanced contribution stressing the necessity, in view of the impending standardization of world literature, for historical syntheses based on studies of the evolution of a concrete phenomenon in world literature (such as Curtius' topoi, specific lines of Dante as interpreted by successive generations, etc.). Rejects syntheses resting on too general, too abstract preformed terms, or on presumed literary periods, or on cooperative efforts.

Höllerer, Walter. "Methoden und Probleme vergleichender Literaturwissenschaft," *Germanisch-Romanische Monatsschrift,* Neue Folge, 2 (1952), 116–31. Dwells on problems facing (especially German) comparatists: demarcation of the field, terminology, methods, approaches (biographical, epochal, typological, textual, stylistic, formal, structural, conceptual, imagistic). Numerous examples.

———. "Die vergleichende Literaturwissenschaft in Deutschland nach dem Kriege," *Rivista di letterature moderne*, 3 (1952), 285–99. Excellent survey of postwar tendencies in German comparative-literature research. Proposes increased emphasis on comparative interpretations of central portions of poetic works (e.g., Balzac-Büchner, Baudelaire-Nietzsche, Döblin-Sartre) and of symbols and images (tears, laughter, the actor, the city, etc.).

PEYRE, HENRI. "A Glance at Comparative Literature in America," *Yearbook of Comparative and General Literature*, 1 (1952), 1–8. Phosphorescent survey of the opportunities and pitfalls of comparative literature in this country. Good general bibliography (pp. 2–3).

GILLIES, ALEXANDER. "Some Thoughts on Comparative Literature," *Yearbook of Comparative and General Literature*, 1 (1952), 15–25. Sensible observations by a British scholar on the problems of comparative-literature research, followed by three overstated but rousing examples of the effect of literature on history (Shakespeare's reception in Germany, Madame de Staël's vision of Germany, Herder as the father of the Slav Renaissance).

LEVIN, HARRY. "La littérature comparée: point de vue d'outre-Atlantique," *Revue de littérature comparée*, 27 (1953), 17–26. Stresses desirability of less source, influence and success, and of more analogy, motif, stylistics, genre, movement and tradition studies in comparative literature. Underlines importance of research dealing with the classical tradition, Baroque and Realism.

HÖLLERER, WALTER. "La littérature comparée en Allemagne depuis la guerre," *Revue de littérature comparée*, 27 (1953), 27–42. While tolerant of various approaches, warns against too limited topics (emitter-receptor-transmitter), cause-and-effect studies, as well as too vast and abstract topics (such as the establishment of general aesthetic "laws" by way of comparative literature, or *Geistesgeschichte*). Favors, somewhere between national literature and world literature, cultivation of *European* literary history within certain geographical units and certain periods, using, among other methods, that of confrontation of central portions of comparable works (see above).

RODDIER, HENRI. "La littérature comparée et l'histoire des idées," *Revue de littérature comparée*, 27 (1953), 43–49. Pleads for transfer to comparative literature of methods used by A. O. Lovejoy to arrive at syntheses in the history of ideas. Argues in favor of cooperative endeavors concerned with semantic clarification and interpretation of central texts. States that the scientifically acceptable coherence of comparative literature as a discipline must be purchased at the price of a self-imposed temporal and geographic limitation to natural groupings of related national cultures (à la Toynbee). This entails increased attention to smaller countries within such units (Holland, Switzerland).

[MUNTEANO, BASIL.] "Conclusion provisoire," in "Orientations en littérature comparée," *Revue de littérature comparée*, 27 (1953), 50–58. For modest, noble, and gently ironic fair-mindedness on the highly controversial question of the orientation of comparative literature, this is a model statement.

WELLEK, RENÉ. "The Concept of Comparative Literature," *Yearbook of Comparative and General Literature*, 2 (1953), 1–5. Keen refutation of Carré's and Guyard's concepts.

MALONE, DAVID H. "The 'Comparative' in Comparative Literature," *Yearbook of Comparative and General Literature*, 3 (1954), 13–20. Continued rebuttal of Carré and Guyard. Long overdue rescue of "pure" comparisons in comparative literature.

FRIEDERICH, WERNER P. "Our Common Purpose," *Yearbook of Comparative and General Literature*, 4 (1955), 55–59. Plea for tolerance among practitioners of comparative literature.

STRUVE, GLEB. "Comparative Literature in the Soviet Union, Today and Yesterday," *Yearbook of Comparative and*

General Literature, 4 (1955), 1–20; 6 (1957), 7–10; 9 (1959), 13–18. Aside from a fascinating account of the repercussions of politics on comparative scholarship, this report calls attention to highly-pertinent, little-known Russian theories (Alexander Veselovsky, Plekhanov, Zhirmunsky) on influences, translations and cultural analogies (stadialism).

GOBBERS, W. "Hoever staan we met het Komparatisme?" *Wetenschappelijke Tijdingen*, 16, no. 1 (January 1956), 11–19. Sane, objective account of the conflicting and complementary currents (literary history, literary criticism) in comparative literature, French and American "schools." Valuable references to little-known, earlier Netherlandic scholarship on comparative literature. Advocates a middle-of-the-road approach.

BAUR, FRANK. "De Philologie van het letterkundige Comparatisme," in *Handelingen van het XXIIe Vlaams Filologencongres*. Leuven (Louvain), 1957, pp. 31–64. Excellent, largely descriptive analysis of *status quo* in comparative-literature scholarship. Very useful bibliographical references.

RODDIER, HENRI. "Littérature comparée et histoire des idées," in *Littérature générale et histoire des idées*. Actes du premier congrès national de littérature comparée. Paris, 1957, pp. 16–19. Plea for the preparation of a dictionary of ideological terms indispensable for the understanding of the evolution of literature, beginning with a specific period and a limited area. Very brief review of conflicting tendencies in present-day comparative-literature research. See Bémol's comment below (Munteano).

MUNTEANO, BASIL. "Littérature générale et histoire des idées," in *Littérature générale et histoire des idées*. Actes du premier congrès national de littérature comparée. Paris, 1957, pp. 20–30. In this lively, searching and challenging paper, a curious mixture of old and new, Munteano proposes complementary synthesis of horizontal "general literature" and vertical "history of ideas." Restricts literary history and comparative literature to *actual, conscious* contacts. Follows essentially Van Tieghem in assigning to "General Literature" assemblage of vaster, mutually relevant data and currents.

General literature would also cover relationship between literature and other arts. Sees philosophy of history as ultimate synthesis. In the ensuing discussion, Bémol demands that artistic nature of literature be recognized along with its ideological importance.

ETIEMBLE, RENÉ. "Littérature comparée, ou comparaison n'est pas raison," in *Savoir et Goût*, vol. 3 of *Hygiène des lettres*. Paris, 1958, pp. 154–73. Argues for emphasis on *literature* (structure, style, intrinsic values) as well as *comparison* (including pure parallelisms between Oriental and Western literatures which may enable us to arrive at literary invariables) without abandoning historical studies. Criticizes conservatism, provincialism and even nationalism in French concepts of comparative literature; calls for more intensive study of Oriental, Slavic, Semitic, Finno-Ugrian, etc., literatures. Seems unaware of Malone's article (see above) and makes no effort to differentiate between comparative literature, general literature, and world literature.

GILLET, J. "Cosmopolitisme et littérature comparée," in *Les Flandres dans les mouvements romantique et symboliste*. Actes du second congrès national de littérature comparée. Paris, 1958, pp. 45–51. In rejecting Höllerer's "vague assimilation between Comparative Literature and Cosmopolitanism," Gillet objects to comparative study of "some works detached from their national context" as a sort of "exercise in virtuosity." He argues that the comparatist must start from historically and geographically restricted, concrete cases within a national framework, but need not necessarily stop there.

VAN DER LEE, A. "Zur Komparatistik im niederländischen Sprachraum," in *Forschungsprobleme der Vergleichenden Literaturgeschichte*, 2. Ed. Fritz Ernst and Kurt Wais. Tübingen, 1958, 173–77. Sketch of the *status quo* in the Dutch-Flemish speaking areas with emphasis on questions of definition and function (particularly Baur's quadripartition of comparative literature into crenology, doxology, genology, and thematology, the perfecting of which leads to a historical-aesthetic synthesis).

FRIEDERICH, WERNER PAUL. "Zur Vergleichenden Literaturgeschichte in den Vereinigten Staaten," in *Forschungsprobleme der Vergleichenden Literaturgeschichte*, 2. Ed. Fritz Ernst and Kurt Wais. Tübingen, 1958, 179–91. Outlines the positions of the three main components of comparative literature in the United States (world literature and great books courses, the "French school" and the "American school"), and offers to reconcile them.

GUÉRARD, ALBERT. "Comparative Literature?" *Yearbook of Comparative and General Literature*, 7 (1958), 1–6. In this more vivacious than circumspect paper, Professor Guérard argues that comparative literature is a makeshift term needed only as long as "the nationalistic heresy has not been extirpated" and should soon be in a position to commit a triumphant suicide.

BLOCK, HASKELL M. "The concept of influence in Comparative Literature," *Yearbook of Comparative and General Literature*, 7 (1958), 30–37. Balanced and persuasive plea for the rehabilitation of the term "influence" in comparative literature as "an intrinsic part of literary experience."

HANKISS, JANOS. "Théorie de la littérature et littérature comparée," in *Comparative Literature*. Proceedings of the Second Congress of the International Comparative Literature Association, Chapel Hill, Vol. 1, 1959, pp. 98–112. Affirms essential unity of national literary history, comparative literature, and the theory of literature.

RODDIER, HENRI. "De l'emploi de la méthode génétique en littérature comparée," in *Comparative Literature*. Proceedings of the Second Congress. 1, 113–24. A spirited French reaction to the dangers of "abstract . . . simplistic . . . intransigeant . . . sterilizing . . . formalism" inherent in too sweeping an application of the New Criticism to comparative literature. Likens the New Criticism to a study of the qualities of the violin without worrying about the violinist. Proposes an extension of the genetic method so fruitful in biographies to literary genres, themes, types, myths, etc., culminating in the juxtaposition of vertical histories of particular literatures resting on systematic researches about the circumstances that have contributed to the uniqueness of this literature, that have limited its possibilities of evolution, with special stress on the language. Such a cooperative endeavor would elucidate the national variations of labels applied to European literature such as *the* Renaissance, *the* Reformation, *the* classicism, etc., but would also show characteristics common to several national literatures.

MUNTEANO, BASIL. "Situation de la littérature comparée. Sa portée humaine et sa légitimité," in *Comparative Literature.* Proceedings of the Second Congress, 1, 124–42. Far-reaching diagnosis of the "crisis" in comparative literature. Rejects the "myth" of the literary work as an absolute self-contained unit and the stringent separation between "extrinsic" and "intrinsic" (Wellek), the task of interpretation being precisely the reconstruction of the transmutation from extrinsic *to* intrinsic. Defends intelligent use of the search for sources, influences, and affinities. Comparison is by necessity dialectic. Considers comparative literature as practical, convenient, necessary subdivision of general science of comparison: dialectic comparatism.

WELLEK, RENÉ. "The Crisis of Comparative Literature," in *Comparative Literature.* Proceedings of the Second Congress. 1, 149–59. Vigorous, even more outspoken and less conciliatory restatement of the critiques leveled previously by Wellek against prevailing comparative-literature research, notably against "an artificial demarcation of subject matter and methodology, a mechanistic concept of sources and influences, (and) a motivation by cultural nationalism, however generous." Reprinted in Wellek, *Concepts of Criticism,* New Haven, 1963, pp. 282–295.

LA DRIÈRE, J. CRAIG. "The Comparative Method in the Study of Prosody," in *Comparative Literature.* Proceedings of the Second Congress. 1, 160–75. Elucidates the comparative method in literary studies from his experiences with the comparative method in the study of prosody. Argues for necessity of variety in comparative studies, that theory, history, and criticism are distinct, though not unrelated, and that, in line wth Baldensperger, Hankiss, and Van Tieghem, comparative literature be viewed as an intermediate step between national and general literature. Advocates collaborative projects in solving comparative questions beyond the reach of any individual scholars.

GUILLÉN, CLAUDIO. "The Aesthetics of Influence Studies in Comparative Literature," in *Comparative Literature*. Proceedings of the Second Congress. 1, 175–92. Aesthetic-genetic theory and classification of influence studies, distinguishing between genuinely genetic "sources vécues," conventions and techniques, and parallelisms. Representative bibliography.

PEYRE, HENRI. "Seventy-five Years of Comparative Literature. A backward and a forward glance," *Yearbook of Comparative and General Literature*, 8 (1959), 18–26. Urges more attention to human values.

WILL, FREDERIC. "Comparative Literature and the Challenge of Modern Criticism," *Yearbook of Comparative and General Literature*, 9 (1960), 29–31. Plea that the comparatist recognize the inaccessibility of the literary work as a private entity, but exploit its public features.

REMAK, HENRY H. H. "Comparative Literature at the crossroads: diagnosis, therapy, and prognosis," *Yearbook of Comparative and General Literature*, 9 (1960), 1–28. Survey and evaluation of the great debate on the essence, function, and purpose of Comparative Literature during the last decade. Bibliography.

TRIOMPHE, ROBERT. "L'URSS et la littérature comparée," *Revue de littérature comparée*, 34 (1960), 304–10. Highly informative account of comparative literature in the Soviet Union. Supplements Struve's essay.

DYSERINCK, HUGO. "Crisis in de Vergelijkende Literatuurwetenschaap? *Spiegel der Letteren*, 4, no. 3 (1960), 175–93. Sensible, comprehensive account of the "crisis" in comparative literature, of French and American trends seen as integral parts of the situation in literary scholarship, and careful suggestions as to areas of agreement. Comparison with trends in music and art scholarship.

SICILIANO, ITALO. "Quelques remarques sur la littérature comparée," in *Venezia nelle letterature moderne*. Ed. Carlo Pellegrini. Venice, 1961, pp. 4–10. Personal, informal, engaging, a bit lukewarm (Croce?) defense of comparative literature by a distinguished Italian scholar. Pitfalls of comparative literature seem to rate more attention in this aperçu than its opportunities. Remarks date from 1955.

BALAKIAN, ANNA. "Influence and Literary Fortune," *Yearbook of Comparative and General Literature*, II (1962), 24–31. Attempt to distinguish between influence (critical) and reception (historical) investigations.

DE DEUGD, CORNELIS. *De Eenheid van het Comparatisme.* Utrechtse Publikaties voor Algemene Literatuurwetenschap, no. 1. Utrecht, 1962. Sound in details, laudable in aims, but somewhat shaky in thesis that there are no dominant trends in French and American comparatism because (obviously) not every French comparatist agrees with Carré or every American comparatist with Wellek. Rather "jumpy" in organization.

GICOVATE, BERNARDO. *Conceptos Fundamentales de Literatura Comparada. Iniciación de la Poesía Modernista.* San Juan de Puerto Rico, 1962. Promise of main title not borne out by this influence study on Spanish and Spanish-American "modernismo." No references to scholarship on fundamental concepts of comparative literature.

GUILLÉN, CLAUDIO. "Perspectivas de la literatura comparada," *Boletín Informativo del Seminario de Derecho Político*, 27, Princeton, (August 1962), 57–70. One of very rare accounts in Spanish of situation in comparative literature, sound, discriminating, clear, with plentiful practical illustrations of theoretical problems.

RÜDIGER, HORST. "Nationalliteraturen und europäische Literatur. Methoden und Ziele der Vergleichenden Literaturwissenschaft," *Schweizer Monatshefte*, 42 (1962), 195–211. Diachronic and synchronic survey of the evolution of comparative literature, with due attention to topics (reception, intermediaries, translations), methods, the present "crisis" in comparative literature, and the integration of national literatures into European literature. Bibliography.

SÖTÉR, ISTVAN, ed. *La Littérature comparée en Europe Orientale.* Proceedings of the Budapest Conference on Comparative Literature, October 26–29, 1962. Budapest, 1963. Exceedingly important collection of papers revealing principles, practice, and aims of comparative literature as seen in Eastern Europe. Contributions in Russian, French, German, etc. Considerable number of papers of high quality.

ETIEMBLE, RENÉ. *Comparaison n'est pas raison. La crise de la Littérature comparée.* Paris, 1963. Refreshing, lively, independent, fair view of comparative literature as practiced in East and West, indicative of prospective trends and changes. Stresses attention to non-Western languages and literatures. Not entirely realistic in all recommendations.

———. *The Crisis in Comparative Literature.* East Lansing, 1966. Translation of preceding item by Herbert Weisinger and Georges Joyaux, with substantial, spirited, somewhat hyperbolic foreword by translators (vii–xxiv). No index.

TEESING, HUBERT P. H. "Literature and the Other Arts: Some Remarks," *Yearbook of Comparative and General Literature,* 12 (1963), 27–35. Observations on the collaboration of several arts in one work of art, on historical relations between literature, the fine arts, and music, and on the problematical systematic relations between the arts.

NEUPOKOEVA, I. G. "Moderne bürgerliche Literaturwissenschaft und reaktionäre Soziologie," in *Wissenschaft am Scheidewege.* Ed. G. Ziegengeist. Berlin, 1964, pp. 161–73. Dogmatic attack against supranational writing of Western European literary history and against intrinsic approach (Curtius, Wais, Wellek).

MATLAW, RALPH E. "Comparative Literature in Eastern Europe," *Yearbook of Comparative and General Literature,* 13 (1964), 49–55. Penetrating survey of the directions of comparative-literature research in the eastern sphere of Europe since 1956.

TROUSSON, RAYMOND. *Un Problème de littérature comparée: les études de thème. Essai de méthodologie.* Paris, 1965. Long overdue, persuasive plea for the disdained field of thematology, highly relevant to the role played by myth and symbol in contemporary literature and scholarship. Rich in thesis subjects (p. 93). Index. Summary of arguments in Trousson, "Plaidoyer pour la *Stoffgeschichte*," *Revue de littérature comparée*, 38 (1964), 101–14.

WELLEK, RENÉ. "Comparative Literature Today," *Comparative Literature*, 17 (1965), 325–37. Play-by-play, personal and personable account of the (often controversial) development of comparative literature as a discipline in Europe (including Russia) and the United States since the 1920's. Eloquent, compelling defense of the importance to the humanities of a *literary* approach to literature, and of a combination of history and criticism. A discussion on the state of comparative literature in the United States (Balakian, de Man, Weisinger, Bergel) follows (pp. 338–40).

Wissenschaftliche Zeitschrift der Ernst-Moritz-Arndt Universität Greifswald, 14 (1965), 405–65. Issue devoted to East German reactions to and recommendations of method and application of world (read: comparative) literature and literary criticism. Heavy layers of propagandistic lingo are not infrequently pierced by scholarly awareness.

SCHWARZ, EGON. "Fragen und Gedanken zur vergleichenden Literaturwissenschaft vom Standpunkt eines Germanisten," *The German Quarterly*, 38 (1965), 318–24. Judicious, eloquent plea for the institutional recognition of comparative literature as well as for a comparative attitude basic to any balanced study of literature.

JOST, FRANÇOIS, ed. *Proceedings of the Fourth Congress of the International Comparative Literature Association (Actes du Quatrième Congrès de l'Association Internationale de Littérature Comparée)*, Fribourg, 1964. The Hague, 1966. 2 vols. Numerous studies on principal questions concerning nationalism, cosmopolitism, imitation, influence, and originality in comparative literature studies. Index.

MCCUTCHION, DAVID. "Comparative Literature in Eastern Europe," *Jadavpur Journal of Comparative Literature*, 5 (1966), 88–100. Aggressive but fair discussion of Budapest Conference (see *La littérature comparée en Europe Orientale*, above) and of *Littérature Hongroise, Littérature Européenne*, I. Sötér and O. Supek, eds. (Budapest, 1964).

Branches out into confrontation between sociohistorical (East) and esthetic-literary (West) approaches to literature. Recognizes relaxation of dogmatic Marxistic approach in several Communist countries, but regrets slowness with which shift in dogma is followed up in specific studies.

FLEISCHMANN, WOLFGANG BERNARD. "Das Arbeitsgebiet der Vergleichenden Literaturwissenschaft," *Arcadia*, 1 (1966), 221–30. Despite some questionable accents and literary judgments (Fontane-Flaubert-Sinclair Lewis), this essay has much stimulating originality. Sees three main tasks of comparative-literature scholarship: 1) the study of the style of literary structures beyond a linguistic area, 2) the history of literary concepts beyond a linguistic area within the history of ideas, 3) literary evaluation on an international basis.

KRUSE, MARGOT, "Die Kunst des literarischen Vergleichs. Wandel und Konstanz im wissenschaftlichen Werk Hellmuth Petriconis," *Romanistisches Jahrbuch*, 17 (1966/67), 23–46. Revealing account of the analogy method developed by the Hispanist Petriconi and its application to problems of European literature. See also Dieter Beyerle, "Hellmuth Petriconi zum Gedächtnis," *Arcadia*, 2 (1967), 103–8.

MUNTEANO, B. *Constantes dialectiques en littérature et en histoire. Problemes, Recherches, Perspectives.* Paris, 1967. Collection of essays and reviews, remarkably substantial, amounting *grosso modo* to a theory of variable constants as a key to the unlocking of ideas in literature, and to the stress on dialectic comparison in the study of comparative literature. Emphasis on the art of synthesis, on rhetoric, convention, and local color. Vivid humanistic philosophy concerned with continuity and change in literature. Numerous footnotes; no bibliography or index.

LEVIN, HARRY. "Thematics and Criticism," in *The Disciplines of Criticism* (in honor of René Wellek). New Haven, 1968, pp. 125–45. Rehabilitation of thematics for literary criticism through a profusion of illustrations ranging widely through European and American literature and scholarship.

HATZFELD, HELMUT. "Comparative Literature as a Necessary Method," in *The Disciplines of Criticism*. Ed. Peter

Demetz et al. New Haven, 1968, pp. 79–92. Identification of epoch styles and style epochs (Baroque, Classicism, Romanticism) through comparative literature. Learned, provocative, somewhat opinionated essay.

ZIEGENGEIST, GERHARD, ed. *Aktuelle Probleme der Vergleichenden Literaturforschung.* Berlin, 1968. Collection of essays reflecting Marxist approach to comparative literature, based on the international colloquium held in East Berlin in 1966. Besides numerous reports on the state of comparative literature in East European countries and comparative, reception, and influence aspects of Slavic literatures in other countries, basic guidelines are proposed by Zhirmunsky (pp. 1–16), Chrapcenko (pp. 17–46; excellent), Durisin (pp. 47–58; interesting chart), and Neupokoeva (pp. 59–65; very general). Western scholarship sparsely utilized. Footnotes and extensive index of names.

"Principy komparatívneho skúmania literatúry [Principles of comparative study of literature], *Slavica Slovaca,* 3 (1968), 113–15 (Russian and English translations, pp. 115–20). Concise, well-balanced, comprehensive twelve-point statement by the Institute of World Literature and Language of the Slovak Academy of Sciences. While based on the premises of national literatures, historical-genetic considerations, mutual relations (translations, reception, influences) and dialectic-typological relationships, it makes allowance for synchronic as well as diachronic points of view, for the studies of genres, movements, and affinities on a supranational scale, for the progression from national to "world" literature, and for an interpenetration of historic and stylistic-typological aesthetics. Favors a relative rather than absolute validity for the comparative method of research.

KRAUSS, WERNER. "Nationale und Vergleichende Literaturgeschichte," in his *Grundprobleme der Literaturwissenschaft.* Hamburg, 1968, pp. 105–18. Qualified plea by the distinguished East German "Romanist" for the dependence of comparative on national literature and against analogies outside causal historical connections. Highly selective and not always reliable documentation. Despite assurance by publisher that this book was written specifically for him, this essay is largely a rephrasing of Krauss, "Probleme der vergleichenden Literaturgeschichte," in *Sitzungsberichte der Deutschen Akademie der Wissenschaften zu Berlin,* Klasse Philosophie, no. 1, Berlin, 1963, 3–17.

MALONE, DAVID H. "Literature and 'Comparative Literature,'" in *Medieval Epic to the "Epic Theater" of Brecht.* Ed. Rosario P. Armato and John M. Spalek. Los Angeles, 1968, pp. 1–7. Rapid sketch of situation of comparative-literature studies in the United States.

JOST, FRANÇOIS. " 'Komparatistik' oder 'Absolutistik'?" *Arcadia,* 3 (1968), 229–34. Sparkling but confusing plea for the absolute (universal) rather than relative (national) values of the "misnomer" comparative literature.

———. "La Littérature comparée, une philosophie des lettres," in his *Essais de littérature comparée.* Fribourg and Urbana, 1968, pp. 313–41. Exuberantly written, learned, somewhat epigrammatic and discursive plea for universality of the study of literature. Rather critical of emphasis on national heritage, comparisons, and sources in comparative-literature scholarship, yet generous in approach.

LEVIN, HARRY. "Comparing the Literature," *Yearbook of Comparative and General Literature,* 17 (1968), 5–16. Beautifully and humanely written, candid yet urbane, committed and controversial survey of recent past and present of comparative-literature studies. Plea to compare the literature rather than to talk about how to do it.

ALDRIDGE, ALFRED OWEN. "The Comparative Literature Syndrome," *Modern Language Journal,* 53 (1969), 110–16. Plainspoken survey of the malaise in comparative-literature methodology accompanying the boom of the discipline through a searching, both objective and subjective, review of the Jeune, Corstius, and Nichols-Vowles volumes. Avows he is somewhat tired of methodological polemics.

Proceedings of the Vth Congress of the International Comparative Literature Association (*Actes,* Belgrade Congress, 1967). Belgrade and Amsterdam, 1969. More than eighty papers on the international character of literary currents, the relationship between oral and written literature, and the interpretation of Slavic letters in other literatures include several general essays (in French, German, English) on international trends by Zhirmunsky, Dolanski, Markiewicz, Neupokoeva, Durisin, and Dimaras. Footnotes but no index. Report on the "History of European Literature" project (pp. 775–94).

3 *Comprehensive International Histories of Literature and Criticism*

Among the many studies of literary history and criticism from the international angle, we have selected only two kinds of samples: histories of literature and criticism spanning vast geographic areas through one or several centuries, and works furnishing a picture of the totality of the foreign literary relations of a particular country.

COMPREHENSIVE HISTORIES

Van Tieghem, Paul. *Histoire littéraire de l'Europe et de l'Amérique de la Renaissance à nos jours.* Paris, 1946 (first printed in 1941). An expanded and revised version of his *Précis de l'Histoire Littéraire de l'Europe depuis la Renaissance,* Paris, 1925, translated into English as *Outline of the Literary History of Europe since the Renaissance,* New York, 1930. In contrast to many so-called comparative histories of literature which are juxtapositions of separate national histories under one cover, this is a genuinely international history organized not by countries but by periods and genres. The mass of names and titles and the impossibility of delving into any one author make this (like the Friederich-Malone) a valuable reference work rather than a readable, connected history.

Friederich, Werner P., and Malone, David H. *Outline of Comparative Literature from Dante to O'Neill.* Chapel Hill, 1954. A supranational, truly comparative history of literature, stressing influences, parallels, and contrasts. Index of names and topics, but no bibliography.

WELLEK, RENÉ. *A History of Modern Criticism: 1750–1950.* 4 vols. New Haven. Volume 1: *The Later Eighteenth Century* (1955). Volume 2: *The Romantic Age* (1955). Volume 3: *The Age of Transition* (1965). Volume 4: *The Later Nineteenth Century* (1965). Indispensable. Primary stress on literary theory, secondary stress on literary taste. All four volumes cover England (and Scotland), France, Germany, and Italy; volumes 3 and 4 add Russia and the United States. Volume 5, "The Twentieth Century," will include Spain. Quotations in English, with original texts in notes. Selective and descriptive bibliography, notes, chronological tables, index of names, topics, and terms in each volume.

Encylopédie de la Pléiade. Histoire des littératures, II: *Littératures occidentales.* Paris, 1956. Despite uneveness of contributions and survival of traditional features of organization along national literature lines, this is one of the very few histories of literature of the Western world with a sophistication adequate for comparative literature scholarship.

WIMSATT, WILLIAM K., and BROOKS, CLEANTH. *Literary Criticism. A Short History.* New York, 1957. A biased, brilliant, brash, uneven, and exceedingly stimulating history of criticism from Socrates to Jung. Many references. Index.

ALBÉRÈS, R.-M. *L'Aventure intellectuelle du XXe siècle. Panorama des littératures européennes: 1900–1959.* 2nd ed., rev. and enl. Paris, 1959. Although not "scholarly" in the traditional sense, being based on primary sources rather than engaging in scholarly polemics, this readable approach to twentieth-century European literature by dominant themes rather than countries could become exemplary for comparative research. National contributions (primarily English, French, Spanish, German, and Italian, incidentally other Romanic, Scandinavian and Slavic literatures) are by no means submerged in this history of European literary sensibility in the twentieth century. Rich mine for comparative topics. Introduction presents clear hypothesis; much overlapping, of course, in actual text. Synoptic chronological table arranged by themes. Index of names.

RODDIER, HENRI. "Principes d'une histoire comparée des

littératures européennes," *Revue de littérature comparée,* 39 (1965), 178–225. Investigation, extraordinary in depth and breadth, of the foundations of the writing of a genetic comparative history of European literatures.

TOTALITY OF FOREIGN RELATIONS OF ONE COUNTRY

MOMIGLIANO, ATTILIO, ed. *Letterature comparate.* Milan, 1948. Collection of surveys by various scholars covering the relations between Italian literature and classical (Sorbelli), French (Pellegrini), Spanish (A. Croce), English (Praz), German and Scandinavian (Santoli), dialect (Sansone), and troubadour (Viscardi) literature. Each survey followed by extensive bibliography.

KOHLSCHMIDT, WERNER, and MOHR, WOLFGANG, eds. *Reallexikon der deutschen Literaturgeschichte.* 2nd ed. Berlin, 1955. Contains succinct, comprehensive, amply annotated accounts of foreign influences (American, English, Finnish, etc.) on German literature.

STAMMLER, WOLFGANG, ed. *Deutsche Philologie im Aufriss.* 3, 2nd ed. Berlin, 1957. Provides, in separate studies, systematic coverage of foreign influences on German literature (Nordic, Finnish, English, American, Dutch, French, Italian, Spanish, Hungarian, Oriental, Indian, East Asian, Russian, Czech, Yugoslav). Bibliographies.

Littérature Hongroise–Littérature Européenne. Budapest, 1964. Collection of essays by various scholars on Hungary's literary relations with other countries, all written in French. Book also contains an account of the history of comparative literature in Hungary. Excellent annotated bibliography, index of persons and things.

Although I have not included in this section of my essay bibliographies of national literatures that contain chapters on their foreign relations, the very inadequate attention that Spanish literature has received from non-Hispanists prompts me to mention the substantial comparative section in José Simón Díaz, *Bibliografía de la literatura hispánica* (Madrid, 1950), 1: 469–517. I owe this reference to the kindness of Professor G. N. G. Orsini. See also 2nd ed. (1960), 1: 531–94.

4 *Comparative Chronological Tables*

VAN TIEGHEM, PAUL, ed. *Répertoire chronologique des littératures modernes.* Paris, 1935. Lists by years (1455 to 1900), subdivided by languages, important works and related facts of all European (except Turkish) and American literatures. Alphabetical index of authors and works.

SPEMANN, ADOLF. *Vergleichende Zeittafel der Weltliteratur.* Stuttgart, 1951. Less elaborate parallel to van Tieghem's *Répertoire,* but covers, in addition, the years 1150 to 1455 (briefly) and 1900 to 1939 (very extensively). Helpful alphabetical index of all authors mentioned, with titles and dates of their works.

BRETT-JAMES, ANTONY. *The Triple Stream. Four centuries of English, French and German literature.* 1531–1930. Cambridge, England, 1953; Philadelphia, 1954. Juxtaposed tabulation, by years, of literary names (birth and death dates) and titles from English, French, and German literature, including Belgium, Austria, and Switzerland. Some nonliterary dates pertinent to literature are listed. Practically no references to translations and intermediaries. Some choices of dates dubious. Index of all authors. (See also Bompiani entry under 7.)

5 *Bibliographies of Comparative Literature*

BALDENSPERGER, FERNAND, and FRIEDERICH, WERNER P. *Bibliography of Comparative Literature.* Chapel Hill, 1950. Indispensable, (too?) comprehensive reference work. Ingenious organization, though not perspicuous at first glance. Stresses emitter. No descriptive or evaluative comments. Lists very few reviews. Addition of index would augment usefulness of work considerably. Supplements published annually since 1952 in *Yearbook of Comparative and General Literature.*

Bibliographie générale de littérature comparée, 5 vols. (published with the aid of UNESCO). Paris, 1950–60. Covers 1949–58. Quarterly bibliographies of the *Revue de littérature comparée* (see section 6) collected in annual volumes. Sections on bibliography, theory, style, literary genres, themes and types, general relations, intermediaries, currents, movements and epochs, "ambiances," influences (the latter arranged by emitting nations). Nondescriptive, noncritical. Some reviews listed. Index.

ROSENBERG, RALPH P. "Bibliographies," *Comparative Literature*, 2 (1950), 189–90. Checklist of bibliographies pertaining, in whole or in part, to Comparative Literature, which appear periodically in American publications. Dated.

FISHER, JOHN H. "Serial Bibliographies in the Modern Languages and Literatures," *PMLA*, 66 (1951), 138–56. Invaluable noncritical survey, although somewhat dated. Has a special section on "Bibliographies of Comparative Literature" (150–51), but some comparative-literature bibliographies are listed under other headings in the survey. Subject index and index of bibliographers. The annual bibliographies in *PMLA* contain a special section on comparative literature and references to comparative-literature items under different headings.

Comparatistische Bibliografie [Comparative Bibliography]. Edited by the Instituut voor Vergelijkend Literatuuronderzok [Institute for Comparative Literature]. University of Utrecht, 1955–61. Bibliographical cards (about four hundred per year), comprising all significant Dutch, Flemish, and Afrikaans publications, books as well as articles, on comparative literature or important for comparative literature. Each card contains a catchword in Dutch, German and French or English (depending upon the linguistic preference of the subscriber) referring to the contents of the publication.

Regesten (Register of the acquisitions of the Institute for Comparative Literature). University of Utrecht, 1956–61. Contains many brief reviews in Dutch, much more descriptive than critical, of recent literary studies in various languages acquired by the Institute. A good many items, though not always the majority, are comparative. Four issues per year.

6 *Periodicals*

Only those periodicals exclusively devoted to Comparative Literature and currently published are covered. For a more general orientation, the rich symposium on "International and New Periodicals in Comparative Literature," *Yearbook of Comparative and General Literature* 17 (1968), 122–35, is recommended.

Revue de littérature comparée, 1921. Scholarly articles. and reviews with marked preference for problems of literary history. Extensive bibliographies, discontinued after January–March, 1960 issue. News and notes. Quarterly.

Comparative Literature, 1949–. Scholarly articles and reviews, inclined toward problems of literary criticism. Lists of "Books received." Brief announcements. Quarterly.

Hikaku Bungaku (Journal of Comparative Literature, Japan), 1951–. Three times a year. Articles in Japanese, French, English, etc., on all aspects of comparative literature. Summaries in English, French, German, or Italian.

Yearbook of Comparative and General Literature, 1952–. Basic questions of definition and function. Extensive reviews of research on broader aspects of comparative literature. Concern with problems of translation. Articles on teaching and organizational aspects of comparative literature. Biographical sketches of great comparatists. Historical documents. Comparative-literature activities here and abroad. Reviews of professional works (mainly for teaching and general orientation purposes), of translations and editions. Bibliography of translations. Supplements to Friederich-Baldensperger's *Bibliography of Comparative Literature.*

Jadavpur Journal of Comparative Literature, 1961–. Annual. Articles on various aspects, topics, and authors related (predominantly) to comparative or (occasionally) to national literature, including the relationship between literature and the arts, music, religion, and science. Notes on development of comparative literature in India and abroad, excerpts from noteworthy articles published elsewhere, selective bibliography of important writings on comparative literature and of important translations into English. Most articles in English.

Comparative Literature Studies, 1964–. Quarterly. Stresses literary history, history of ideas, European literary relations

COLLEGE OF THE SEQUOIAS
LIBRARY

with North and South America. Certain issues are devoted to single topics. Reviews.

Arcadia, 1966–. Three times a year. Articles in German (mostly), English, and French. While open to various topics and aspects, stress on historical studies and on revitalization of humanistic tradition in comparative literature. Reviews.

Cahiers algériens de littérature comparée, 1966–. Annual. Articles, bibliographies, reports, with special reference to Arab (particularly Algerian) questions and the impact of Marxism on literary scholarship.

7 *Other Useful Reference Works*

Shipley, Joseph T., ed. *Dictionary of World Literature.* New York, 1943. 2nd rev. ed. New York, 1953. 3rd ed., unchanged, Paterson, New Jersey, 1960 (paperback). Encyclopedia of literary terms, forms, techniques, methods, problems, schools, and criticism (only exceptionally authors and critics). Signed contributions of considerable originality. Both editions should be consulted.

———., ed. *Encyclopedia of Literature.* 2 vols. New York, 1946. Condensed surveys of the literary history of the nations of the world, arranged alphabetically according to names of nations. Each survey followed by a bibliography of pertinent literary histories. Biographical notices about most important writers at the end of the second volume.

Smith, Horatio, ed. *Columbia Dictionary of Modern European Literature.* New York, 1947. Signed, informative, and refreshingly written articles on authors, national literatures (thirty-one), critics and movements (uneven coverage) from about 1870 to date of publication. Great Britain and Ireland are excluded. English translations, and English (including American) criticism of continental literature (in the concise bibliography following each article) given particular attention.

Eppelsheimer, Hanns W. *Handbuch der Weltliteratur.* 2 vols. Frankfurt, 1947–50. Volume 1: to the end of the eighteenth century; Volume 2: nineteenth and twentieth centuries.

Covers oriental, classical, medieval, and modern literature. Organized by great epochs subdivided by countries, genres or movements. Brief descriptive introduction to epochs, genres, works, writers followed by bibliography accompanied by numerous short but helpful descriptive and/or critical remarks. Concise biography for main authors. Each volume has index of names, terms, and anonymous works. Volume 2 contains general bibliographies pertaining to literary scholarship, national literatures and genres, forms, themes, and problems of literature; also errata and addenda. Handy reference, despite shortcomings.

Dizionario letterario Bompiani. Milan, 1947–52. Comprehensive, rich, and magnificently illustrated reference work on world literature in nine volumes, arranged alphabetically within its main sections (artistic movements, works, persons appearing in works, and index). Comparative chronological tables from Ancient Greece to 1914 in volume 9 (1950). Updated appendix in two volumes: 1, 1964; 2, 1966.

Dictionnaire des oeuvres de tous les temps et de tous les pays. Ed. Laffont and Bompiani. 2nd ed. Paris, 1955. 5 vols. Contains an analysis of and commentary on more than twenty thousand works, with the stress on world literature. Profusely illustrated. Magnificent achievement. Last volume contains indices of authors and illustrations, and synoptic chronological tables. Based on *Dizionario Letterario Bompiani.*

Index Translationum. International Bibliography of Translations. Published by UNESCO. Paris, since 1949. Appears annually, covering the literature of the preceding year. Contains also alphabetical list of authors, and (but only until vol. 6, 1954, for 1953) of translators and publishers by country. From volume 4 (1952, for 1951) on, supplements for previous years.

LEACH, MARIA, ed. *Dictionary of Folklore, Mythology and Legend.* New York, 1949–50. Volume 1 (A–I); Volume 2 (J–Z). Standard reference work. In addition to articles on some 8,000 folklore terms, contains surveys of American, Basque, French, German, etc., folklore, and biographies of important folklorists.

LAIRD, CHARLTON, ed. *The World Through Literature.* New York, 1951. Generally competent, well-written surveys of Primitive (Radin), Far Eastern (Chinese by Shao Chang Lee, Japanese by Younghill Kang and John Morrison), Indian (Buck), Near Eastern (Koran by Calverley, Arabic by Jurji), Hebrew (Silberschlag), Greek and Latin (Benham), Italian (Prezzolini), French (Huse), Spanish and Portuguese (Schevill), German (Morgan), Scandinavian (Benson), Slavic (almost exclusively Russian, by Posin) and Latin American (Nichols) literatures. Bibliography, often with descriptive and critical comments, is appended to each essay. Index of names and titles.

PEI, MARIO A., and GAYNOR, FRANK, eds. *Liberal Arts Dictionary.* New York, 1952. Definition of artistic, literary, and philosophical terms, with corresponding French, German, and Spanish terms. Comprehensive index of the foreign language words.

STEINBERG, S. H., ed. Cassell's *Encyclopedia of World Literature.* New York, 1954. First published as Cassell's *Encyclopedia of Literature,* London, 1953. Two volumes. Volume 1, part 1: histories of the literatures of the world from oral traditions to the present. Articles on literary forms, literary schools, contemporary trends, special subjects, and particular aspects of literature throughout all times and countries. Volume 2, part 2: biographies of writers from earliest times to 1914 (A–H). Volume 2, part 2: same (I–Z). Volume 2, part 3: biographies of contemporary writers, 1914 to present (A–Z). Articles and biographies written in a lively individualistic style. Entries followed by selective bibliographies.

Dictionnaire biographique des auteurs de tous les temps et de tous les pays. Paris, 1957–58. 2 vols. Contains surprisingly extensive, interesting appreciations of (particularly literary) authors of all times and countries, the more ambitious entries signed by reputable scholars. Many illustrations, references to sources, and significant quotations on these authors.

Lexikon der Weltliteratur im 20. Jahrhundert. 2 vols. Freiburg, 1960–61. Dictionary of twentieth-century authors, genres, and terms, as well as succinct comprehensive treatments of the twentieth-century evolution of national literatures. Distinguished international collaborators. Primary and secondary sources listed, with dates. Significant quotations from historians and critics often appended to specific articles. Some (catholic) bias. Comprehensive index of persons in vol. 2. Substantially revised and updated American edition in 3 vols. *Encyclopedia of World Literature in the Twentieth Century*. Ed. Wolfgang B. Fleischmann. New York, 1 (1967), 2 (1969).

Third Conference on Oriental-Western Literary and Cultural Relations. Supplement to *Yearbook of Comparative and General Literature*, 11 (1962), 119–236. Papers and symposia presented at Indiana University Conference (1962). See also *Asia and the Humanities* (ed. Frenz), Bloomington, Ind., 1959, and *Indiana University Conference on Oriental-Western Relations* (ed. Frenz and Anderson), Chapel Hill, 1955.

FRENZEL, ELISABETH. *Stoffe der Weltliteratur*. Stuttgart 1962. Dictionary of main motifs (Antigone, Don Juan, Medea, etc.) of world literature, with particular attention to German literature. Indispensable reference tool.

———. *Stoff-, Motiv-und Symbolforschung*. Stuttgart, 1963. Comprehensive review of research on themes, motifs, and symbols in literature. Index. Though main stress is on German literature, comparative research is not neglected. Considerable overlapping with Frenzel, "Stoff- und Motivgeschichte," in *Deutsche Philologie im Aufriss* 1 (Berlin, 1957–60), 281–332.

———. *Stoff- und Motivgeschichte*. Berlin, 1966. Theme and motif as structural elements of literature. Relationship to author, nation, time, genre. Review of research. Illustrations from German literature predominate, but many international examples given as well. Extensive bibliography, no index.

The Concise Encyclopedia of Modern World Literature. London, 1963. Urbane, literate (rather than factual) and uneven, but very readable. Accent on literature rather than philosophy and criticism, on the twentieth century, and on importance and availability to readers of English.

WILPERT, GERO VON. *Lexikon der Weltliteratur*. Stuttgart, 1963. Important authors and anonymous works of all times and places. Belles-lettres only. Literary terms, movements, genres, themes, and national literature accounts are excluded. Biographies, works, evaluations, primary and secondary bibliographies.

Sainz De Robles, F. C. de *Ensayo de un diccionario de la literatura*, 3 vols. 3rd ed. Madrid, 1964–65. Covers general aspects and terms (vol. 1), Spanish and Spanish-American authors (vol. 2), and foreign authors (vol. 3). Descriptive and (moderately) critical. Gives primary and secondary sources.

Hermand, Jost. *Literaturwissenschaft und Kunstwissenschaft.* Stuttgart, 1965. Review of (almost exclusively German) research on the reciprocal relations of literature and art since 1900. Index of names.

Encyclopedia of Poetry and Poetics. Princeton, 1965. History, theory, technique, and criticism of poetry regardless of time and place. National and ethnic histories of poetry (American, Armenian, Canadian, etc.). Consideration of relationship of poetry with fine arts, music, religion, philosophy. No proper names as entries (not even Aristotle).

Comparatists at Work. Studies in Comparative Literature. Ed. Stephen G. Nichols, Jr., and Richard B. Vowles. Waltham, 1968. Based on a rather loose idea of comparative literature, this eclectic volume offers a collection of disconnected essays on critical theory (Wellek, Guillén, Szili), theory of the novel (Oxenhandler, Gibian, Ziolkowski), literature and the other arts (Hagstrum), poetics (Levin, Block), and history of ideas (Fleischmann). Footnotes, index.

Thorlby, A., ed. *The Penguin Companion to Literature 2. European.* Harmondsworth, Eng. and Baltimore, 1969. Up-to-date, comprehensive, informative, and critical encyclopedia of continental European writers of all time. Good balance between biographical, bibliographical (primary and secondary), and critical coverage. Personal touch. Reasonably priced paperback. Criteria of inclusion and exclusion of nonauthor items are not stated and therefore confusing; included are Acmeism and Expressionism (exceedingly brief) but not Formalism, Romansh literature but not Roumanian, Symbolism but not Realism or Romanticism, *Athenäum* but not *Die Horen*, etc.

RUTTKOWSKI, W. V., and BLAKE, R. E. *Glossary of Literary Terms in English, German and French for the Study of General and Comparative Literature.* Berne and Munich, 1969. Sections on metrics, style and rhetoric, structure, genres, and periods. Index.

MAYO, ROBERT S. *Herder and the Beginnings of Comparative Literature.* Chapel Hill, 1969. Valuable contribution to an urgently needed history of comparative literature, restricted to French, English, and German comparatists (from the sixteenth century on) which Herder drew on, and to Herder's own comparatistic activities. Clear presentation. Quotations in the original language. Bibliography, no index.

2

ON DEFINING TERMS

EDWARD D. SEEBER

MOST TERMS commonly encountered in traditional literary history and criticism—for example, "dramatic irony" or "terza rima"—are adequately explained in special reference works[1] if not in dictionaries, and present no special problems of interpretation. At the same time there are many others, often deceptively simple, that are not susceptible of such facile definition, and it is to this more complicated order that attention is here directed by means of a few examples, practical suggestions, and illustrative references.

In specific contexts, terms may demand close study for different reasons; indeed, they sometimes must be considered simultaneously in more than one of the following categories:

1] *Terms that may undergo a change of meaning in different eras.* The adjective "Gothic" had, in the seventeenth century, a pejorative sense suggesting the phrase "of the time of the Goths"; it commonly meant "archaic," "uncouth," "barbarous," "ugly," even "formidable" (as in "a Gothic alp"). It was applied with similar connotation to Gothic architecture. These meanings persist through the eighteenth century: Shenstone, alluding to the intrusion of art into nature, used the phrase "otherwise night, gothicism, confusion, and absolute chaos are come again";[2] the *Encyclopédie méthodique* in 1788 belittled the "barbarous inflexibility" of Gothic artisans, the defects of their sculpture and paintings, and their "complete renunciation of nature";[3] and the Charleston (S. C.) *City Gazette* of December 5, 1792, spoke of "the Gothic inviolability in the supreme executive." But in the same century the term also becomes tempered; it means "that which is not practiced by fashionable people" or "old-fashioned," and is eventually associated with melancholy and nostalgia. This change reflects the growing interest in olden times and the so-called Gothic Revival, when many popular authors with marked antiquarian interests (Blair, the Wartons, Young, Mathew Lewis, Ann Radcliffe, etc.) stirred public appreciation of a hitherto despised architectural style, and transformed Gothicism into a much cultivated aspect of Romantic literature.

Similarly "nature" meant quite different things to Rabelais, Pascal, Rousseau, and Balzac, just as the bald precept "follow nature" was persistently followed, but variously construed, by successive generations of English poets.

2] Terms that may mean different things within the same era. In his *Essay on Criticism* Alexander Pope equated nature with common sense, reason, the universal, and the rules of classical composition:

> *Learn hence for ancient rules a just esteem;*
> *To copy Nature, is to copy them.*
>
> . . . .
>
> *These rules of old discover'd, not devis'd,*
> *Are Nature still, but Nature methodis'd.*

Within the same era, needless to say, "follow nature" and terms like "reason" and "imitation" were interpreted differently by the Classicists and the Romanticists. Another example is the term "natural religion," which had two disparate meanings in the eighteenth century: it was applied to similarities with Christian practices discovered by early explorers and travelers among primitive peoples, and at the same time it was, for freethinkers, a synonym of deism or religion according to nature.

3] *Terms that may have different meanings in different countries.* This group includes innumerable cognates that embody various degrees of deceptiveness. Experience soon teaches us that "Romanticism" did not mean the same thing in, say, France and Germany; that, with respect to form, there are important differences between the Italian and English sonnet, the French *ballade* and the English ballad, or English drama and the French *drame.* But there are more insidious cognates that call for constant alertness and wariness, for they present serious pitfalls even to those who profess some competency in handling foreign-language texts. Many of these are words that have preserved an original meaning that has become either lost or rare in the English cognate. Thus Italian *melodramma* connotes a *dramma in musica;* French *industrie* commonly means "dexterity," "skill," "ingenuity," and the adjective *fastidieux,* "tedious," "dull." Abridged dictionaries will, of course, supply most of these meanings; but they are likely to exclude others if they are archaic or obsolete, e.g., the primary sense of "a learned man" once embodied in German *Poet.*

4] *Terms that may mean different things to the same writer using them.* Some terms used repeatedly by an author must be studied carefully to detect variations in meaning or even contradictions in usage. Striking examples are "virtue" and "natural goodness," so common in the writings of Rousseau.

The use of "Romanticism" suggests that a certain number of everyday terms are by nature so complex as to defy specific and adequate definition—although this has been attempted repeatedly. Obviously a movement marked by sharp differences in method, subject matter, and personalities, in which one encounters, as in English Romanticism, such varied components as external nature, the Lyric Revival, medievalism, subjectivity, humanitarianism, melancholy, orientalism—to name only a few—precludes a simple definition.

Two other good examples are "Baroque" and "Classicism." "Baroque," widely discussed in recent years, began as a relatively simple concept and then expanded to a considerable degree; and its close study is now yielding a broader understanding of its meaning with respect to eras, authors, and literary productions. The full sense of "Classicism" depends, among other things, on a knowledge of the meaning attached to "reason," which is in turn associated with the concept of "common sense," "the universal," and "nature." At this point one is confronted with terms requiring further definition as well as the understanding of several basic assumptions that appealed to the neoclassic mind. One must account for other, related terms, for example "imitation" and "creation" as opposed to "invention," and even the derivative term "original genius"—a gift precious to the Romanticist who considers himself above all rules. This kind of circuitous probing is often profitable: Havens found, for example, that Rousseau's "natural goodness" is better understood in reference to its opposite, "natural perversity." Terms, then, must often be studied both in their context of a given moment and in their changing and altered meanings; and it must be remembered not only that Classicists and Romanticists sometimes used a given term in different ways, but also that both Classical and Romantic traits often coexisted in the same writer, as they did in Balzac.[4]

The older dictionaries, to which one may turn hopefully for insight into meanings, at a given period, of terms and other lexical matters, will provide remarks that are often interesting, occasionally useful, but rarely definitive. For example, *pittoresque* is not found in the 1734 edition of the *Dictionnaire de Trévoux,* though it appears in the 1771 edition as a term applied to painting—something invented by, or imagined by, the artist, relating to the disposition or attitude of his figures, their unusual or original expressions, and so forth. The same sources give curious and confused definitions of the novel, reflecting the reputation of this genre before Rousseau's day. According to the 1734 edition, novels are "livres fabuleux" containing stories or adventures of love and chivalry, invented to divert and amuse. "Novels are prose-poems" (Fontenelle); "novels are lies in the guise of probability, and ingenious fictions written to occupy the time of decent lazy folk . . . [the reading of which] inspires indolence and love" (Huet). Bourdaloue's sermon on worldly pastimes is cited for its fine passage condemning novel-reading. The expanded article of 1771 declares that "novels ruin the taste of young people who come to prefer their extravagant, wondrous elements to the natural simplicity of truth."

But caution is needed in using such works. The *Dictionnaire de Trévoux* was a Jesuit publication and, in many respects, merely a continuation of earlier dictionaries, notably that of Furetière, therefore one cannot assume that the articles are uniformly unbiased or even up to date. Similarly the eighteenth-century dictionaries that bore the name of Pierre Richelet, compiler of the *Dictionnaire français* of 1680, are unreliable sources for usage at that time. And the dictionary of the French Academy is notoriously slow in admitting new words: Balzac's coinage *humanitarisme,* of 1838, did not appear until 1931. One must remember that many concepts and abstractions have not, in the past, become matters of lexicographical record until long after they were well known or even commonplace. Gas, for example, was certainly known before the term was invented by Helmont in the seventeenth century, and humanitarianism was a familiar sentiment before the word itself came into being in the mid-nineteenth. Similarly, a feeling for the picturesque did not wait upon the dictionaries to give it approbation and currency, and its history is best studied elsewhere.[5]

It follows that one must cultivate not only the practice of scanning original texts, but also the ability to recognize a concept that may not be labeled by a familiar term. Thus a prose passage may reveal characteristics of the "prose-poem," as in the case of Rousseau's *La Nouvelle Héloïse* (part 6, Letter 7), where textual alterations were deliberately made to affect the rhythm, resulting in ornaments like the Alexandrine "Malheureux qui se livre à ton calme trompeur." One must be able to distinguish the Gothic in lines like these, from the *Faerie Queene:*

> *Low in a hollow cave,*
> *Far underneath a craggy cliff ypight,*
> *Darke, doleful, dreary, like a greedy grave,*
> *That still for carrion carcasses doth crave,*
> *On top whereof there dwelt the ghastly Owle*
> *Shrieking his baleful note . . .*

and, in the following passage from the first chapter of Samuel Johnson's *Rasselas,* the neoclassic feeling for the universal, for "nature" which is everywhere and at all times the same, as opposed to the individualistic, the particular, and the eccentric:

From the mountains on every side, rivulets descended, that filled all the valley with verdure and fertility, and formed a lake in the middle, inhabited by fish of every species, and frequented by every fowl whom nature has taught to dip the wing in water. This lake discharged its superfluities by a stream which fell with dreadful noise from precipice to precipice till it was heard no more.

The sides of the mountains were covered with trees, the banks of the brooks were diversified with flowers; every blast shook spices from the rocks, and every month dripped fruits upon the ground. All animals that bite the grass or browse the shrub, whether wild or tame, wandered in this extensive circuit, secured from beasts of prey by the mountains which confined them.

Turning now from particular terms to a necessarily rambling survey of a discrete group of words and phrases culled from English and French literature, we can look closely at some of the problems of identification, provenance, shift of meaning, and reconciliation common to the more complex orders of terms. Around 1728, following a sojourn in England, Voltaire wrote an amusing account of his visit to a tavern where he had met on the previous day a group of gay and affable Englishmen, now, gloomy and taciturn, their laconic remarks turned to the subject of suicide and the baleful effect of the east wind. Most contemporary French readers would have recognized in this scene the ravages of that common English affliction known as the spleen—although the term was not yet current on the continent.

In 1621 Robert Burton had published his *Anatomy of Melancholy*, a scholarly and exhaustive compendium of earlier views on the kinds, causes, and cures of those "black humours" that plague mankind. "Melancholy" is Burton's common term, subdivided into types such as "flegmatick melancholy," "head melancholy," "love melancholy," and "religious melancholy." Older writers, he says, referred to it variously as "a bad and pievish disease," "a commotion of the mind," "a perpetual anguish of the soul," "a kind of dotage without fever," etc.:

The most received division is into three kinds. The first proceeds from the sole fault of the *brain*, and is called *head melancholy*: the second sympathetically proceeds from the *whole body*, when the whole temperature is melancholy: the third ariseth from the bowels, liver, spleen, or membrane called *mesenterium*, named *hypochondriacal* or *windy melancholy*, which Laurentius subdivides into three parts, from those three members, *hepatick, splenetick, mesaraick*.[6]

The physiological connection between disorders of the spleen (or vapors arising therefrom) and human behavior was a matter of longstanding concern: the term "spleen," it will be recalled, was used by Shakespeare to denote a whim or caprice, hot temper, high spirit, or violent ill-nature. Sometime during the seventeenth century, "spleen" superseded "melancholy" and other terms as the common name for the "English distemper." "Only some fumes from his heart, Madam, makes his head addle," wrote Killigrew in *Pandora* (1664). " 'Tis called the spleen of late, and much in fashion."[7]

In 1653 Sir William Denny had labeled this affliction "the Dumps" and "a melancholy Fitt"; and thereafter, even when "spleen" was the well-established term, synonyms were numerous: on through the eighteenth century we find "black jaundice," "a wise distemper" (or "disease"), "vapors" or "hysteric disorders" (in women), "hypochondriacism," "hypochondriack malice," "the hipp," "fits of chagrin," an "infection," "tyrannical distemper," "perturbation of mind," "the disease," "the dumps" or "dumbs," "a fit of the sullens," "the mopes," and *taedium vitae*.

In France also the particular type of hypochondria issuing from *la rate* (the spleen) was recognized; indeed, the Latin adjective *spleneticus* had become French *splénique* as early as the sixteenth century, and Molière later cites "les vapeurs de la rate" and "le *parenchyme splénique*, c'est-à-dire la rate."[7] But the term "spleen," for the affliction itself, was slow in passing into the French vocabulary, in spite of numerous travelers and other continental writers who, by 1725, had widely publicized the "English malady." Its first appearance, as a borrowed substantive, was probably in the abbé Leblanc's *Lettres d'un Français* (La Haye, 1745), which made several important contributions to the current of eighteenth-century Anglomania. The word soon became popular in the many plays and novels that depicted the typical melancholy *milord*, and with Voltaire and Diderot (who used the form *splin*).

As in England, synonyms and paraphrases are also found, such as "la maladie anglaise," "mélancolie hypocondriaque," "affection vaporeuse," and, especially, "vapeurs," in both males and females. Among the more interesting terms identified with spleen is "consomption," defined by Guérineau de Saint-Péravi in his *Epître sur la consomption* (1761) as the English equivalent of French "vapeurs." Caylus, a contemporary, says in his story *Les Deux Anglois* that the English "sont sujets à une noire mélancolie qui dégénère en un mal incurable qu'ils appellent *consomption*." Diderot's *Encyclopédie*, article "Phtisie" (1765), defines "phtisie hypocondriaque ou hystérique" (also called "phtisie nerveuse" and "vapeurs") as a "*consomption* of the whole body, without fever, cough, or difficulty of respiration," and adds that the disease is prevalent in England "in recent times," as in France.

During the first half of the nineteenth century, the

terms "spleen," "consomption," "vapeurs," and "melancholia anglica" are very common; Vigny and later Flaubert use the English term "blue devils" (female vapors), and medical treatises introduce special and related terms like "lypémanie" and "mélancolie suicidique intermittente."

The frequent allusions to spleen in French literature of the eighteenth century concerned in part the English, and, especially after 1750, the French themselves; for they eventually acknowledged its inroads as a baneful effect of Anglomania, even blaming it for their supposedly increasing rate of suicides. It was with genuine anxiety that the abbé Gérard wrote in *Le Comte de Valmont* (1774): "What have we gained from this Anglomania, so contagious and so universal in our day? Spleen, consumption, disgust with life . . . [and] suicide, that barbaric craze which has become a system and a principle. . . . Fine presents, indeed!"

The unprecedented outpouring of melancholy literature from the end of the French Revolution through the Romantic period invites speculation concerning the persistence of "spleen." Its identification is both complicated and obscured by that convenient label *mal du siècle* which we now relate specifically to the pernicious *maladie morale* (Burton's "head melancholy") that infected the generation born or maturing in the midst of the disquieting events of 1793 and 1814 and influenced unquestionably the lives and works of Chateaubriand, Sénancour, Musset, Constant, and others.

At the same time, other strains of melancholy were pervading French literature and creating new terms: "le youngisme," from Edward Young's *Night Thoughts;* "le mal de René," from Chateaubriand (which, Sainte-Beuve said, merely superceded "le mal de Rousseau"); "le byronisme," from the poet whom Musset called "the great prophet of melancholy"; and "le werthérisme," from Goethe's novel. But anyone familiar with the frequent discussions, in eighteenth-century England and France, of the various causes, symptoms, and cures of the "English malady," can easily trace its robust survival in the first half of the nineteenth century.

For example, there is no plainer case of acute spleen than that of Chateaubriand's René (both in *Les Natchez* and in the later story). This is apparent from his oppressive melancholy and *taedium vitae,* his attempted cure by traveling (a commonplace, especially among Englishmen, for more than a century), his hypersensitivity to sights and sounds, his visions and involuntary cries, and his determination in the fall of the year (when suicides in England were allegedly at their peak) to end his life. Indeed, Chateaubriand's own René-like childhood and English influences, as reported in his *Mémoires d'Outre-Tombe,* are revealing: He studied English in his youth, composed his *René* largely in England, and returned to France "English in manners, in taste, and, to a certain point, in opinions." His early melancholy led to the most extravagant behavior, visions, and exaltation; he attempted suicide, and exclaimed on at least one occasion: "I have the spleen."

Sainte-Beuve remarked in an essay on Sénancour (1832) that *Obermann* (1804) reflects this author's "psychology, melancholy disposition, and ennui," and that this ennui constituted, in part, the *mal du siècle.*[8] It is generally agreed that Sénancour's melancholy was, indeed, personal, sincere, and intellectual. Yet the influence of Sterne, Young, and Goethe had been remarked;[9] Sénancour's "stupor, apathy, and torpor" contributing to his "great misery" have been described as a neurosis inherited from his parents,[10] and in 1837 George Sand actually referred to his "spleen."[11] Young Obermann, it will be noted, is in some respects a conventional splenetic type: Consumed with boredom, melancholy, and suicidal impulses, he attempts a cure by traveling to Switzerland, where his neighbors take him to be either a lunatic or a splenetic Englishman, and expect him momentarily to add another "beau suicide" to the village annals.

Raphaël, in Balzac's *La Peau de chagrin* (1831), is plainly splenetic, as is the hero of Lamartine's *Raphaël* (1849) with his dejection, desire to travel, and thoughts of suicide; George Sand refers repeatedly, in her letters and autobiographical works,[12] to her own "terrible disposition au spleen"; and many other writers occupy themselves with this affliction down to Baudelaire, whose poem "Spleen" (first published in *Fleurs du mal*, 1857) begins with the lines

> *Quand le ciel bas et lourd pèse comme un couvercle*
> *Sur l'esprit gémissant en proie aux longs ennuis,*

introducing the familiar detail of climatic influence, long blamed as a prime cause of English spleen.

It seems, then, that the popular term "mal du siècle," though quite properly associated with certain Romantic sensibilities discomposed by events growing out of the Revolution, may easily obscure and underrate other important aspects of melancholy. This *mal* had larger implications: If "la jeunesse a besoin de pleurer" [13] during the early nineteenth century, it is equally true that many youths assiduously cultivated *la mode romantique,* just as their forebears had made of spleen a "fashionable disease." [14] André Monglond not only refers astutely to Mme du Deffand, who died in 1780, as a writer who "offers us an early case of the *mal du siècle,*" but finds its "first form" much earlier in Prévost's novel *Cleveland* (1732); [15] and as early as 1827 Antoine Caillot recognized the broad implications of this term in an epitome of the *mal du siècle*. Certain conditions, he said, have produced in many individuals

> a sad, morose nature which makes them impervious to all that gentle and consoling emotions can communicate to the heart. Nothing pleases these unfortunates; everything, on the contrary, is for them a source of ennui and disgust. Unbearable to themselves, as to others, they seek continually to be avoided and to flee from themselves. But their imagination endeavors in vain to wander from object to object; always coming back to itself, it finds there only the same images that sadden it. They love only solitude, and solitude only adds to their black melancholy, the burden of which they drag about with them everywhere. . . . For a few years they drink from the cup of bitterness; and when it is almost empty, they throw themselves with barbaric joy into the arms of a voluntary death. This malady, which the English call *spleen*, and the French *consomption*, has become, since the Revolution, commoner than people think, and is possibly, in our land, the principal cause of suicides.[16]

In conclusion, these remarks support the view that the nineteenth century, with its striking new patterns of literature, is the crowning point of the involved and progressive history of the melancholy genre, in which two centuries of preoccupation with the spleen—often encountered under the guise of innumerable terms—played a large part.

Prior to the second quarter of our century, scant attention was directed to a better understanding of literary terms and to a more discriminating use of them—excluding of course the formalized terminology of academic areas like rhetoric and prosody. But ever since the publication in 1924 of Logan Pearsall Smith's exemplary study "Four Words" (cited later in this chapter) our critical vocabulary has been sharpened by burgeoning articles, special glossaries, and divers treatises such as William Elton's *A Guide to the New Criticism* (Chicago, 1953), René Wellek's *Concepts of Criticism* (New Haven, 1963), and I. A. Richards' *Principles of Literary Criticism* (New York, 1965), in which a number of important terms are defined and discussed.

An important counterpart of the matter treated thus far is represented by Elton's *Aesthetics and Language* (Oxford, 1954). This collection of essays by various authors emphasizes the need for scrupulous attention to the language of criticism—the employment of *all* words and phrases in a manner that is definite, concise, and readable. Novelists and short-story writers must of necessity and through self-discipline demonstrate both the desire and the ability to communicate intelligibly if they are to produce marketable manuscripts; but writers engaged in the more recondite branches of literature enjoy, it would seem, a somewhat greater degree of freedom that allows their language now and then to take a direction that readers may well find puzzling, frustrating, even annoying. A fair example of this is seen in a passage from Jacques Maritain quoted by J. A. Passmore, a contributor to the aforementioned Elton volume: "The music of Lourié," says Maritain, "is an ontological music; in the Kirkegaardian style, one would say 'existential.' It is born in the singular roots of being, the nearest possible juncture of the soul and the spirit, spoken of by St. Paul." Passmore's reaction to this kind of writing is a heartfelt "Oh, for the *Journal of Agriculture* on pigs!" which must surely reflect the view of all who support the movement to free the language of aesthetics and literary criticism from the confusion and obscurity that have plagued it in the past. This movement has been given direction and vigor by Elton's volume and by other helpful works [17] that show how words, when properly used, can become effective tools of thought.

The broad miscellany that follows presents selected examples of studies of common terms published in recent years. For other titles and other terms see the annual bibliographies of *PMLA* and *YCGL*.

Baroque

CAPUA, A[NGELO] G. de. "Baroque and Mannerism: Reassessment 1965." *Colloquia Germanica*, 1 (1967), 101–10.

CARR, C. T. "Two Words in Art History: I. *Baroque*; II. *Rococo*." *Forum for Modern Language Studies* (Univ. of St. Andrews, Scotland), 1 (1965), 175–90, 266–81.

HATZFELD, HELMUT. "Use and Misuse of *Baroque* as a Critical Term in Literary History." *Univ. of Toronto Quarterly*, 31 (1962), 180–200.

HEYL, BERNARD C. "Meanings of Baroque." *JAAC*, 19 (1960), 275–87.

ROUSSET, JEAN. "La Définition du terme 'Baroque,'" in *Actes du IIIe Congrès de l'Association Internationale de Littérature Comparée*. 's Gravenhage, 1962.

Burlesque

WEISSTEIN, ULRICH (see under Parody).

Catharsis

BURKE, KENNETH. "On Catharsis, or Resolution." *Kenyon Review*, 21 (1959), 337–75.

HILL, D. M. "'*Catharsis*': *An Excision from the Dictionary* of Critical Terms." *Essays in Criticism* (Oxford), 8 (1958), 113–19 (with comment by F. W. Bateson, pp. 119–20).

Classicism

MOREAU, PIERRE. *Le Classicisme des romantiques*. Paris, 1932.

PEYRE, HENRI. *Qu'est-ce que le classicisme?* Paris, 1965.
RANSOM, JOHN C. "Classical and Romantic," *Saturday Review of Literature*, Sept. 14, 1929, pp. 125–27.
VAN TIEGHEM, PAUL. "Classique," *Revue de synthèse historique*, 41 (1931), 238–41.
WELLEK, RENÉ. "The Term and Concept of 'Classicism' in Literary History," in *Aspects of the Eighteenth Century*, ed. Earl R. Wasserman. Baltimore, 1965.

Conceit

POTTER, G. R. "Protest Against the Term 'Conceit.'" *PQ*, 20 (1941), 474–83.

Creative

SMITH, LOGAN PEARSALL. "Four Words," *Society for Pure English*, Tract no. 17 (1924); reprinted in his *Words and Idioms*. London, 1948.

Enthusiasm

BABCOCK, R. W. "A Note on Genius, Imagination and Enthusiasm in Some Late Eighteenth-Century Periodicals." *N & Q*, 192 (1947), 93–95.
ELTON, O. "Reason and Enthusiasm in the Eighteenth Century," in *Essays and Studies by Members of the English Association*. Vol. 10. Oxford, 1924.

Expressionism

MITTNER, L. *L'Espressionismo*. Bari, 1965.
MODERN, R. E. *El expresionismo literario*. Buenos Aires, 1958.
SELLE, C. M. "Notes on Expressionism." *The Carrell: Journal of the Friends of the Univ. of Miami* [Fla.] *Library*, 3 (1962), 13–20.
TURBEVILLE, F. S. (see under Surrealism).

WEISSTEIN, ULRICH. "Expressionism: Style or 'Weltanschauung'?" *Criticism*, 9 (1967), 42–62.

Fancy

BULLITT, JOHN, and W. JACKSON BATE. "Distinctions Between Fancy and Imagination in Eighteenth-Century English Criticism." *MLN*, 60 (1945), 8–15.

BUNDY, MURRAY W. *Theory and Imagination in Classical and Medieval Thought*. Urbana, 1927.

KALLICH, MARTIN. "The Association of Ideas and Critical Theory: Hobbes, Locke, and Addison." *ELH*, 12 (1945), 290–315.

Futurism

FOLEJEWSKI, Z. "Futurism East and West." *YCGL*, 14 (1965), 61–64.

GERSHMAN, H. S. "Futurism and the Origins of Surrealism." *Italica*, 39 (1962), 114–23.

TURBEVILLE, F. S. (see under Surrealism).

Genius; Original Genius

BABCOCK, R. W. (see under Enthusiasm).

KAUFMAN, PAUL. *Essays in Memory of Barrett Wendell*. Cambridge, Mass., 1926.

SMITH, L. P. (see under Creative).

Gothic

CLARK, KENNETH. *The Gothic Revival. An Essay in the History of Taste*. New York, 1929.

FRANKL, P. *The Gothic: Literary Sources and Interpretations through Eight Centuries*. Princeton, 1960.

HOLBROOK, WILLIAM C. "The Adjective *Gothique* in the XVIIIth Century." *MLN*, 56 (1941), 498–503.

KAUFMAN, PAUL (see under Genius).

KLIGER, SAMUEL. "The 'Goths' in England: An Introduction to the Gothic Vogue in Eighteenth-Century Aesthetic Discussion." *MP*, 43 (1945), 107–17.

LONGUEIL, ALFRED E. "The Word 'Gothic' in Eighteenth Century Criticism." *MLN*, 38 (1923), 453–60.

Grotesque

BARASCH, FRANCES K. "The 'Grotesque': Its History as a Literary Term." *DA*, 25 (1965), 5923–24 (New York Univ.).

KAYSER, WOLFGANG. *The Grotesque in Art and Literature*. New York, 1966.

Idea

MCRAE, ROBERT. " 'Idea' as a Philosophical Term in the Seventeenth Century." *JHI*, 26 (1965), 175–90.

Imagination

BABCOCK, R. W. (see under Enthusiasm).

BOND, DONALD F. " 'Distrust' of Imagination in English Neo-Classicism." *PQ*, 14 (1935), 54–69.

———. "The Neo-Classic Psychology of the Imagination." *ELH*, 4 (1937), 245–64.

BULLITT, JOHN, and W. JACKSON BATE (see under Fancy).

BUNDY, MURRAY W. "Invention and Imagination in the Renaissance." *JEGP*, 29 (1930), 535–45 (see also under Fancy).

HAMM, V. M. "The Imagination in English Neo-Classical Thought and Literature (1650–1780)." *Harvard University . . . Summaries of Theses*. Cambridge, 1932.

Imitation

BULLITT, JOHN, and W. JACKSON BATE (see under Fancy).

CARAPETYAN, ARMEN. "The Concept of the *imitazione*

della natura in the Sixteenth Century." *Jl. of Renaissance and Baroque Music*, 1 (1946), 47–67.

Impressionism

SOMMERHALDER, H. *Zum Begriff des literarischen Impressionismus*. Zurich, 1961.

Influence

HASSAN, IHAB H. "The Problem of Influence in Literary History: Notes Towards a Definition." *JAAC*, 14 (1955), 66–76.

Invention

BUNDY, MURRAY W. (see under Imagination).
KALLICH, MARTIN (see under Fancy).

Mannerism

BOASE, A. M. "The Definition of Mannerism," in *Actes du IIIe Congrès de l'Association Internationale de Littérature Comparée*. 's Gravenhage, 1962.

BRAHMER, M. "Le 'Maniérisme': terme d'histoire littéraire," in *La Littérature comparée en Europe orientale*. Ed. I. Sötér. Budapest, 1963.

CAPUA, A. G. de (see under Baroque).

HAUSER, A. *Mannerism: The Crisis of the Renaissance and the Origin of Modern Art*. New York, 1965.

KUNISCH, H. "Zum Problem des Manierismus: Einführung." *Literaturwissenschaftliches Jahrbuch*, 2 (1961), 173–76.

SCRIVANO, R. "La Discussione sul manierismo." *Rassegna della letteratura italiana*, 67 (1963), 200–231.

Metaphysical Poets

NETHERCOT, ARTHUR H. "The Term 'Metaphysical Poets' before Johnson." *MLN*, 37 (1922), 11–17.

Myth

DOUGLAS, WALLACE W. "The Meaning of 'Myth' in Modern Criticism." *MP*, 50 (1953), 232–42.

Natural Goodness

HAVENS, GEORGE R. "Rousseau's Doctrine of Goodness According to Nature." *PMLA*, 44 (1929), 1239–45.

Naturalism

CARGILL, OSCAR (see under Realism).

DENNES, WILLIAM R. *Some Dilemmas of Naturalism.* New York and London, 1960.

DUMESNIL, RENÉ. *Le Réalisme et le naturalisme.* Paris, 1955.

LINDEN, WALTHER. *Naturalismus.* Leipzig, 1936.

MUNRO, THOMAS. "Meanings of 'Naturalism' in Philosophy and Aesthetics." *JAAC*, 19 (1960), 133–37.

POSSO, GIANNI M. "Le Origini del naturalismo contemporaneo." *Dialoghi*, 11 (1963), 256–66.

STONE, E., ed. *What Was Naturalism?* New York, 1959.

Nature

LOVEJOY, ARTHUR O. " 'Nature' as Aesthetic Norm." *MLN*, 42 (1927), 444–50.

MATTINGLY, ALETHEA SMITH. "Follow Nature: A Synthesis of Eighteenth-Century Views." *Speech Monographs*, 31 (1964), 80–84.

Priestley, F. E. L. "Newton and the Romantic Concept of Nature." *Univ. of Toronto Quarterly*, 17 (1948), 323–36.

Schinz, Albert. "The Concept of Nature in Philosophy and Literature; a Consideration of Recent Discussion." *Proceedings of the American Philosophical Society*, 68 (1929), 207–25.

Novel

Grant, Douglas. "The Novel and its Critical Terms." *Essays in Criticism*, 1 (1951), 421–29.

Long, Richard A., and Iva G. Jones. "Toward a Definition of the 'Decadent Novel.'" *College English*, 22 (1961), 245–49.

Originality

Smith, Logan Pearsall (see under Creative).

Parody

Hempel, W. "Parodie, Travestie und Pastiche: zur Geschichte von Wort und Sache." *Germanisch-romanische Monatsschrift*, 15, n.s. (1965), 150–75.

Shlonsky, T. "Literary Parody: Remarks on its Method and Function," in *Proceedings of the IVth Congress of the International Comparative Literature Association*, ed. F. Jost. 2 vols. The Hague, 1966.

Weisstein, Ulrich. "Parody, Travesty, and Burlesque." *Proceedings of the IVth Congress of the International Comparative Literature Association*, ed. F. Jost. 2 vols. The Hague, 1966.

Pastiche

Hempel, W. (see under Parody).

Picaresque

GUILLÉN, CLAUDIO. "Toward a Definition of the Picaresque," in *Actes du IIIe Congrès de l'Association Internationale de Littérature Comparée.* 's Gravenhage, 1962.

Picturesque

HUSSEY, CHRISTOPHER. *The Picturesque.* London and New York, 1927.

Pre-Raphaelitism

DE ARMOND, ANNA. "What is Pre-Raphaelitism in Poetry?" *Delaware Notes,* 19th series (1946), 67–86.

Progress

BURY, J. B. *The Idea of Progress.* London, 1920.

Realism

BECKER, GEORGE J. "Realism: An Essay in Definition." *MLQ,* 10 (1949), 184–97.

CARGILL, OSCAR. "A Confusion of Major Critical Terms." *Ohio Univ. Review,* 9 (1967), 31–38.

DEMETZ, PETER. "Zur Definition des Realismus." *Literatur und Kritik* (Wien), 16/17 (1967), 333–45.

DUMESNIL, RENÉ. *Le Réalisme.* Paris, 1936 (see also under Naturalism).

GREENWOOD, E. B. "Reflections on Professor Wellek's Concept of Realism." *Neophilologus* (Groningen), 46 (1962), 89–97.

LEVIN, HARRY. "What is Realism?" *CL,* 3 (1951), 193–99.

SASTRE, A. *Anatomîa del realismo.* Barcelona, 1965.

WELLEK, RENÉ. "The Concept of Realism in Literary Scholarship." *Neophilologus* (Groningen), 45 (1961), 1–20.

———. "A Reply to E. B. Greenwood's Reflections." *Neophilologus* (Groningen), 46 (1962), 194–96.

Reason

ELTON, O. (see under Enthusiasm).

MICHÉA, R. "Les Variations de la raison au XVIIe siècle. Essai sur la valeur du langage employé en histoire littéraire." *Revue philosophique*, 126 (1938), 183–201.

Relativism

HEYL, BERNARD C. "Relativism Again." *JAAC*, 5 (1946), 54–61.

Rococo

BRADY, F. "Rococo and Neo-Classicism." *Studi francesi*, 8 (1964), 34–49.

CARR, C. T. (see under Baroque).

KIMBALL, SIDNEY F. *Le Style Louis XV: Origine et évolution du rococo.* Paris, 1949.

SYPHER, WYLIE. *Rococo to Cubism in Art and Literature.* New York, 1960.

Satire

ELLIOTT, R. C. "The Definition of Satire." *YCGL*, 11 (1962), 19–23.

HIGHET, GILBERT. *The Anatomy of Satire.* Princeton, 1962.

Sense

KRAPP, ROBERT M. "Class Analysis of a Literary Controversy: Wit and Sense in Seventeenth-Century English Literature." *Science & Society*, 10 (1946), 80–92.

Situation

LANCASTER, H. C. " 'Situation' as a Term in Literary Criticism." *MLN*, 59 (1944), 392–95.

SPITZER, LEO. "*Situation* as a Term in Literary Criticism Again." *MLN*, 72 (1957), 124–28.

Stream of Consciousness

BOWLING, L. E. "What is the Stream of Consciousness Technique?" *PMLA*, 65 (1950), 333–45.

Sublime

MONK, S. H. *The Sublime: A Study of Critical Theories in Eighteenth-Century England*. New York, 1935.

WOOD, THEODORE E. B. "The Word *Sublime* and its Context, 1650–1760." *DA*, 26 (1966), 5421 (Univ. of Pennsylvania).

Surrealism

CHAMPIGNY, ROBERT. "Analyse d'une définition du surréalisme." *PMLA*, 81 (1966), 139–44.

DEL NOCE, A. "Interpretazione filosofica del surrealismo." *Rivista di estetica* (Univ. of Padova), 10 (1965), 22–54.

GERSHMAN, HERBERT S. "Toward Defining the Surrealist Aesthetic." *Papers on Language and Literature*, 2 (1966), 47–56.

TURBEVILLE, F. S. "Surrealist Theories of Literature." *DA*, 21 (1960), 2724 (Indiana Univ.).

Symbol

MISCHEL, THEODORE. "The Meaning of 'Symbol' in Literature." *Arizona Quarterly*, 8 (1952), 69–79.

Taste

ARONSON, A. "The Anatomy of Taste. A Note on Eighteenth-Century Periodical Literature." *MLN*, 61 (1946), 228–36.

HAVENS, RAYMOND D. "Changing Taste in the Eighteenth Century." *PMLA*, 44 (1929), 501–36.

HOOKER, EDWARD N. "The Discussion of Taste, from 1750 to 1770, and the New Trends in Literary Criticism." *PMLA*, 49 (1934), 577–92.

Travesty

HEMPEL, W. (see under Parody).

WEISSTEIN, U. (see under Parody).

Ut Pictura Poesis

FOLKIERSKI, WLADYSLAW. "*Ut pictura poesis:* ou l'étrange fortune du *De arte graphica* de Du Fresnoy en Angleterre." *RLC*, 27 (1953), 385–402.

HAGSTRUM, JEAN H. *The Sister Arts.* Chicago, 1958.

HAIGHT, ELIZABETH H. "Horace on Art: *ut pictura poesis.*" *Classical Journal*, 47 (1952), 157–62.

Virtue

SCHINZ, ALBERT. "La Notion de vertu dans le *Premier Discours* de J.-J. Rousseau." *Mercure de France*, 97 (1912), 532–55.

Vorticism

WEES, W. C. "Vorticism: The Movement and its Meaning." *DA*, 25 (1965), 6640 (Northwestern Univ.).
WEISSTEIN, ULRICH. "Vorticism: Expressionism English Style." *YCGL*, 13 (1964), 28–40.

Wit

KALLICH, MARTIN (see under Fancy).
KRAPP, ROBERT M. (see under Sense).

3

LITERARY INDEBTEDNESS AND COMPARATIVE LITERARY STUDIES

J. T. SHAW

THE STUDY of literary indebtedness has never given up its place as an important branch of literary research within particular literatures, and especially in comparative literature. However, its value and validity have been so questioned [1] that it has recently been on the defensive. Source hunting has been deprecated as having been too frequently practiced incautiously and as an end in itself. The study of literary influence has been under attack from several directions. Some consider the concept of influence "positivistic" and reject it on that ground.[2] Other, deterministic schools have rejected it: One contends that meaningful determinism is national-social-economic rather than international and literary; [3] another, arguing for determinism in purely literary matters, has maintained that the study of literature should be merely of the craft as such and that "historical necessity" in a native literary tradition determines all within it, including any foreign importations, and that hence the concept of foreign influence is meaningless.[4] Another recent interpretation insists that influence may properly be considered only with regard to the personality and psychology of the author as a person, but that his literary works are properly studied only in terms of the literary tradition, considered as largely autonomous.[5]

At the same time, studies of direct literary relationships and indebtedness continue to provide a staple of literary scholarship, and their place in comparative literature has hardly diminished, as any bibliography of recent literary studies will show.[6] Suggested substitute fields of research, whether of study of parallel manifestations, or of the "isms," or artistic analysis of particular works, or studies of themes and their treatment in various times and literatures do not remove the *raison d'être* of studies of direct literary relationships. Any serious study or analysis of any author includes consideration of the component parts of his work, their meaning and relationship, how they were suggested to the author, and what they mean to him and to his work. No one who has deprecated study of sources or influences has suggested that it is not of interest and value to know how Shakespeare transmutes materials taken from Boccaccio or from Holinshed. No one has argued that the popularity of Shakespeare, Byron, and Scott in Europe in the nineteenth century was not followed in various literatures by the production of works which it is difficult—to put it mildly—to imagine having been written as they were, either in form or content, if these English authors had not written or had not become known. Questions of biographical or social development or of literary genre or tradition simply do not adequately account for such relationships as those between *Don Quixote* and the novels of Henry Fielding.[7]

Some scholars and critics, including many who have studied literary indebtedness, seem to feel that to suggest an author's literary debts diminishes his originality. But originality should not be understood in terms of innovation. Many great authors have not been ashamed to admit that others have influenced them, and many have even paraded their indebtedness to others. They seem to have felt that originality consists, not exclusively or even primarily in innovations in materials or of style and manner, but in the genuineness and effectiveness of the artistic moving power of the creative work. The innovation which does not move aesthetically is of interest only to the formalist. What genuinely moves the reader aesthetically and produces an independent artistic effect has artistic originality, whatever its debts. The *original* author is not necessarily the innovator or the most inventive, but rather the one who succeeds in making all his own, in subordinating what he takes from others to the new complex of his own artistic work.

Direct interrelationships between literatures exist in a context of the reception and popularity of an author or authors of one country in another. The reception of foreign authors in a particular literature and time forms a direct and integral part of the literary taste and hence the shaping of an audience for a native author, as well as the native author's own artistic and critical consciousness. Elaborate and still usable methods of studying reception and popularity have been developed.[8] It can be traced through critical and other comment in newspapers, journals, diaries, and by mentions and allusions in literary works. It can be partially measured by the sales of an author's works, by the number and size of the editions published, and by translations.

One aspect of popularity and reception may be insufficiently taken into account—the availability of an author's works in a language understood in a particular country. For example, English literature can be directly received by Americans, and vice versa. Similarly, French literature could be directly received in Russia during the eighteenth and nineteenth centuries, and authors who wrote in still other languages were made accessible through French translations to the Russian public interested in literature. Thus English, German, and Italian literature were known to Russian cultivated society in the nineteenth century largely through French translations. An intermediate language—and consideration of what works may have been translated into that language, and of what changes works may have undergone in these translations—must often enter into the study of reception.

Particular authors or even literary movements may produce a non- or extraliterary effect upon a whole society or a significant part of it. For example, Voltairean, Byronic, or Tolstoyan modes of thought, action, or even dress may have a broad reflection in various societies of their own and later times. And this social action may contribute to forming the social consciousness of a writer who may then embody it in literature, whether or not there is a direct connection between his works and the foreign author's.

One author's reception may lead to that of much of a whole literature in another country. Byron's popularity in Europe had something to do with that of Thomas Moore and other writers of his time, and perhaps indirectly, in various countries, even contributed to the cult of Shakespeare in the nineteenth century. Turgenev's acceptance in the West led to that of Tolstoy, Dostoevsky, and of modern Russian literature as a whole. One may seek answers to the fascinating question why some authors are exportable while others are not—why Byron was so much better received abroad than any of his English contemporaries. At the same time, reception of an author or his works by an individual or national culture must be sharply differentiated from literary influence, though to be sure it may provide the impetus or intermediaries through which an influence may come to operate. An author could be quite popular in another country but produce no noteworthy effect within its literature.

Curiously enough, there seems to be no readily

available juxtaposition of the various terms which may indicate literary indebtedness, with an attempt to define them and discriminate among them. The terms which most need such definition and discussion appear to be translations, imitations, stylizations, borrowings, sources, parallels, and influence.

Translation is itself a creative act; the translator brings into his contemporary native literary tradition a work written in another language and often at a different time. Translations have perhaps been insufficiently studied as literary works in their own right because of the modern translator's usual attempt to give himself up entirely to the form and matter of the original work and to reproduce it to the best of his ability in the new language. Nevertheless, any translator to a greater or lesser degree adapts the translated work to the taste of his own time, and he modernizes the older work he undertakes to translate. Old theory and practice of translation admitted relative freedom of excision, addition, paraphrase, and change of form and often of style. And in any case the selection of a work for translation, if not the execution, is likely to reflect what Professor Poggioli has called the elective affinity of the translator for the work.[9] Thus translations belong not only to the study of the reception of a foreign author in a particular literature, but to the study of the literature itself. They provide the best intermediaries between the work of the foreign and native authors, and it is often the form and content of its transmuted, translated form which has the greatest effect upon the native literature, for in this form it is directly assimilable into, and indeed already a part of, the literary tradition.

In the case of *imitations* the author gives up, to the degree he can, his creative personality to that of another author, and usually a particular work, while at the same time being freed from the detailed fidelity expected in translation. Imitations have often been used as a pedagogic device in an artist's development. They have often been contemned by scholars and critics, but they may have independent aesthetic merit of their own. As Pushkin points out, imitations do not necessarily indicate "intellectual poverty," but they may show a "noble trust in one's own strength, the hope of discovering new worlds, following in the footsteps of a genius, or a feeling in its humility even more elevated, the desire to master one's model and give it a second life." [10] An imitation may be of an entire work or a part; occasionally it may be in the general style and manner of another writer, without specific debts.

Related to an imitation but perhaps best considered separately is a *stylization*, in which an author suggests for an artistic purpose another author or literary work, or even the style of an entire period, by a combination of style and materials. For example, Pushkin often stylizes to convey a particular mood or background. He slightly stylizes after the eighteen-century heroic manner to present Peter the Great in *Poltava*. Pushkin's only poetic epitaph for Byron is in his "To the Sea," where he in part celebrates Byron by having a passage suggestive of him, though the entire poem is quite un-Byronic and though Pushkin had by this time modified his early admiration for his English contemporary.

In the case of *borrowings*, the writer helps himself to materials or methods, especially to aphorisms, images, figures of speech, motifs, plot elements. One may discover the *source* of a borrowing in newspapers, reported conversations, in critical reviews, as well as within artistic works. A borrowing may be an *allusion*, more or less clearly pointing to the literary source; it may or may not be *stylized*. Many sophisticated authors—ancient and modern—have assumed that their readers will read them in literary contexts. The critic's and scholar's task with borrowings is to discover the relationships of the use of the material in the new work to that of the old—the artistic use to which the borrowing is put.

The term *source* is perhaps most frequently used to indicate the place from which a borrowing is taken; it would seem that in literary scholarship this use of "source" should be clearly distinguished from "source" in the sense of a work providing the materials or the basic part of the materials—especially the plot—for a particular work. The source in this sense may or may not provide or even suggest the form for a particular work. In the usual case the source materials and the form involved are quite separate. The source of Pushkin's *Boris Godunov* is Karamzin's *History*, and Shakespeare found sources in Holinshed and Boccaccio, but in each case the artistic use of the materials came from elsewhere.

The various terms cited above all indicate a direct connection between literary works. *Parallels* provide a further subject of interest and value. In cases where there may be some question of the direct source of borrowings, because of comparable materials being present in several available works, a definite source may be determined when there are sufficient exclusive parallels, as Professor Zhirmunsky has argued in demonstrating that Pushkin's use of the genre of the Byronic or romantic verse tale was taken directly from Byron.[11] In addition to this type of parallel, there are comparable manifestations in form or content in different authors, literatures, and perhaps at different times, and with no demonstrable direct relationship to each other. Juxtaposition of comparable works may have great interest and value in the criticism of each of them. These parallels may or may not go back to a common source. Often they are involved in literary movements and may be produced apparently by different literatures operating on the basis largely if not entirely of their own literary tradition, as in the case of Dickens and Gogol. The value of the study of parallels, as with other literary phenomena, is in the light they cast on the qualities and merit of the individual works; they may also be of interest in indicating similarities and differences in national literary traditions. When one studies parallels in this sense he nevertheless should consider the possibility of direct relationships. The author of a recent comparative study of Lermontov's *Demon* and Vigny's *Éloa* failed even to consider whether Lermontov was acquainted with Vigny's work, and hence whether similarities or differences indicate conscious reactions.[12]

An author may be considered to have been *influenced* by a foreign author when something from without can be demonstrated to have produced upon him and/or his artistic works an effect his native literary tradition and personal development do not explain. In contrast to imitation, influence shows the influenced author producing work which is essentially his own. Influence is not confined to individual details or images or borrowings or even sources—though it may include them—but is something pervasive, something organically involved in and presented through artistic works. In the case of Pushkin's *Boris Godunov*, again, the principal influence is not the source —Karamzin's *History*—but Shakespeare's handling of characterization, action, and the dramatic form. Literary influence on an author will result in his literary works as such having pervasive, organic qualities in their essential inspiration or artistic presentation which they otherwise would not have had, either in this form or at this stage of his development. The seed of literary influence must fall on fallow land. The author and the tradition must be ready to accept, transmute, react to the influence. Many seeds from various possible influences may fall, but only the ones for which the soil is ready will germinate, and each will be affected by the particular quality of the soil and climate where it takes root, or, to shift the image, to the shoot to which it is grafted.

Literary influence appears to be most frequent and most fruitful at the times of emergence of national literatures and of radical change of direction of a particular literary tradition in a given literature. In addition, it may accompany or follow social or political movements or, especially, upheavals. Thus, like all literary phenomena, it has a social and often also a meaningful political context, in addition to the literary one. When literary forms and aesthetics appear to be outworn, earlier manifestations within the same literature may provide an answer to authors' present needs, or they may discover abroad what exemplifies or satisfies their inclinations. In the case of emerging national literatures, authors may seek in form or ideology that which they can adapt or transmute for their own consciousness, time, and nation. Usually there will be conflicting domestic and foreign literary movements and figures; there will usually be foreign influences of varying kinds available for assimilation. For example, French, German, and English authors and literatures in turn and even concurrently influenced Russian authors and literary traditions of the eighteenth and nineteenth centuries.

Influence, to be meaningful, must be manifested in an intrinsic form, upon or within the literary works themselves. It may be shown in style, images, characters, themes, mannerisms, and it may also be shown in content, thought, ideas, the general *Weltanschauung* presented by particular works. Of course it is necessary to adduce satisfactory external evidence that the hypothetically influenced author *could* have been influenced by the influencing author; for this purpose, mentions, allusions, quotations, diaries, the evidence of contemporaries, and evidences of an author's reading must be used. But the essential test must be within the works themselves. Whether particular borrowings are interpreted as showing influence depends upon their effect and importance in the new work; but influence need not include any specific borrowings. Influence study can be particularly interesting when it can be traced through an author's development, as when Pushkin, at various stages of his career, acclimatized and adapted and later developed in his own way the genre of the romantic verse tale from Byron, the chronicle-play-tragedy from Shakespeare, and the form of the historical novel from Scott. Influence may occur within or across genre lines. There may be a juxtaposition of influences in a particular work, as when Dostoevsky in *The Brothers Karamazov* uses Schiller for the characterization of Dmitri, Goethe for Ivan, and *The Wanderings of the Monk Parfeny* for Father Zosima; but the total work is completely his own, enriched by the influences utilized.

The influence of literary works upon literary works is perhaps the most convincingly demonstrable type, and perhaps aesthetically the most interesting. In addition, there is influence upon the writer as a man. Here the influence may be from a literary or nonliterary man; it will usually be upon content, rather than directly upon genre and style, upon *Weltanschauung* rather than upon artistic form. As Truman Capote recently pointed out to an audience of Russian writers, a nonliterary man, Freud, has been one of the most potent influences on modern Western literature. Philosophers and thinkers have often exerted influence upon writers, from Plato and Aristotle, to Thomas Aquinas, Hegel, Alfred North Whitehead, and Karl Marx. Personal and literary influence may coincide, as in the case of Mallarmé and Valéry.[13] The international fame and influence of particular authors may to a considerable extent depend upon answers they provide—or are interpreted as providing—to the *Weltanschauung*, as well as to the literary tradition within a particular country and time.

One of the most complex problems in the study of literary influence is that of direct and indirect influence. An author may introduce the influence of a foreign author into a literary tradition, and then, as in the case of the Byronic tradition in Russia, it may proceed largely from the influence of the native author. But as the tradition continues, it may be enriched by another native author going back to the foreign author for materials or tonalities or images or effects which were not adopted by the first author. Thus Lermontov was influenced by the Byronic verse tale of Pushkin and other Russian authors, but then went directly to Byron for qualities which Pushkin had omitted or modified.[14]

Literary influence has a number of aspects which have particular manifestations in comparative literature. The first of these has to do with translations, which we have already discussed, but to which we must return. Even when there is a general public which can read a foreign work in the original or some intermediate language, the work does not really belong to the native tradition until it has been translated—until appropriate style, form, and diction have been found for it within the native tradition. Thus translations, not only in the conscious changes of a literary work which they often produce, but in the adaptation which any translation provides, play a special role in the inception and the transmission of literary influences. The direct influence is often produced by the translation rather than the original work. And in any case they may emphasize certain works of an author, certain sides of his creative personality, to the exclusion or at least deprecation of others. For example, that the first verse translations of Byron were Zhukovsky's version of

The Prisoner of Chillon and Kozlov's of *The Bride of Abydos* had great importance in the further development of the Byronic tradition in Russia.

The question of the influence of literary diction and style across languages has hitherto been perhaps insufficiently studied. Each age creates its own literary language, partly in furtherance of the native literary tradition, and partly in opposition to it. In imitating or translating a foreign author, an author gives himself the task of adapting directly the author's style and language to the needs of his own time, language, and literary tradition. In this adapting, the translator or imitator often brings something new into his literary tradition, not only in genre and content, but also in style and diction. Phrase, metaphor, similes, and general style and diction cannot simply be borrowed from another language, but must be reshaped to fit them into the native literary tradition.

A special problem of influence in comparative literature has to do with the time of reception and influence. In the nineteenth century Shakespeare influenced English literature as well as many foreign literatures, and there may be common points of contact in the appreciation and reinterpretation which resulted in this influence. Nevertheless, the influence of Shakespeare in France or in Russia in the nineteenth century was quite different from that in England, because Shakespeare had always been known and exerted a measure of influence in his native land. Revaluation is not discovery. Shakespeare fitted quite differently into nineteenth-century English literary tradition from the way he fitted into the traditions of other countries. The influencing author must be studied in relationship to the literary traditions where he wrote and where he exerts an influence. The literary background of each age and country varies, and hence the influence exerted by an author or literature will vary in accordance with what a given age feels it needs. A new element in a literature is qualitatively different from one that has been there and known, but has been relatively inactive.

I trust this brief survey of literary relationships has shown that there is still need for study of reception and popularity and for all the varieties of direct literary indebtedness including literary influence. With proper caution and safeguards, illumination can be cast upon authors, works, and literary movements. Perhaps the most fruitful immediate fields for further study are those of the recently or presently emerging national literatures. Sufficient data may become available, as has been recently suggested, to push these studies further back into the past; it has been rightly asked why such studies usually begin only with the Renaissance or even later.[15]

It seems to me that even the best studies of literary indebtedness have all too often paid insufficient attention to detailed study of the interrelationships between particular works. For example, Estève's monumental study of Byron in France, certainly one of the best comparative studies of reception and influence—with its excellent account of Byron's reception in France and its intelligent discussion of which aspects of Byron were influential upon what French authors—is nevertheless far less satisfying when one wishes to discover the relationships between individual works, when one wishes to evaluate or analyze the French work influenced.[16] In even the most frequently studied literary contacts, the general conclusions may prove accurate, but many valuable insights remain to be discovered.

The influences upon an author or a literature should be studied, for understanding both. Such studies should take into account what qualities were taken, what were transmuted, what were rejected. The center of interest should be what the borrowing or influenced author does with what he takes, what effect it has upon the finished literary work. The study of direct literary relationships and literary indebtedness can be indispensible to understanding and evaluating the individual work of art, not only for placing it in the literary tradition, but also for defining what it is and what it essentially attempts and for determining wherein it succeeds.

4

THE ART OF TRANSLATION

HORST FRENZ

THROUGHOUT THE CENTURIES grave doubts have been raised over the feasibility of translations of literary works. Again and again it has been maintained that it is not possible for anyone to combine in another language the thoughts, the emotions, the style, and the form of an epic, a lyric poem, a poetic drama, or even a prose novel. Yet the fact remains that the art of translation has been practiced everywhere in the world. Through this art many of the literary achievements of one country have found a hearing and even become "naturalized" in other countries. Their people have been able to share the experiences and emotions expressed in foreign works, and men of letters have been stimulated and even profoundly influenced by them.

Most readers must depend upon the translator if they are to know and appreciate the literature of the world. His role is more important than is often realized. One of the most striking illustrations is probably the case of the German Shakespeare translation commonly referred to as the Schlegel-Tieck translation. Between 1797 and 1810 August Wilhelm Schlegel published seventeen of Shakespeare's plays, and the remaining ones were translated by Count von Baudissin and Dorothea Tieck under supervision and with the cooperation of her father, Ludwig Tieck. The principle on which these translations were based was faithfulness. Schlegel, realizing the importance of Shakespeare's fondness for mixing poetic and prose elements, preserved Shakespeare's verse forms; he differentiated between rhetorical and conversational prose and attempted in many other ways to reproduce the original.

The Schlegel-Tieck version transformed Shakespeare into a German classic poet who was read, played, and quoted as widely as the German masters themselves. In his lecture on "Shakespeare and Germany,"[1] Alois Brandl cited as one of the qualities of this version that "the obsolete words and the quaint meanings of words which often puzzle his English readers, and sometimes even demand comment, are replaced by current phrases." "In our classical translation by Schlegel-Tieck," Brandl continues, "the meaning is put forth so clearly that, when I had to reprint it in a popular edition, there was sometimes not even one passage to be explained in a whole play—so perfectly had the Tudor words been recast in lucid and up-to-date German." Thus, a German reader and spectator might come closer to an understanding of Shakespeare than "a Londoner, who has no other choice than to take him in the original." Schlegel's poetic gift produced a work of art which, while it was faithful to the original, could stand on its own as an original work. He was an "Umdichter," a poet able to use his imaginative powers freely and at the same time willing to accept the Englishman as his master.

It must be kept in mind that Schlegel was the disciple of a great poet, Goethe, and the representative of an important movement, Romanticism. The romanticists worshipped Shakespeare, for they found in him a universality not only of content but also of form. The time was ripe for a complete transmission of Shakespeare's work to Germany, and Schlegel was the ideal translator to accomplish the task. Here was an act of cooperation—

Goethe's extension of the German language, the romanticists' interest in the Englishman, and Schlegel's talent as a translator. The Schlegel-Tieck version captured the German mind so thoroughly and satisfyingly that no other translation has been able to take its place. Many of those who have since tried their hand at translating Shakespeare into German have either used this "standard" translation as a point of departure or have limited themselves to improving the Tieck contributions.[2]

Today the name of the American poet Bayard Taylor is known more for his translation of Goethe's *Faust* than for his own writings. A true disciple of the German poet he undertook the tremendous task of rendering both parts of *Faust* into English and was the first American to try his hand at translating the second part. In order to do justice to the original, he delved into the mysteries of early Greek mythology, studied certain geological theories, and extended his research to editions and critical works throughout the world. Understanding clearly the relationships between the two parts of *Faust* he delighted in the second part because of "its wealth of illustration, and the almost inexhaustible variety and beauty of its rhythmical forms." [3] Taylor, like Schlegel before him, believed in utter fidelity to the sense of the original work of art, in reproducing the verse forms and even, as far as possible, the rhythm and rhyme. A poet in his own right, he was willing to subordinate his poetic powers to the work of his master and thus created a standard work which has lasted far beyond his own time. His *Faust* translation was not only recognized as a significant literary production at the time of its publication but also became the model for many later versions.

Miss Anna Swanwick thought it necessary to revise and improve her first translation of *Faust* by introducing feminine rhymes.[4] In the preface to his rendition Professor van der Smissen acknowledged his indebtedness to Anna Swanwick and Bayard Taylor for often "suggesting a rhyme or a turn of phrase, or pointing the way out of an apparently hopeless impasse." [5] In more than one respect van der Smissen followed the method employed by Taylor, and in the problems dealing with the art of translating he agreed with Taylor. He, like Taylor, saw the task in reproducing the original text, both as to the substance and form, "with utmost fidelity to the sense, rhythm, metre and rhyme, as far as is possible in transferring from one language to another within the narrow limits prescribed by a line of verse." [6] In his translation of both parts of Goethe's *Faust* George Madison Priest has adhered to Taylor's principle and preserved the metrical and rhyming schemes of the original. Based upon the conviction that Goethe cannot be improved upon, Priest's aim was "to change nothing, to omit nothing, and above all, to add nothing." [7] Taylor's influence is also noticeable in Alice Raphael's *Faust* translation (1930). After she had written at first in loose and rhymeless verses, her deeper penetration into the masterpiece seemed to dictate the use of rhyme and of Goethe's original meter. In the foreword to her revised translation of 1955,[8] she points out that she "learned to meet the demands established once for all time by Bayard Taylor," namely, neither to add nor omit lines, to maintain "the strictest discipline . . . in wrestling with the essential meaning of words," and to follow the original meters as closely as possible. Yet at the same time she proposes to go beyond Taylor by producing a "version that would meet the demands both of the modern reader and of the modern stage."

Just as Schlegel's Shakespeare translations contain for some modern Germans too much of the Romantic, Taylor's *Faust* has been found by modern Americans to be too Victorian in the use of idiom and rhetoric. However, both men have done invaluable service in presenting a great foreign literary figure to their countrymen. Their translations are still alive today, even if, as particularly in Taylor's case, only as an inspiration to new attempts at translation in the light of recent scholarship and new insights.

In England, too, a number of translations have found a permanent place and exerted their influence throughout the ages. Besides the Authorized Version of the Bible might be mentioned Chapman's Homeric poems, Pope's *Iliad*, Dryden's Vergil, and in the nineteenth century Edward FitzGerald's *Rubaiyyat*. The last work is particularly interesting, for in this case an obscure Persian poet was brought to the attention of the English-speaking world. FitzGerald's important place in the development of English literature has been secured not through any of his original works but through this translation, which, in the opinion of one authority, is "probably quoted more frequently than any other work in English literature." [9] In this country Charles Eliot Norton, editor of the *North American Review*, first recognized the quality of FitzGerald's work—without actually knowing the identity of the translator. He spoke of the "poetic transfusion of a poetic spirit from one language to another, and the representation of the ideas and images of the original in a form not altogether diverse from their own, but perfectly adapted to the new conditions of time, place, custom, and habit of mind in which they reappear." He called the *Rubaiyyat* "the work of a poet inspired by the work of a poet; not a copy, but a reproduction, not a translation, but the redelivery of a poetic inspiration," and concluded that "there is probably nothing in the mass of English translations or reproductions of the poetry of the East to be compared with this little volume in point of value as *English* poetry." [10]

FitzGerald concerned himself little with theological

or philosophical problems but found in the epigrammatic stanzas of the Persian poet some answers to his own feelings of doubt, to his questions concerning life after death, and to the complexities of modern life. The consensus of recent scholarly opinion is that most of FitzGerald's quatrains were either "faithful . . . paraphrases" or "composite" stanzas "traceable to more than one quatrain" and that the English poet after the first two editions eliminated most of those quatrains for which there had been no particular ones in the original.[11] He selected from Khayyam, regrouped the quatrains, and thus gave a certain form to the whole. Even if he created a somewhat different mood, as some critics maintain, there is no justification in going so far as to conclude that the *Rubaiyyat* is no more than "an English poem with Persian allusions."[12] Whatever changes FitzGerald made in transferring the *Rubaiyyat* from Persia to England and whatever method of translating he used to convey the ideas and the emotions of the Oriental poet the fact remains that he has succeeded in making this work known not only in England but also in the whole Western world.

These three examples cited at random reveal some interesting similarities. In each case, a poet attempted to translate another poet's work and made a great success of it. All three—Schlegel, Taylor, and FitzGerald—became well-known figures in world literature largely because of their work as translators. All three did a great deal of preliminary or supplementary labor in connection with the work they were translating. While the first two transplanted two giants of literature, FitzGerald brought a little-known writer of the East to the attention of his countrymen and proved how effectively the translator can open new lanes in the literary-world traffic. Furthermore, these illustrations are by no means exceptional. Translation has flourished during many of the great epochs of literature, and there seems to be general agreement that the Elizabethan age, for instance, "was also the first great age of translation in England."[13] A host of writers owe their standing in world literature to international fame which they have gained through translation, at times in spite of an insecure foothold in their own literature. The foreign reputation of Heine has kept him respected in Germany, even if sometimes rather reluctantly; it is abroad that the literary rank of Edgar Allan Poe has been established beyond doubt.

To be sure, some countries have depended on translation more than others. It is perhaps true that "German is a language into which others . . . can be more faithfully and successfully translated than into any other";[14] and that "l'Allemagne est le plus grand pays traducteur du monde."[15] But in many other countries the novels of Cooper, Scott, and Dickens, for instance, were more popular than any contemporaneous local fiction. The novels of Balzac and Zola almost immediately became the expression of the "modern" Western world, to the degree of making in many a country the growth of an indigenous *cosmopolitan* fiction supernumerary. Ibsen's fame in Germany and Europe had to silence the opposition at home; and the worldwide popularity of other Scandinavians such as Strindberg, Jacobsen, Lagerlöf, Undset, Hamsun, to what else can it be attributed than to the potency of translation? The case of the great Russian novelists is particularly revealing. Long before Russian was widely understood, Turgenev, Tolstoy, and finally Dostoevsky outranked native novelists in some highly literary countries.

The twentieth century is far from revising the trend. "Le xxe siècle, l'âge de la traduction par excellence," a French authority maintains.[16] Even in France, so long notoriously self-sufficient in literary matters, translation now exceeds 10 percent of the total printed production. It is hardly an exaggeration to assert that the "monde moderne apparaît comme une immense machine à traduire."[17] The task of the translator is increasing in importance and he is contributing in a large measure to a one-world concept.

One must also admit that the translator may do a great deal of harm in several ways. First, he may translate the wrong works, that is unknowingly or intentionally ignore certain literary achievements which are worthy of becoming better known. Here fads and fashions play a role, too, and a translator may submit to them in selecting his subjects. It has been claimed again and again that great literary works have a way of attracting attention abroad, but it is very doubtful that this optimistic point of view can be applied to literatures in less well-known languages or in culturally and politically less important areas. Also, ideological curtains of all kinds, political and economic barriers, and racial prejudices are formidable enough to interfere with the task of the translator which should be, above all, to acquaint his own country with the best literature that has been produced in foreign languages.

Then, there is the harm that can be done by a translator who distorts a literary work and thus becomes responsible for presenting an idea or a point of view or a mood which was actually not expressed by the foreign writer. Rabelais, for instance, has become known in the English-speaking world as "a bibulous, gormandizing 'philosopher' shaking his sides in laughter at the follies of humankind and the essential vanity of life"[18] as the result of Sir Thomas Urquhart's translation. By injecting an "amiable scepticism," by implying erotic undertones where there were none in the original, Urquhart created, according to Samuel Putnam, "a false or grossly distorted conception of Rabelais." Urquhart's difficult seventeenth-century style helped to obscure the real Rabelais whose works, after all, were best sellers enjoyed "alike by the learned and the unlearned of his time," whose sentence structure is "prevailingly short, simple, and direct." It was the style of the English translator which prevented many from reading Rabelais and encouraged a "cult on the part of a select few." [19] An aura was created which the original never had.

While in the case just mentioned it cannot be said that the translator intentionally distorted the original, there are other instances in which the translator is fully aware of what he is doing. When the German version of the American war play, *What Price Glory?* (German title: *Rivalen*), by Maxwell Anderson and Laurence Stallings was presented in Berlin in 1929, it did not, as most critics seemed to think, preserve the American point of view. Instead, it had become a play which used the Americans' plot as a vehicle for Carl Zuckmayer's own feelings against militarism, to express his ideas of the "Etappe," to give his conception of the experiences in the front lines, and to portray French and Jewish characters according to his own whims. Zuckmayer did the two playwrights a disservice by introducing his own ideas into the American war play. Interestingly enough, it never had the success that the British war play, *Journey's End,* experienced in Germany at about the same time; that play had been translated very faithfully. One may venture the conjecture that the German audiences found nothing in the American play they could not find in their own war plays.[20]

In the past, it has often been common practice for translators to delete from or add to a work indiscriminately, in line with their own religious bias or because they were shocked and embarrassed by statements which struck them as immoral or obscene. Peter Motteux, who continued the Rabelais translation begun by Sir Thomas Urquhart, was a "rabid Protestant" and showed his religious bias when he simply deleted a significant passage which shows the Calvinists in an unfavorable light.[21] In Edith Wharton's translation of Sudermann's play, *Es lebe das Leben,* a nobleman's line, "Wenn ich mit einer gesunden Kuhmagd Kinder zeugen dürfte," becomes "If only I could marry a healthy dairymaid." The suggestion of marriage to a dairymaid is made, I assume, out of moral consideration; it hardly conveys the caste concept of the nobility expressed in the original statement.[22]

Such changes for religious or moral reasons have been somewhat less frequent in recent times, but the history of the last few decades has shown many cases of distortions arising out of political considerations. I need only refer to the Russian translations of Eugene O'Neill's *All God's Chillun Got Wings* and *The Hairy Ape* in which certain changes were made in order to bring the plays more in line with the current social thinking of the Soviet Union. Thus, in the former play, the racial and economic implications were stressed at the expense of the emotional impact. In *The Hairy Ape,* the lack of concerted labor action rather than his own inner upheaval was made responsible for Yank's downfall.[23] It goes without saying that this kind of editing or "improving" is hardly justifiable.

Likewise, plain mistranslations made either out of ignorance of the foreign language or out of carelessness cannot be condoned. The recent translation of Hermann Hesse's *Das Glasperlenspiel* by Mervyn Savill (English title: *Magister Ludi*) contains so many errors that frequently the meaning of a sentence or thought is completely distorted. At the end of the introductory chapter, for example, the relationship of the bead game and religion is discussed, and Hesse tells us that the game was very much like a religious service, "während es sich jeder eigenen Theologie enthielt," which is exactly the opposite of the statement found in the translation that "it contained its own theology." And any translator should know that "eine Spielsprache" is a "game-language" and not "a game of speech." [24]

In his version of *What Price Glory?* Zuckmayer obviously shows ignorance of an American colloquialism when he renders the sentence, "parks his dogs in Flagg's bed" literally as "lässt seine Hunde in Flaggs Bett liegen" instead of realizing that "dogs" is slang for "feet." In this case, the result is amusing, but at times a mistranslation can have rather serious consequences. Instead of being a means of bringing two nations together, a wrong translation may have the opposite effect, may tear them apart. Aesthetically, wrong as well as bad translations do harm to the original author and to his and his country's reputation. As Gilbert Highet put it, "A badly written book is only a blunder. A bad translation of a good book is a crime." [25]

Perhaps it should be added that the real dangers of translation do not arise from mere ignorance or incompetence, that they lie not so much in the translator as in translation itself. The very prophets of translation made it plain that theirs was a problematical job. The author of the translation that has been read more than any other book in the world, St. Jerome's Vulgate, said "Non verbum e verbo, sed sensum exprimere de sensu," enunciating thereby the principle of nonliteralness which has been accepted for all higher translation. And one of the most powerful of all translators, Martin Luther, in stating "Man muss . . . dem gemeinen Mann aufs Maul sehen," found the principle most widely claimed as guide and goal: to arrive at the living common language of the day. Both principles have created more problems than they have settled. The main questions have always been: how far away from literalness can a good translation go? How far can the transposition into current speech be carried? These are the questions which every age has answered differently; but the most important answers for us must be those given in our own age.

Since in recent years English and American translations of the world classics have been appearing at an accelerated pace, it seems appropriate to study the comments of modern translators on the problems of translating into English. Fortunately, most modern translators feel impelled to justify their efforts and thus have created a substantial body of critical material. Let us therefore examine the various principles for the most widely used translations of the present, largely college, popular, or paperback editions—and the gigantic scale on which translations have invaded the colleges and drugstore counters may well be a very important phenomenon of our present cultural life.

Considerable agreement exists that poetry should be translated into poetic form, but there is less agreement on the question whether or not the same verse form, rhyme scheme, etc., should be used in the translation. Edna St. Vincent Millay in her introduction to George Dillon's and her own translations of Baudelaire,[26] feels very strongly that it should, pointing out that to most poets the shape of a poem is of real significance: "To many poets, the physical characters of their poem, its rhythm, its rhyme, its music, the way it looks on the page, is quite as important as the thing they wish to say; to some it is vastly more important." Therefore she feels it is unfair to force a foreign poet into a different meter or form just because the translator may be more familiar with that particular form.

Likewise, Dorothy Sayers for her Dante version chooses the original *terza rima* in spite of certain objections to it, simply because she feels that blank verse, "with its insidious temptation to be literal at the expense of the verse, has little advantage over prose and, though easier to write badly, is far more difficult to write well." Miss Sayers accepts Maurice Hewlett's contention that the translator of Dante can only choose between "*terza rima* or nothing." [27]

John Ciardi, on the other hand, does not follow Dante's complicated rhyme scheme, for he finds he might be able to preserve either the rhyme or "the tone of the language, but not both." His decision is based on the argument that English does not lend itself to rhyme as easily as Italian and that consequently "the language must be inverted, distorted, padded, and made unspeakable in order to force the line to come out on that third all-consuming rhyme." Although Ciardi departs from the *terza rima* and at times uses "deficient" rhymes—in order not to force "an exact rhyme" at the expense of naturalness—he keeps the three-line stanza with the first and third lines rhyming.[28]

However, Rolfe Humphries, in his translation of the *Aeneid,* does not hesitate to change Vergil's meter, for he finds that a loose iambic pentameter would be "the most convenient medium" to take the place of the Latin hexameter.[29] C. Day Lewis, another translator of the *Aeneid,* seems to show equally small concern for meter and form as long as the epic form is in verse which, he contends, will move a translator a little closer to the original.[30]

Theodore Howard Banks, who in translating Sophocles' *The Theban Plays* for stage presentation is particularly concerned with catching "the idioms and cadences of spoken, rather than written, language," [31] writes most of the dialogue in blank verse, while for some parts of it he employs "heroic couplet, heroic quatrains, or irregular rhymed stanzas" in order to indicate a change of meter in the original. On the other hand, the choruses and a number of lyric passages in the dialogue are reproduced in pairs of rhymed stanzas. The choruses, Banks explains, "are distinguished from the dialogue in two other ways. Because they are lyric poems, in which people are not so much speaking as singing, their vocabulary is somewhat fuller and more elaborate. Also, in them, the translation is of necessity less close, since the thought must be paraphrased or expanded to provide rhymes. Rhymed stanzas contrast sharply with the dialogue, however, and this contrast provides an aesthetic effect comparable to that of the Greek." Philip Vellacott, translator of Euripides' plays, tries "to represent faithfully, by one device or another, every idea, image, and association expressed in the poet's original words," [32] and yet he does not attempt the same meters Euripides had employed; rather he alternates between prose and verse, for instance, to make clear the distinction between dialogue and lyric passages or indicates a change in Greek meters by a change from rhymed to unrhymed lines. Similarly, F. Kinchen Smith in his stage version of *Antigone*, chooses prose for the dialogue—partly because he thinks that prose would give "greater faithfulness to the original"—and renders the choral passages into free verse.[33] Stating that their purpose is "to reach—and, if possible, to render precisely—the emotional and sensible meaning in every speech in the play," Dudley Fitts and Robert Fitzgerald, the translators of *Alcestis* and *Antigone*, find occasionally "the best English equivalent in a literalness which extended to the texture and rhythm of the Greek phrasing." However, they would "not follow the Greek word for word, when to do so would have been weak and therefore false." And so they feel justified in using "a more or less free paraphrase" to allow "alterations, suppressions, and expansions." [34]

Almost all authorities maintain that faithfulness should be adhered to in the process of translating, but they do not always mean the same thing by faithfulness.

They agree that faithfulness does not imply word-by-word translation, but there the agreement ends. It has already been pointed out that some, like Edna St. Vincent Millay and Dorothy Sayers, insist on preserving the original meter and form of a poem while others find it sufficient to translate into whatever verse form may seem most appropriate. Humphries maintains that he has tried "to be faithful to the meaning of the poem" as he understands it and "to make it sound" to the reader "the way it feels" to him. That does not prevent Humphries from taking "all kinds of liberties" such as transposing lines, cutting "proper names and allusions where . . . they would excessively slow down reader interest," substituting "the general for the specific or the specific for the general." [35]

The translators of *The Song of God: Bhagavad-Gita,* Swami Prabhavananda and Christopher Isherwood, too, maintain that their work is not a paraphrase, that "except in a very few difficult passages, it faithfully follows the original." And yet they admit freely that, without finding any particular justification for such a procedure in the original text they have "translated the Gita in a variety of styles, partly prose, partly verse" and that "the transitions from one style to another are quite arbitrary." [36]

"To translate poetry into prose, no matter how faithfully and even subtly the words are reproduced, is to betray the poem." [37] This verdict by Miss Millay is interesting in the light of some significant recent attempts at rendering Greek epic poetry into English prose. W. H. D. Rouse, E. V. Rieu, and T. E. Lawrence, three significant translators of *The Odyssey,* have advocated or implied that prose is the appropriate vehicle for the classical epic, since the modern prose novel has taken over the place in literature once held by the epic. Maintaining that most translations of Homer "are filled with affectations and attempts at poetic language which Homer himself is quite free from," Rouse feels that a translator must speak just as "naturally" as Homer did: "In these dialogues, and in most of the narrative, I have used Homer's words. I have left something out, but if you read the Greek words without prejudice, you will see that they are as natural and simple as mine. There is absolutely nothing of poetic embellishment in the words; they are the same words which ordinary human beings would use in these conditions . . . in the simplest English the same nobility and beauty is found when the thing said is noble and beautiful." [38] When Rouse claims that he wants to have his version judged "simply as a story," [39] he gives basically the same reason for using prose as did Lawrence and Rieu. *The Odyssey* is considered as a novel, "the first novel of Europe" (Lawrence) [40] and Homer is looked upon as "the world's best story-teller" (Rieu).[41]

While there is some justification for rendering classical epic poetry into English prose, it is more difficult to accept Rieu's contention, expressed in the preface to his translation of Vergil's *Pastoral Poems*, that more is lost than gained "by squeezing Virgil into the mould of alien design" and that the result would have been "less like Virgil" if he had "laboured to render the music of his hexameters in some traditional form of English verse." [42] H. R. Huse, prose translator of Dante's *The Divine Comedy*, does not think that the loss of rhyme and meter is very important and suggests that "rhyme and the division into a certain number of syllables (the meter) are less vital than the style or rhythm of the phrases." [43]

Most of those who favor the translation of poetry into prose do it in an attempt to get at the meaning of the original work. Bayard Quincy Morgan believes that the important message Goethe presents in *Faust* deserves a translation "which should endeavor to focus the reader's attention exclusively, or as nearly as the English language will permit, upon the meaning of the text." A prose version, he suggests, could combine fidelity to the sense with freedom of style while a verse translation is likely to misrepresent "the thought of the original" with the result that "in crucial passages . . . an actual falsification of the poet's intent" may occur.[44]

So far we have spoken only of the rendering of poetry into another language. What about prose literature? Are there no problems involved in the transmission of prose works? George Bull, translator of Benvenuto Cellini's *Autobiography*, speaks of "the extravagance of the original and its frequent changes in tempo and emphasis" and quotes finally the statement by Cellini's French translator, Eugène Plon, who spoke of Cellini's language as "the dialect of the Florentine people, so pure, so original, and so witty, that it defies translation." [45] Rex Warner finds Thucydides' *The Peloponnesian War* difficult–and at the same time pleasurable–to translate into English because of his "style which, in its sudden illuminations and in its abrupt strength, can never, I think, be reproduced in English." [46] Warner thinks that Plato would be easier to translate. H. D. P. Lee, however, in translating Plato's *Republic* faces the problem of "preserving the conversational atmosphere of the original dialogue" particularly in the very long passages. He encounters difficulties in translating Plato's terminology. Since a literal translation of moral and abstract terms might well be misleading or at least clumsy, he feels that a translator "must go behind what Plato said and discover what he means" and then express the thought as it "would be expressed today." [47]

Samuel Putnam saw two basic problems facing the translator of *Don Quixote:* "that of attaining a style which, like the original, shall be free of affectation–colloquial and modern without being flagrantly 'modernized'; and that of combining textual and linguistic fidelity with a readable prose." He maintains that an antiquated style and vocabulary should be avoided in a modern translation of Cervantes just as much as "any modernism that would be out of place and savor of flippancy." And while he, in his translation of Rabelais, intends to give "as faithful as possible a presentation of Rabelais' writings," he objects, here also, to "an unduly modernized version." He feels present-day slang expressions and colloquialisms would be out of keeping with the spirit of the work and would too quickly make the translation obsolete; at the same time, he rejects "unnecessary archaisms employed merely for the sake of effect." [48] John Butt, the translator of *Candide*, holds "the difference of economy and rhythm between French and English" responsible for some of the difficulties in translating. He finds that Voltaire's style needs to be expanded here and there so that it may not "offend an English ear by its very baldness" and continues: "Voltaire's economy in ligatures has an important effect on his rhythm. It allows him to vary the number of clauses and sentences which could be linked together in a rhythmical period. A literal rendering would sound harsh, and a translator must therefore abandon something of Voltaire's rhythm in the effort to make him speak modern English." [49]

Even a modern prose writer such as Balzac poses certain difficulties because, as his translator Marion Ayton Crawford points out, his long sentences are so "packed with meaning, crammed with metaphor and allusion" that they "require to be disentangled and unwound into even longer English sentences." Thus the conclusion is drawn that "a word for word translation of Balzac would be even more incomprehensible than *most* word for word translations" of other writers.[50]

What then is the primary intent of present-day English and American translators? It is, it seems to me, to present to their readers modern versions of the world classics, modern simply meaning easily readable and intelligible to the English or American reader. As J. M. Cohen puts it, the translator's task lies in "reconciling faithfulness to Cervantes with the writing of contemporary English." [51] Ciardi wants to write "idiomatic English." [52] Thomas G. Bergin's aim is "readability." [53] Rieu intends "to present the modern reader with a rendering of the *Odyssey* which he may understand with ease and read with appreciation." And as he explains in another passage, when he speaks of modern readers, he thinks primarily of "those who are unfamiliar with the Greek world." [54] Michael Grant, in his preface to the translation of *The Annals of Imperial Rome,* thinks the first task of the translator is to render the meaning of a literary text, "to convey, as faithfully as possible, the essential thought and significance of what Tacitus wrote." Then he adds that a translator should also attempt to reproduce "expression"—in the case of Tacitus to bring out the conciseness of his style—but that it is most important that the translation be readable. He sees no point in imitating Tacitus' style, if it should result in an "unreadable translation." [55]

Una Ellis-Fermer writes in the introduction to the translation of three Ibsen plays that her "volume attempts the impossible task of pretending that Ibsen wrote his plays in the English of 1950." [56] And L. W. Tancock, who espouses "the principle of fidelity to the *tone* of the original," goes one step further when he states that it is "the duty of a translator to try to reproduce on English readers the effect which the original had upon its readers when it was published." [57] Since it is in some cases very difficult to ascertain what the effect of a poem has been on its readers, this is hardly a criterion that can seriously be considered. Nevertheless it seems clear that what is meant is simply that the translated work should stand as a modern work, with modern vocabulary and word order, in the idiom of our time, and should *not* read like a translation.

If this survey of contemporary opinions held by the best practitioners seems confusing and often contradictory, it only mirrors the true state of affairs. Still, it is not quite the final word on our subject. The theory of translation seems to have come of age in the last two decades. A few books may be singled out as representative: Edmond Cary's *La Traduction dans le monde moderne* (Geneva, 1956); Theodore Savory's *The Art of Translation* (London, 1957); a German anthology entitled *Das Problem des Uebersetzens* and edited by Hans Joachim Störig (Darmstadt, 1963); and two symposia, *On Translation* edited by R. A. Brower (Cambridge, Mass., 1959) and *The Craft and Context of Translation* edited by William Arrowsmith and Roger Shattuck (Anchor Books A358, New York, 1964).[58] Edmond Cary starts out with the sentence "Il n'existe pas d'ouvrage d'ensemble consacré à la traduction." Fortunately, this is the only completely erroneous statement in an otherwise very well documented and most practical volume, which gives much attention to nonliterary fields of translation, as it behooves the Ecole d'Interprètes of Geneva.

In Savory's book one finds an altogether reasonable and scholarly exposition of especially the literary problems involved. Of particular interest is the page (49) where the author sets forth six instructions and their *opposites*, "because the only people qualified to formulate them have never agreed among themselves." Two of the contrasting points read as follows: "A translation should read like an original work." "A translation should read like a translation." "A translation of verse should be in prose." "A translation of verse should be in verse." Mr. Savory is extremely liberal in allowing for *all* the contradictions and justifying them all by the needs of different kinds of readers.

It is H. J. Störig's intention to prove the importance of the field of literary translation by offering twenty-seven essays by writers and thinkers, critics and translators from various countries and ages (ranging from Luther to Ortega y Gasset and Heidegger). R. A. Brower's volume represents the diversity of opinion on translation today;[59] it concludes with "A Critical Bibliography of Works on Translation" (by B. Q. Morgan) which quotes from some two hundred items and is in itself a comprehensive historical treatise on translation. The "critical symposium" by Arrowsmith and Shattuck is significant because the editors are connected with the national Translation Institute at the University of Texas (which, in 1968, began the publication of its journal, *Delos*). The book does not repeat the usual arguments concerning principles but contains essays on different translation problems, e.g., Robert W. Corrigan's "Translation for Actors" and Joseph Kerman's "Translation for Music" as well as Robert Fitzgerald's penetrating analysis of passages from his translation of Homer.

Mr. Savory's unprincipled principle, namely that a good translation is the one which the contemporary reader expects and accepts, is also shared by the majority of contributors to the American symposia. It is not an evasion. It is the necessary latitude within a field which the good translators have created for themselves. Moreover, it is only the profession as a whole which seems to enjoy it, not the individual translator. From all the heated controversies of past and present the fact emerges that the individual translator can translate one work only in one way, his best way, and that his best way is always a tension between the precise idiom of the original and the very personal idiom of the translator. The loving rivalry between the original and the new idiom can never be eliminated, nor can the tension between imitation and reproduction, between closeness and naturalness, between form and meaning, between poetry and prose. These things represent divergent ideals, but in translation they have to be reconciled, for translation is a matter of compromise.

It is not true, however, that the happy medium is the one and only solution. Even in this field one-sided ideals have produced fine results, although it has generally been true that the freest translations have won the widest popularity, while the closest are appreciated most by those who are able to go to the originals themselves. Moreover, the present trend toward the naturalized and the vernacular is not necessarily a perennial one. The most "contemporary" versions may well age the quickest. In general, translations date more quickly than their original. But apart from this, the natural revolution of taste should cause a future generation to prefer translations that transmit a maximum of the historic, or the exotic, to relish the strange originalness (Ezra Pound excels in this type) rather than the slick naturalization.

In the last few decades we have become increasingly concerned with historical antecedents and theoretical complexities of the translator's work. Perhaps Dryden would even today be right to complain "that there is so little Praise and so small Encouragement for so considerable a part of Learning." But the theoretical attention has certainly increased enormously, in quantity, and this development is by no means confined to the West.[60] As with everything in the field of the arts, there is no straight progress in quality. It would take a good deal of complacency to proclaim that our age is producing the best translations. It would hardly be more safe to maintain that it has reached new clarity or new validity in formulating its theories. The impression is rather that of a greater diversity and greater tolerance of viewpoints.

In conclusion, let us ask if there is any justification for calling translating an art. It is clear that a translator must bring sympathy and understanding to the work he is to translate. He must be the original author's most intimate, most exact, in short, his best reader. But he must do more than read. He must attempt to see what the author saw, to hear what he heard, to dig into his own life in order to experience anew what the author experienced. No nation sees even a simple incident in the same way as another and thus a translator has to express a phrase, an event, a situation as it should be said in his own language. At times he may be able to stay close to the foreign word, but what is more important is that he be able to imagine the situation—that he understand what a German translator has called the "lebendige Zusammenhang." [61] The translator as well as the writer must be sensitive to the mythological, historical, and social traditions reflected in a language and must use words to convey not only sounds but also rhythm, gesture, expression, melody, color, and association.

However, it should be pointed out that translating is neither a creative art nor an imitative art, but stands somewhere between the two. It is not creative because it does not follow the inspirations of the translator, but rather undertakes to create in the manner of another that which is already created. But neither is it an imitative art, for it must not only convey the idea of the work translated, but must also transform it.[62] The translator must be creative, a "maker"; at the same time, he must submit to the reality of the writer whom he is translating. Thus translating is a matter of continuous subconscious association with the original, a matter of meditation. Two spheres of languages move closer together through the medium of the translator to fuse at the moment of the contact into a new form, a new *Gestalt*. Here we recognize signs of an artistic process. The fact that the perfect fusion is not always reached should not prevent us from calling translating an art. After all, in the other arts there are amateurs, craftsmen, and masters, too.

André Gide has expressed the point of view that every creative writer owes it to his country to translate at least one foreign work, to which his talent and his temperament are particularly suited, and thus to enrich his own literature.[63] Let us hope that our present writers will feel obligated to follow this dictum. Only then will the position of the translator become more respected, will the quality of translations improve, and we will be less hesitant to speak of translating as an art.

5

LITERATURE AND PSYCHOLOGY

LEON EDEL

LITERATURE AND PSYCHOLOGY—and in particular psychoanalysis—have come to recognize in our century that they stand upon common ground. Both are concerned with human motivations and behavior and with man's capacity to create myths and to use symbols. In this process, both have become involved in the study of the subjective side of man. With the incorporation of psychoanalysis into psychology, that is the study of the unconscious from the symbols it projects, literature has found itself calling increasingly upon the knowledge derived from Sigmund Freud's explorations of the psyche at the turn of the century. Any examination of literature and psychology must concern itself alike with the direct fertilization of imaginative writing by psychoanalysis and the use which literary criticism and biography have made of the psychological and psychoanalytical tools.

Man's observation of his inner self and his emotions is as old as Aristotle. But it was not until the Romantic Movement that creative artists showed a deeper awareness of the existence of an unconscious dream-making faculty in the poet. Rousseau, in seeking to recover and examine his early experience; Goethe, in his belief that fiction must occupy itself with the inner thoughts of man; Blake, with his personal mythology and his symbolic sense; Coleridge, in perceiving man's involuntary "flights of lawless speculation"—that is day-dream as well as night-dream—and his "modes of inmost being"—all these writers found themselves by this process engaged in psychological exploration. German romantic critics, such as Friedrich Schlegel or Jean Paul, in searching for the laws of man's nature which result in the writing of poetry, were pursuing, on a critical level, similar ends. Balzac, in his introduction to the *Comédie Humaine,* recognized that there existed "phenomena of brain and nerves which prove the existence of an undiscovered world of psychology," and in this country Hawthorne spoke of the "topsy-turvy commonwealth of sleep." The American novelist expressed the belief that modern psychology would reduce the dream worlds to a system "instead of rejecting them as altogether fabulous." During the nineteenth century the works of Dostoevsky, Strindberg, Ibsen, and Henry James, showed a profound awareness of unconscious motivation in human beings akin to the insights of Coleridge: while the Symbolist movement in France, with its insistence on impressionism and intuition, and its attachment to sensory experience anticipated observations of the psychologists. But it was not until 1900, with the publication of Sigmund Freud's *The Interpretation of Dreams,* that students of literature began to recognize the relation between the poet's dream-work and his actual creativity.

In subsequent years, Freud's writings on certain non-literary problems served to illuminate such questions as wit and its relation to the Unconscious, the concept of wish-fulfillment, the problems of neurosis and the associative character of symbols—all applicable to literary study. Even more important for literary criticism and biography were his actual writings on the nature of art and the artist (collected in 1924 under the title *Psychoanalytische Studien an Werken der Dichtung und Kunst*). These included his psychoanalytic study of a minor novel by Wilhelm Jensen,

Gradiva, his essay on Leonardo da Vinci, with its speculation on a memory of Leonardo's childhood, and his study of Dostoevsky and parricide. Freud believed that art represents an attempt to gratify certain wishes in the artist; that it is a kind of "love affair" with the world, a quest for approval and acceptance, but that the artist in turn gratifies certain universal desires in his audience. He thus extended the concept of katharsis. Freud conceived of art as "an intermediate territory between the wish-denying reality and the wish-fulfilling world of fantasy." However, he always affirmed that psychoanalysis cannot explain the mysteries of creation.

Freud's view of creativity is now recognized to have been limited and speculative. The development of ego psychology has shown how artists use their art to confront and resolve states of disequilibrium in their inner being; and Ernst Kris's important concept of "regression in the service of the ego" suggests that art can often serve as a creative impulse leading to unconscious "self-therapy," even as dreams have been shown to play a role in resolving inner conflicts and anxieties. Art thus is not necessarily a product of neurosis, as Freud in essence postulated, but may even be an expression of the artist's will to health. Freud's essays on literature are the brilliant speculations of a humane healer; they suffer however from having their boundaries within a therapeutic system. This therapeutic approach continues to obscure the fundamental relation between literature and psychology.

As early as 1910 Wilhelm Stekel in *Dichtung und Neurose* began the application of Freud's ideas to artistic creativity, with the artist consistently treated as a patient in need of therapy. Notable exponents of "applied psychoanalysis" have been C. G. Jung, Otto Rank, Ernest Jones, Hans Sachs, Oskar Pfister, Ernst Kris, Franz Alexander, Erich Fromm, Phyllis Greenacre, Erik Erikson, while in the camp of literature are to be found such diverse figures as Louis Cazamian, Charles Baudouin, Gaston Bachelard, Robert Graves, and Northrop Frye. In the United States Van Wyck Brooks, Joseph Wood Krutch, and Ludwig Lewisohn used primitive Freudian ideas; and in more recent decades Edmund Wilson, Kenneth Burke, Frederick C. Crews, and Lionel Trilling, among others have adapted psychoanalytic concepts to criticism. Leon Edel has sought to reconcile the two disciplines in the writing of literary biography.

The most direct early influence of psychoanalysis on literature and literary experiment is to be found in the surrealist movement. André Breton, its founder, came under Freud's influence during the First World War. After an interview in Vienna with Freud, Breton gave up medical studies to devote himself to exploring the role of the unconscious in art. The name *surrealism* was given by him to his concept of a marriage between dream states and reality to form what he believed was an "absolute reality." Surrealism concerned itself with "tapping" the unconscious—recording of dream states, automatic writing and exploration of the hypnagogic movement, that is the attempt to capture the half-formed inchoate fantasies of falling asleep. Literary historians have pointed out that surrealism began as an inquiry into the involuntary poetic imagination and ended as a study of "total subjectivity." Language was considered as the artist's personal property and, as with abstract painting, the writers dealt with personal symbols. The external world was often denied at the expense of the inner world of the individual. Freud opposed this application of psychoanalysis to art, pointing out that the unconscious merely contains the raw materials of art; these still must be submitted to conscious disciplines. The artist, Freud said, knows how to make his works "lose what is too personal . . . and to make it possible for others to share in the enjoyment of them."

Parallel to the early Freudian explorations of the role

of the unconscious in art, what might be called man's inner consciousness, we find analogous explorations undertaken on the ground of literature in the so-called "stream of consciousness" or "internal monologue" writers—certain novelists in various countries who tried to tell their stories "from the inside" by lodging the reader within the thoughts of the character. The reader was thus made a direct participant in the mental and sensory experience of the fictitious personality.

This represented, in the novel, an extraordinary revolution in narrative technique: Time becomes "psychological," since the reader is always experiencing the thoughts of the character at the very moment of experience, that is in present time. The material, moreover, is presented without the order or chronology of the conventional novel, the data being given in the disordered state in which they come into consciousness through the operation of sensory stimuli, memory, association. The result, in terms of narration, was the removal of the omniscient author from the actual work. The reader moreover is required to deduce the story and the characters from the mental and emotional data furnished, without the author's seeming directly to assist in the progress of the story. The novel of subjectivity was influenced in part by the writings of Henri Bergson and notably his exploration of human time (as distinct from mechanical time) and the processes of memory. In the United States, William James's *Principles of Psychology* offered certain illuminating pages on the psychology of thought. It was he who first employed the metaphor "stream of consciousness." While these philosophical and psychological observations and theories were being advanced, the French and German symbolists, stimulated by the use of the thematic material in the Wagnerian operas, had attempted to use language associatively and evocatively in order to give verbal representation of what might be termed the thematic material of the consciousness, including the operation of the senses. This resulted in many literary attempts to capture momentary experience and to frame and preserve these moments in language. The difference between "stream of consciousness" or "internal monologue" and the soliloquies of the classic dramas was that the conventional monologue was wholly intellectual and given in a logical and ordered sequence, whereas the Symbolists and their successors sought to convey the actual "flow" of consciousness, and to create an illusion of thought with the impingement of external stimuli upon the inner man—in its unsorted condition: the flotsam and jetsam as it might be found in the "stream" of the subjective life.

The earliest attempt to tell a story wholly "from within" is now regarded to have been made by Édouard Dujardin in his 1888 experiment, *Les lauriers sont coupés*, a work which he said was inspired by Richard Wagner's use of the leitmotiv in his music. So, in thought, he explained, themes occur and recur and these can be set down in a language designed to capture the innermost thoughts, those which he believed to be closest to the unconscious. In his seminal essay on the art of fiction (1884), Henry James had echoed the ideas of Goethe and urged upon novelists the recreation of the "atmosphere of the mind."

In England, on the eve of the First World War, Dorothy M. Richardson began writing a long subjective novel which she entitled *Pilgrimage*. She arranged it in twelve parts, each published separately between 1915 and 1938, and then brought out the entire work in four volumes. A thirteenth part was published posthumously in 1967. In this long novel the reader, if he can translate himself into the mind of the protagonist, is posted wholly in the consciousness of a woman named Miriam Henderson whose pilgrimage, mental and emotional, takes her from her adolescence to her middle years. Miss Richardson's effort, less searching and imaginative, yet of unfailing realism, paralleled that of Marcel Proust in France. His novel, however, was not so much stream of consciousness or internal monologue as a continual probing of memory and association and their relation to human time—carried out by a first-person narrator.

The fountainhead of the subjective movement in fiction was James Joyce, the Irish novelist, whose *A Portrait of the Artist as a Young Man* projected the developing mind and consciousness of the artist on five distinct levels: sensation, emotion, physical passion, religious passion, and finally the level of intellectual awareness. Told with a remarkable symbolic use of language, this novel represented a turning point in modern English fiction. It was followed by *Ulysses* in 1922 in which Joyce's verbal mastery enabled him to create a series of streams of consciousness of certain individuals in Dublin during a single day. At the same time he used the Odyssey myth to represent modern man's voyage and adventures during the one day in the one city. The book had a profound influence upon such writers as Virginia Woolf and William Faulkner during the late 1920's. Joyce's final work, *Finnegans Wake* in 1939, derived from the Jungian hypothesis of racial memory and the "collective unconscious." It is an attempt to suggest the cyclical nature of history, building upon the postulates of Giambattista Vico, and the role of myth and symbol as an ever-recurring and repetitive phenomenon in human life. *Finnegans Wake* is the only work of fiction—and it might be argued whether it can actually be called a novel—in the whole of literature in which its four principal characters, H. C. Earwicker (Here Comes Everybody), his wife and two children, are asleep from beginning to end. Around their sleeping figures is the swirl of all time and all history; the Liffey river at their doorstep is in reality all rivers, and they are also Adam and Eve and Cain and Abel, the eternal family. In this way James Joyce produced a book which is a kind of composite of all myths and that portion of eternity in which thinking man, historically aware, functions. By that token the book is poem-epic-drama-novel rolled into one, like its characters and the mythic time-stuff of its texture.

While the novel of the "inner vision" achieved its particular technical development at the hands of Joyce, analogous experiments had been carried out in other literatures. In Vienna, Arthur Schnitzler had experimented with a modified internal monologue and in his *Fräulein Else,* both in its technique and the substance of the story, unravels a psychotic episode through the inner vision of the person who suffers it. Alfred Döblin, in *Alexanderplatz,* was the chief exponent in Germany of the Joycean experiments; and imitators have been legion during the succeeding decades.

This "inward turning" in literature, in its first phase, must be recognized as having occurred largely without the benefit of psychoanalysis. It paralleled rather than derived from the Freudian development and influence. But there came a moment after the First World War when literature and psychology increasingly erased the boundaries between them, and psychoanalysis began directly to fertilize imaginative writing. Thus Italo Svevo's *La Coscienza di Zeno* written in Trieste (Svevo was a personal friend of James Joyce) is an account of a psychoanalysis. There are signs in the novels of William Faulkner of his direct exposure to certain psychological ideas. In *Light in August,* we have what might be considered a textbook account of the protagonist's "conditioning." During the 1920's one of the most successful plays produced in New York was *Strange Interlude* in which the characters, through continual soliloquizing, reveal to us their inner thoughts. O'Neill followed this with a distinctly Freudian play, *Mourning Becomes Electra,* applying primitive pychoanalysis to a New

England version of the Sophoclean tragedy. It showed also, as much of O'Neill's work did, exposure to the psychological plays of a pre-Freudian dramatist, August Strindberg.

More directly, the work of Thomas Mann derived much from Freud. The German master acknowledged his debt in an essay "Freud and the Future" published in 1936 in which he discussed certain of the ideas and themes used by him in the Joseph novels which stemmed from the psychoanalytic movement. But where Mann used Freud as illumination of the romantic self-discovery of man, Franz Kafka found in him the means of constructing eerie writings which contain some of the macabre qualities of a Poe and the grotesqueries of a Gogol. Kafka hit upon the idea of treating subjective material as if it were wholly objective: his narratives of dream states are told as if the dream had actually occurred in reality. The result is the creation of an often terrible sense of day-nightmare, rendered acutely vivid by the matter-of-fact method of narration.

It would be a large undertaking to chronicle the full impact of the psychoanalytic movement upon contemporary literature. Few writers of any eminence have escaped being exposed directly or indirectly to some of its ideas. Certain writers have actually had the experience of analysis; most, however, have imbibed psychoanalytic ideas by reading the leading theorists and the numerous commentaries and popularizations.

Psychoanalysis has contributed important aids to three facets of literary study: 1] to criticism itself, 2] to the study of the creative process in literature, and 3] to the writing of biography. In addition it is helping to illuminate a tangential literary problem which belongs essentially to the fields of aesthetics and sociology: the relation of the reader to the work.

1] Psychology and criticism. While psychology can be applied with considerable success in biography, it is more difficult to use it in literary criticism. Most psychological critics begin with the study of a given work but all too soon end by discussing it as a product of a given personality—an extended dream or fantasy of its author. In criticism, however, it is possible for psychology to be used in the analysis of the human situations and characters which have been created in fiction and drama; and also in the study of forms of metaphor and the symbolic imagination particularly in relation to the emotions as expressed in poetry. Certain psychological concepts have in a quiet and pervasive way been taken over in the analysis of poetry; it must be remembered that the exploration of meaning by I. A. Richards or of ambiguity by William Empson have their roots in the psychological recognition earlier of man's ambivalence and his ability to create a personal iconography.

A) Seen in this light, Ernest Jones's reading of Hamlet's "oedipal" problem in his essay on *Hamlet and Oedipus,* while an imaginative piece of extrapolation, may be regarded as perhaps too speculative and too limited to explain the full appeal and universality of Shakespeare's play. The danger in this kind of reconstruction resides in treating characters composed of language and emotion as if they existed in flesh and blood. The psychology within a given work must maintain an illusion of reality: and it is useful to see Raskolnikov in *Crime and Punishment* as an embodiment of irrational violence, caged in a rational being; even the dream material with which Dostoevsky endows him makes it possible for us to grasp how man builds allegories of the emotions for himself. Tolstoy's *Anna Kerenin* affords us not only a picture of the way in which life interferes with high romance: it is, in essence, a documented picture of two states of melancholy—that of Anna, who will in the end take her life, and Levin who, though filled with despair, will reach an existentialist solution. And while Anna and Levin must also not be treated as case histories, and must not be expected to have the psychological consistency of flesh-and-blood characters, they embody certain fundamental truths of behavior which psychology can illuminate. Similarly a complex tale like "The Turn of the Screw" by Henry James lends itself to psychological explorations, since its narrator, a governess, is not a credible witness. Her testimony, however, provides sufficient data to suggest that it is she who is haunted by ghosts and in turn haunts the children placed in her charge, even though she believes that the phantoms seek to possess the children. James can be shown to have rendered, in a remarkable way, the state of mind of a young woman frightened by her own imaginings. Psychological criticism should also be able, ultimately, to make critics aware of pathology in literature, and might perhaps give them a better perspective when they must cope with the imaginations of writers whose verbal skill gives expression to states of being reflecting violence and destruction. What used to be called "morbid" by critics may now be more accurately labeled.

B) The explorations of Dr. C. G. Jung, who broke with Freud over the libido theory as early as 1912, have a particular appeal to literary criticism and to students of myth. In Jung's study of myths, his search for parallels between primordial images and fantasies and dream material derived from his patients, he touched some of the wellsprings of the poetic experience. Jung came to believe that the experience of an individual's ancestors embodied in mythical themes are ultimately transmitted as a "racial unconscious." He saw these images as archetypes common to whole epochs of society. Rejecting Freud's emphasis on the instincts, Jung insisted that man seeks not only the gratification of his appetites, but from the beginning of history, required a religion, and a philosophy of history, which he embodied in his myths. Of particular interest to poets and critics was Jung's concept of the *persona*. Jung argued that the *persona* represents "the uniqueness of the combination of collective psychological elements." His appeal to those concerned with literary creation resided in his allowing for the reflection in the work of the total artist, rather than some fragmented part of him. Jung insisted also upon mystical experience within art for which no explanation has yet been offered. This concept can in part be related to the postclassical formulations in psychoanalysis of ego psychology.

A striking adaptation to criticism of some of Jung's ideas is to be found in the highly original critical writings of Northrop Frye, notable in his *Anatomy of Criticism* (1957). The central and longest essay in the book is devoted to archetypal criticism and a theory of myths, while the essay on theory of symbols contains within it a discussion of symbolic archetypes. Frye has carried over Jung's idea of the collective or racial unconscious to a concept of the collective literary imagination, and the idea that literature in its totality is a record of the subjective experience of mankind. As he puts it in an essay on *Literature and Myth* (1968), "Individual myths form a mythology; individual works of literature form an imaginative body for which (as Aristotle remarked two thousand years ago) there is no word. If there were such a word, it would be much easier to understand that literature, conceived as such a total imaginative body, is in fact a civilized, expanded and developed mythology." In his writings Frye has explained how the typical forms of myth become the conventions and genres of literature.

Earlier, Maud Bodkin, in her book *Archetypal Patterns in Poetry* (1934) developed the hypothesis that archetypal patterns or images are "present within the experience communicated through poetry, and may be discovered by reflective analysis." While Miss Bodkin took her point of departure from Jung she also derived from Sir

James Frazer's *The Golden Bough* and other primary studies of mythology. The criticism of her work and of "myth studies" in general has been that in seeking underlying myths and archetypes within a given literary work, the study of the individual qualities of that work may be obscured in favor of universal patterns. The critical exegesis becomes so general, it is argued, as to be almost without meaning since it is applicable to so many other works as well.

Directing his attention to the universal symbols rather than archetypal forms, a French physicist-philosopher, Gaston Bachelard, produced a series of studies on what he called *l'imagination matérielle*: the thematic use made by poets and novelists of air, water, fire, earth. His *Psychanalyse du feu* was written as early as 1937 and was followed by *L'eau et les rêves* (1942), *L'air et les songes* (1943), and *La terre et les rêveries du repos* (1948). These constitute a valuable contribution to the literature of dream symbolism as manifested in works of the imagination.

2] Psychology and the creative process. Much literary scholarship in the pre-Freudian period was devoted to tracking down the sources, both biographical and literary, of a given work. A vast literature exists in which the books read by certain writers and the events of their lives have been explored to demonstrate how these influenced the works created. Since the advent of psychoanalysis, criticism has turned from such primitive attempts to penetrate the artistic consciousness, and has sought a more systematic study of the imaginative process, that is the nature of the artist's fantasies and the underlying patterns these take in his work, whether poetry, drama or prose. It is now increasingly recognized that most creative writers do not live in a library; if they are bookish men, the books they read serve largely as stimulus to their imaginative faculty—that it is this faculty and not the food it feeds upon which is all-important. If literary sources are discovered today, and the methods of psychoanalysis are applied to them, the scholar seeks to determine how these sources melted together in the creative unconscious to produce the new work of art. The psychoanalytic approach searches out why a given writer attaches himself to certain sources rather than to others. The study of the creative process inevitably involves looking into biographical material; but it involves certain larger questions which have preoccupied many literary critics as well as psychoanalytical theorists. Thus certain literary critics have pointed out that when psychoanalysts study literary works and their creators they nearly always end up with a description of the neurotic character of the artist. They make art seem the product of certain infantilisms lingering in the artist's consciousness. It is to this type of study that Lionel Trilling alludes in his essay on "Art and Neurosis." Trilling reaches the conclusion that the artist "whatever elements of neurosis he has in common with his fellow-mortals" is nevertheless healthy "by any conceivable definition of health," in that he is given the power to plan, to work, and to bring his work to a conclusion. Applied to the study of the creative process in literature, psychoanalysis can best be employed in showing precisely, as Charles Lamb put it in an essay on the sanity of genius, that "the true poet dreams being awake. He is not possessed by his subject but has dominion over it." The psychoanalytic critic might be inclined to modify this to the statement that the artist is usually possessed by his subject but is capable of gaining possession over it.

Certain psychoanalysts, in developing their studies of ego psychology—notably Ernst Kris—have helped to modify in recent years the trend toward "reductive" analysis. While the revelation of unconscious processes in art has largely interested the psychoanalysts who have used "applied psychoanalysis" to diagnose the personality of the artist, most literary critics and biographers who have used it have been concerned with the actual fabric of the artist's creation, the means by which his verbal imagination gives form and structure to his materials. The development of ego psychology has enabled literary students to recognize that a given poem or story may contain within it unconscious autobiographical material not only from childhood, as Freud often showed, but from other stages of maturation. These ideas have been developed by Erik Erikson in his studies of developmental stages and "crises of identity" in given lives. Although he has focused on religious and political rather than literary figures—Luther, Gandhi, Hitler, among others—Erikson's ideas have had a marked influence in recent years on some literary biographers.

3] Psychology and Biography. The tendencies discussed above under the heading of "creative process" apply inevitably to the writing of biographies of men who were themselves writers. There have been biographies of writers by professional psychoanalysts, such as Marie Bonaparte's E. A. Poe or Phyllis Greenacre's study of Swift, which are more clinical than literary studies, preoccupied with deducing the workings of the unconscious from the writings and the biographical evidence. Literary biographers have tended, when using psychoanalytical theories, to concern themselves with the gaining of certain insights capable of being assimilated within their own rather than the psychoanalytic discipline. Thus the biographer may learn from a slip of the pen in a manuscript or letter much about the subject under study; but where the psychoanalytically trained writer would use the slip as guide to the unconscious, the literary biographer would be inclined to apply this particular slip to the revelation of verifiable facts. The use of psychoanalytic concepts in biography can enable the biographer to escape from the web of his subject's rationalizations; and it can help to explain his predilection for certain subjects and themes. The psychologically-oriented biographer also can note the small and seemingly insignificant detail, which in the past would have been discarded, and use it to illuminate personality. Above all, such a biographer differs from his predecessors by grasping the contradictions and ambiguities within the subject where the old-time biographer sought to efface contradiction and to make his figure more consistent—that is less ambivalent—than people really are. Betty Miller's portrait of Robert Browning or this writer's life of Henry James exemplify the use of psychoanalytical tools so employed as to submerge the clinical and diagnostic aspect and keep in the forefront the living personality in terms of common literary reference. An unique example of psychoanalytical biography—unique because its subject was the founder of psychoanalysis and because it was written by his co-worker—is Ernest Jones's biography of Sigmund Freud. This is remarkable both as biography and as a lucid explanation of Freud's inner life and its relation to the genesis and history of the psychoanalytic movement. But it suffers, in part, from being written in the language of the profession, and within the systems of psychoanalytic therapy.

A notable early venture into psychoanalytic biography was the series of portraits which Stefan Zweig projected as *Die Baumeister der Welt, Versuch einer Typologie des Geistes*. Zweig grouped the types he chose in four volumes: "master builders" such as Balzac, Dickens, Dostoevsky; the demoniacal genius represented by Hölderlin, Kleist, and Nietzsche, figures exalted to creation but driven to self-destruction; adepts at self-portraiture, Casanova, Stendhal, and Tolstoy; and finally mental healers such as Mesmer, Mary Baker Eddy, and Freud. These are not always successful in their analysis, and are outdated in terms of psychoanalytic thinking of recent years; but the literary gift possessed by Zweig gives the portraits vividness nevertheless, and they will be read as pioneering attempts to bring to biography the illumination of psychoanalysis.

The reader and the work. Here psychology and criticism come together on ground which belongs to the study of aesthetics. The question of reader and work goes back to the beginnings of literature. Even in Homer we may discern the devices by which the poet sought to keep his listeners attentive and engaged. In modern times we can find in Proust a close and analytical discussion of how a reader becomes subjectively involved in the novel he is reading and his process of identification with certain characters and scenes in the story. In his ghostly tale, "The Turn of the Screw," Henry James deliberately created certain ambiguities which, he explained, were so many blanks which the reader's imagination would fill in. Each reader thus brings to the story's ambiguities his own particular and private data. In clinical psychology valuable experiments have been carried out from which the literary critic may derive considerable guidance: These involve using "unstructured" material, such as the ink blots of the Rorschach test, or highly structured materials such as works of art, in order to study the effect of their stimulus upon the viewer —as related to the viewer's specific needs and his character structure.

Notable critical studies have been the works of I. A. Richards and also of the semanticists, disciples of Alfred Korzybski. Richards, in collaboration with C. K. Ogden, published as early as 1923 *The Meaning of Meaning,* a study of language designed to link criticism more closely to verbal meaning. In *The Principles of Literary Criticism* (1924) and *Science and Poetry* (1926) Richards developed certain ideas which have had a profound effect on contemporary criticism in the Anglo-American world. He focused his search upon the nature and value of poetry, investigating what occurs within a poem and the way in which a reader may be affected by it. His approach was perforce on the ground of psychology, and his method was descriptive. Richards believed that readers can be trained to read properly and when trained can then appreciate works otherwise generally incommunicable or "difficult." This line of reasoning, pursued by other critics, has led to widespread insistence, particularly in America, upon the importance of explication of text as the primary function of the critical act. It has led, also, to a great deal of "fantasy-reading" of texts.

In general it may be said that while there is a great—and ever-growing—awareness of the illumination offered by psychoanalysis in studying human behavior and the mental processes, the relations between this discipline and the disciplines of literary study are still blurred and uncharted. There is a natural resistance among men of letters, and the Academies, to "psychologizing," a strong feeling that human perception into the psyche, already so profound in the works of the master writers, requires no further aid, especially of scientifically-oriented psychological exploration. It is further argued that the divergences among the psychoanalytic schools in themselves are sufficiently contradictory to call for great caution—and may render ambiguous and highly arbitrary the uses to which a given theory is put in literature.

The use of symbolism by the Freudians in a fixed and rigid manner has been much criticized, most students of literature knowing that while symbols are often universal they have particular associative meanings for every individual. Otto Rank's theory of anxiety as resultant of the birth trauma offers little to literary study, and the "inferiority complex" school of Alfred Adler has much more to do with therapeutic problems than with offering any particular ground of interest for the literary scholar, save in the valuable light Adler cast on the human struggle for power. The Jungians have supplied, as indicated above, much material for literary study because of their orientation toward religion and mysticism. Of great significance, in the view of some, has been the American school of Harry Stack Sullivan which sees the individual as a product of "interpersonal relations" and argues that the pattern of a child's early and not specifically sexual relationship with significant figures plays a major role in the individual's personality formation. Because the novel deals in great measure with interpersonal relations, this school has much to offer to the literary student. Also valuable have been some of the approaches of Karen Horney and Erich Fromm, who draw upon sociological and anthropological thought in formulating their theories. They emphasize the immediate—and the cultural—problems in the life of an individual rather than the biological instinctual emphasis of Freud.

There is little doubt that much of the literary use of psychoanalysis has been to date rather crude and primitive, tending to simplify material highly complex and to make stereotypes of creative personality. It has tended to imitate psychoanalytic use of literary material rather than adapting psychoanalytic insights and methods to literary usage. The cross-fertilization of the disciplines has been inevitably richest in the case of those writers who have a thorough grounding in both disciplines—and largely in the fields of criticism and biography. There is little evidence today that imaginative writers, relying upon their own observation and feeling, have been able to integrate in a satisfactory fashion the theoretical concepts of psychoanalysis. Where this has been done, the results have been mechanical, unless they have been used by creative writers not so much for the psychoanalytic process itself as for certain broad insights, as T. S. Eliot has done in his poems and plays. The number of literary critics and biographers thoroughly familiar with psychoanalysis is small; and the result is that only a few works, among the many published, can be said to have anything more than an ephemeral and superficial value. The literary scholar who "gets up" his psychoanalytic knowledge from books will have highly theoretical concepts and perhaps an *intellectual* grasp of the psychoanalytic tool, but it is not likely to understand sufficiently well—as Freud warned—the role of the unconscious, and in particular its relation to that of the emotions. The difference might be described as analogous to the difference between the novels of a writer like André Gide, which stress intelligence and rationality, and the work of Proust, which uses association and emotion.

One distinct advantage which those critics and biographers who have firsthand experience of the psychoanalytic process enjoy is that they are less likely to project ideas and fantasies from their own psyche into the work or the life they are writing. In this respect they have an attitude of self-observation similar to that which the psychoanalyst himself must have in order to deal objectively with his patients.

Psychology has already shown that in literary works it can find many fertile examples of the creative imagination which illustrates the psychology of thought and the workings of the unconscious. Literature on its side is still absorbing and learning to use the psychological tool and in particular the concepts of psychoanalysis. The problem for literature has been in part one of terminology, the technical terms of psychoanalysis being ill-adapted to the needs of literary criticism. The most successful users of psychoanalysis in the study of literature have been those biographers and critics who have found ways of *translating* the specialized terms into the more familiar vocabulary of their own discipline.

What may be expected in the future will be a further clarification of the respective roles of the two disciplines and a better definition of the uses to which psychoanalysis may be put in literature. As the very word "analysis" suggests, it will be most useful on the critical-analytic level. And it will quite likely have its greatest usefulness in the continued study of the creative process and therefore in the writing of biography: that is, in that part of literary study which relates the work to the man and treats the work as a part of the creating mind which put it forth into the world.

The basic factors which must be considered in defining the relationship between literature and psychology may be stated as follows:

1] Literary psychology is concerned with man's myth-making and symbol-creating imagination and his unremitting effort to find the language and form to express these myths.

2] Literary psychology is the study of the structure and content of a literary work, the imagination that has given it form and pattern, the fantasy that it embodies, the modes of human behavior it describes—a study of all this in the light of what we know of the unconscious and the integrative functions of the personality.

3] The integrity of the literary work as a creative outcome of a personality must be recognized as distinct from the biography of the personality, although both may be studied in pursuit of "creative process."

4] Therapeutic systems used in psychiatry and the psychoanalytic methods of treatment are largely irrelevant in literary psychology.

BIBLIOGRAPHICAL NOTE

For applications of psychoanalysis to literature see the studies in applied psychoanalysis to be found in the works of Sigmund Freud, C. G. Jung, Ernest Jones, and other leading explorers of the psyche. The various journals of the psychoanalytic movement, in different countries, yield a wide range of articles dealing with literature. Basic to the study of literature and psychology are Freud's books on the interpretation of dreams and his study of wit and its relation to the unconscious. Other works to consult are Wilhelm Stekel's *Dichtung und Neurose* (Wiesbaden, 1909) and Otto Rank's *Das Inzest-Motiv in Dichtung und Sage* (Leipzig, 1926) and *Art and the Artist* (New York, 1932); I. D. Suttie, *The Origins of Love and Hate* (London, 1935); W. Muschg, *Psychoanalyse und Literaturwissenschaft* (Berlin, 1930); F. L. Sack, *Die Psychoanalyse im modernen englischen Roman* (Zürich, 1930); Louis Cazamian, *Études de Psychologie Littéraire* (Paris, 1913); and Charles Baudouin, *Psychoanalysis and Aesthetics* (New York, 1924).

In more recent years some of the significant works have been Edmund Wilson's *The Wound and the Bow* (Boston, 1941); Mario Praz, *The Romantic Agony* (London, 1933); W. H. Auden, *The Enchafèd Flood* (New York, 1950); Ernst Kris, *Psychoanalytical Explorations in Art* (New York, 1952); Lionel Trilling, *Freud and the Crisis of Our Culture* (Boston, 1955); Joseph Campbell, *The Hero with the Thousand Faces* (New York, 1949); Herbert Marcuse, *Eros and Civilization* (Boston, 1955); Leon Edel, *The Modern Psychological Novel* (New York, 1955) and *Literary Biography* (London, 1957); Louis Fraiberg, *Psychoanalysis and American Literary Criticism* (Detroit 1960); Frederick J. Hoffmann, *Freudianism and the Literary Mind* (Baton Rouge, 1957); and Simon O. Lesser, *Fiction and the Unconscious* (Boston, 1957). See also Frederick Clarke Prescott, *The Poetic Mind* (New York, 1932); Roy P. Basler, *Sex, Symbolism and Psychology* (New Brunswick, N. J., 1948); Northrop Frye, *Anatomy of Criticism* (Princeton, N. J., 1957); Erich Neumann, *Art and the Creative Unconscious* (London, 1959); Norman Kiell, *Psychoanalysis, Psychology and Literature* (Madison, Wis., 1963); Philip Weisman, *Creativity in the Theatre* (New York, 1965); Norman Holland, *Psychoanalysis and Shakespeare* (New York, 1966); Leon Edel, "Psychoanalysis and the 'Creative' Arts," in *Modern Psychoanalysis*, ed. Judd Marmor (New York, 1968), pp. 624–41. *Relations of Literary Study*, ed. James Thorpe, published by the Modern Language Association (New York, 1967), contains three relevant essays: Northrop Frye, "Literature and Myth," pp. 27–56, Leon Edel, "Literature and Biography," pp. 57–72 and Frederick C. Crews, "Literature and Psychology," pp. 73–87. The quarterly bulletin of the "Literature and Psychology Group" of the Modern Language Association has for some years published a continuing bibliography of works relating to the two disciplines.

6

IDEAS AND LITERATURE

NEWTON P. STALLKNECHT

THE LATE R. G. COLLINGWOOD, a philosopher whose work has proved helpful to many students of literature, once wrote

> We are all, though many of us are snobbish enough to wish to deny it, in far closer sympathy with the art of the music-hall and picture-palace than with Chaucer and Cimabue, or even Shakespeare and Titian. By an effort of historical sympathy we can cast our minds back into the art of a remote past or an alien present, and enjoy the carvings of cavemen and Japanese colour-prints; but the possibility of this effort is bound up with that development of historical thought which is the greatest achievement of our civilization in the last two centuries, and it is utterly impossible to people in whom this development has not taken place. The natural and primary aesthetic attitude is to enjoy contemporary art, to despise and dislike the art of the recent past, and wholly to ignore everything else.[1]

One might argue that the ultimate purpose of literary scholarship is to correct this spontaneous provincialism that is likely to obscure the horizons of the general public, of the newspaper critic, and of the creative artist himself. There results a study of literature freed from the tyranny of the contemporary. Such study may take many forms. The study of ideas in literature is one of these. Of course, it goes without saying that no student of ideas can justifiably ignore the contemporary scene. He will frequently return to it. The continuities, contrasts, and similarities discernible when past and present are surveyed together are inexhaustible and the one is often understood through the other.

When we assert the value of such study, we find ourselves committed to an important assumption. Most students of literature, whether they call themselves scholars or critics, are ready to argue that it is possible to understand literary works as well as to enjoy them. Many will add that we may find our enjoyment heightened by our understanding. This understanding, of course, may in its turn take many forms and some of these—especially those most interesting to the student of comparative literature—are essentially historical. But the historian of literature need not confine his attention to biography or to stylistic questions of form, "texture," or technique. He may also consider ideas. It is true that this distinction between style and idea often approaches the arbitrary since in the end we must admit that style and content frequently influence or interpenetrate one another and sometimes appear as expressions of the same insight. But, in general, we may argue that the student can direct the primary emphasis of his attention toward one or the other.

At this point a working definition of *idea* is in order, although our first definition will have to be qualified somewhat as we proceed. The term *idea* refers to our more reflective or thoughtful consciousness as opposed to the immediacies of sensuous or emotional experience. It is through such reflection that literature approaches philosophy. An idea, let us say, may be roughly defined as a theme or topic with which our reflection may be concerned. In this essay, we are, along with most historians, interested in the more general or more inclusive ideas, that are so to speak "writ large" in history of literature where they recur continually. Outstanding among these is the idea of human nature itself, including the many definitions that have been advanced over the centuries; also secondary notions such as the perfectibility of man, the depravity of man, and the dignity of man. One might, indeed, argue that the history of ideas, in so far as it includes the literatures, must center on characterizations of human nature and that the great periods of literary achievement may be distinguished from one another by reference to the images of human nature that they succeed in fashioning.

We need not, to be sure, expect to find such ideas in every piece of literature. An idea, of the sort that we have in mind, although of necessity readily available to imagination, is more general in connotation than most poetic or literary images, especially those appearing in lyric poems that seek to capture a moment of personal experience. Thus Burns's

My love is like a red, red rose

and Hopkins'

The thunder-purple sea-beach, pluméd purple of thunder

although clearly intelligible in content, hardly present ideas of the sort with which we are here concerned. On the other hand, Arnold's

The unplumbed, salt, estranging sea,

taken in its context, certainly does so.

Understanding a work of art involves recognition of the ideas that it reflects or embodies. Thus the student of literature may sometimes find it helpful to classify a poem or an essay as being in idea or in ideal content or subject matter typical or atypical of its period. Again, he may discover embodied within its texture a theme or idea that has been presented elsewhere and at other times in various ways. Our understanding will very probably require both these commentaries. Very likely it will also include a recognition that the work we are reading reflects or "belongs to" some way of thought labeled as a "school" or an "ism," i.e., a complex or "syndrome" of ideas occurring together with sufficient prominence to warrant identification. Thus ideas like "grace," "salvation," and "providence" cluster together in traditional Christianity. Usually the work studied offers us a special or even an individualized rendering or treatment of the ideas in question, so that the student finds it necessary to distinguish carefully between the several expressions of an "ism" or mode of thought. Accordingly we may speak of the Platonism peculiar to Shelley's poems or the type of Stoicism present in Henley's "Invictus," and we may find that describing such Platonism or such Stoicism and contrasting each with other expressions of the same attitude or mode of thought is a difficult and challenging enterprise. After all, Shelley is no "orthodox" or Hellenic Platonist, and even his "romantic" Platonism can be distinguished from that of his contemporaries. Again, Henley's attitude of defiance which colors his ideal of self-mastery is far from characteristic of a Stoic thinker like Marcus Aurelius, whose gentle acquiescence is almost Christian, comparable to the patience expressed in Milton's sonnet on his own blindness.

In recent years, we have come increasingly to recognize that ideas have a history and that not the least important chapters of this history have to do with thematic or conceptual aspects of literature and the arts, although these aspects should be studied in conjunction with the history of philosophy, of religion, and of the sciences. When these fields are surveyed together, important patterns of relationship emerge indicating a vast community of reciprocal influence, a continuity of thought and expression including many traditions, primarily literary, religious, and philosophical, but frequently including contact with the fine arts and even, to some extent, with science.

Here we may observe that at least one modern philosophy of history is built on the assumption that ideas are the primary objectives of the historian's research. Let us quote once more from R. G. Collingwood:

> History is properly concerned with the actions of human beings . . . Regarded from the outside, an action is an event or series of events occurring in the physical world; regarded from the inside, it is the carrying into action of a certain thought . . . The historian's business is to penetrate to the inside of the actions with which he is dealing and reconstruct or rather rethink the thoughts which constituted them. It is a characteristic of thoughts that . . . in re-thinking them we come, *ipso facto*, to understand why they were thought.[2]

Such an understanding, although it must seek to be sympathetic, is not a matter of intuition.

> History has this in common with every other science: that the historian is not allowed to claim any single piece of knowledge, except where he can justify his claim by exhibiting to himself in the first place, and secondly to any one else who is both able and willing to follow his demonstration, the grounds upon which it is based. This is what was meant, above, by describing history as inferential. The knowledge in virtue of which a man is an historian is a knowledge of what the evidence at his disposal proves about certain events.

It is obvious that the historian who seeks to recapture the ideas that have motivated human behavior throughout a given period will find the art and literature of that age one of his central and major concerns, by no means a mere supplement or adjunct of significant historical research.

The student of ideas and their place in history will always be concerned with the patterns of transition, which are at the same time patterns of transformation, whereby ideas pass from one area of activity to another. Let us survey for a moment the development of modern thought—turning our attention from the Reformation toward the revolutionary and romantic movements that follow and dwelling finally on more recent decades. We may thus trace the notion of individual autonomy from its manifestation in religious practice and theological reflection through practical politics and political theory into literature and the arts. Finally we may note that the idea appears in educational theory where its influence is at present widespread. No one will deny that such broad developments and transitions are of great intrinsic interest and the study of ideas in literature would be woefully incomplete without frequent reference to them. Still, we must remember that we cannot construct and justify generalizations of this sort unless we are ready to consider many special instances of influence moving between such areas as theology, philosophy, political thought, and literature. The actual moments of contact are vitally important. These moments are historical events in the lives of individual authors with which the student of comparative literature must be frequently concerned.

Perhaps the most powerful and most frequently recurring literary influence on the Western world has been that of the Old and New Testament. Certainly one of the most important comments that can be made upon the spiritual and cultural life of any period of Western civilization during the past sixteen or seventeen centuries has to do with the way in which its leaders have read and interpreted the Bible. This reading and the comments that it evoked constitute the influence. A contrast of the scripture reading of, let us say, St. Augustine, John Bunyan, and Thomas Jefferson, all three of whom found in such study a real source of enlightenment, can tell us a great deal about these three men and the age that each represented and helped bring to conscious expression. In much the same way, we recognize the importance of Shakespeare's familiarity with Plutarch and Montaigne, of Shelley's study of Plato's dialogues, and of Coleridge's enthusiastic plundering of the writings of many philosophers and theologians from Plato to Schelling and William Godwin, through which so many abstract ideas were brought to the attention of English men of letters.

We may also recognize cases in which the poets have influenced the philosophers and even indirectly the scientists. English philosopher Samuel Alexander's debt to Wordsworth and Meredith is a recent interesting example, as also A. N. Whitehead's understanding of the English romantics, chiefly Shelley and Wordsworth. Hegel's profound admiration for the insights of the Greek tragedians indicates a broad channel of classical influence upon nineteenth-century philosophy. Again the student of evolutionary biology will find a fascinating, if to our minds grotesque, anticipation of the theory of chance variations and the natural elimination of the unfit in Lucretius, who in turn seems to have borrowed the concept from the philosopher Empedocles.

Here an important caveat is in order. We must avoid the notion, suggested to some people by examples such as those just mentioned, that ideas are "units" [3] in some way comparable to coins or counters that can be passed intact from one group of people to another or even, for that matter, from one individual to another. Our description of an idea's influence must not be oversimplified. It is always a delicate and complicated business. Ideas have usually to be expressed in words and must be so expressed in literature as opposed to music and the fine arts. Words must not only be heard or read, they must be interpreted in contextual groupings, and it is only through such acts of interpretation that ideas become available to our attention.

COLLEGE OF THE SEQUOIAS
LIBRARY

Ideas exist not as readymade commodities but primarily—and here we must step beyond the definition already offered—as the "meaning" latent in human efforts to communicate. Their status is neither "subjective" nor "objective" in the usual sense, but *intersubjective*, communicative, or conversational. Once removed from the give and take of actual communication, ideas lose their vitality. Their genuine existence is transitive. They pass continually from one context to another and, even within the mind of a single individual, ideas must be frequently restated, in fact continually paraphrased, if they are to retain any vitality or even genuine significance. A set formula has little more than mnemonic value and is out of place except in the most elementary textbook.

Thus the term "unit-idea" can hardly be described as referring to any recognizable entity, to say nothing of its being usefully employed by the student of literature. We can, to be sure, redefine it with A. O. Lovejoy as a tendency on the part of certain people to enjoy hearing certain propositions such as "the real is One" or "the world is full of a number of things," thus recognizing philosophical *monism* and *pluralism* as unit-ideas. However, on this level of generality, we would probably do better not to use the term "unit-idea" even as a figure of speech since its connotations are, as already pointed out, often unfortunate, but to content ourselves with the more direct expressions "tendencies," "inclinations," or "dispositions" of "thought and feeling." These tendencies may express themselves in various ways that differ greatly from one period to another. But the notion of a unit-idea interpreted as reappearing or as being transferred from one author to another or from period to period is usually an oversimplification.

In passing from author to author and from age to age, these dispositions of thought and feeling undergo continual restatement, reinterpretation, and transformation. The history of ideas is essentially a commentary upon this process, which is after all the very life of the human spirit that fashions and refashions the ideas through which it becomes conscious of itself and of its environment. As Hegel tried to show in his first great work, *The Phenomenology of the Spirit,* the history of ideas may be considered as an index of the growth of self-consciousness whereby human individuals interpret and reinterpret their position in society and in the world. It goes without saying that the emergence of this self-consciousness transforms the life of the individual, influences his social relations, and profoundly alters his attitude toward nature. Such reorientation as it appears in documentary form is a primary subject-matter of history. Thus the historian must consider all the turns of thought whereby one period of human life is distinguished from its forerunners and from its successors. He may also find himself recognizing parallels and analogies where no notion of historical continuity, involving an actual influence or contact, is likely to develop. An interesting relation of this sort may be discerned as we compare the writings of the Chinese Taoists, especially those of Lao-Tsu himself, with the utterances of European romantics, as for example, Wordsworth's "Lines Written in Early Spring." Both of these may be compared with certain passages of the Neoplatonic philosopher, Plotinus. Some scholars find great importance in such analogies and try by means of them to outline parallel cycles of development in distant cultures. These speculations, such as those of Oswald Spengler, who "identified" ancient Stoicism with modern socialism, and saw Pythagoras, Mahomet, and Cromwell as "contemporaries," or historical analogues, are nearly always interesting and suggestive and sometimes open important paths of investigation. But like all reasoning that rests on intuited analogies, such argument must be evaluated very cautiously and never recognized as conclusive without detailed study of a more pedestrian character.

We have argued that the student of the great "isms" of literary and philosophical history, must proceed with discretion, always recognizing that as ideas pass from one mind to another, change, and often a radical change, is bound to take place in their structure, orientation, and mode of reception. There are many instances of such contrast. Prominent among these stand the mutations that ideas most usually undergo as they pass from thinker to artist. The poet and the philosopher may be said to entertain the "same" idea, but it is most important to remember that the poetic or literary development of an idea is often imaginative, figurative, or metaphorical in nature and that this contrasts sharply with an intellectual or scientific treatment that emphasizes definition and precision even at the risk of pedantry. The thinker is concerned with implications and seeks to preserve a more or less rigorous consistency, while the imaginative writer is usually more eager to make clear how an idea affects the life and colors the emotion of the person who entertains it. He need not be greatly concerned to convince his readers that his notion is a true one or that it excludes every alternative. In any case, he is not likely to construct an argument. In this respect the polemical and controversial energy of a Bernard Shaw, manifest in his prefaces and elsewhere, is unusual. The literary artist does not usually draw distinctions. He does not aim at definitions or at conclusions. Nonetheless his mind may be as completely possessed by an idea as is the rigorous thinking of a geometer.

Thus Shelley's sonnet "Ozymandias" is an intense exemplification of an idea although, since the poet cites but a single instance, one would hardly call the poem an argument or a proof. His "Adonais" brings vividly to mind the Platonic notions of time, eternity, and immortality without retracing Plato's often intricate dialectic. On the other hand, there are passages in the *Divine Comedy,* in *Paradise Lost,* and in Wordsworth's *Excursion* where philosophical and theological ideas are presented within a discursive pattern that approaches a logical argument. Lucretius often goes even further in his exposition of the atomic and Epicurean philosophies and works his way toward something comparable to a *Quod erat demonstrandum,* although to be sure, following an argument borrowed from the philosophers. But such an approach to formal reasoning is unusual in literature. The man of letters is generally more concerned to call our attention to ideas than he is to demonstrate or analyze them. In philosophy, however, reflection upon ideas generally takes the form of knowledge, opinion, or belief, i.e., there is usually some sort of positive assertion involved. But it is often the case in literature that the presence of an idea before our attention does not call for any logical evaluation. In such a case sheer *enjoyment* takes the place of acceptance or rejection. The idea in its embodiment is admired rather than defended. Poets, it would seem, have a way of enjoying an idea without feeling any obligation to demonstrate or verify. Thus they may readily share the experience of the mythmaker who does not pass beyond imagination into argument. The attitude of the philosopher is always less congenial.

For this reason we may argue that mythology lends itself more readily to literary treatment than does science or even philosophy, and that in the conflict which often arises between myth and science, the literary man will sometimes fall into mythological modes of thought and experience almost despite himself, as Lucretius did in his glowing invocation to Venus, that introduces a poem devoted to a materialist account of man and the world, or as Wordsworth in "The Recluse" fragment, where, despite his dislike of "gaudy verse," he invokes Urania and calls upon a prophetic "spirit" to support him in defending a philosophy of humanism. In many instances, the poet tries to retain or regain something of the imaginative appeal of a mythology even though he is intellectually committed to a scientific, or humanist, or even a materialist, view of things. After all, mythology has been at times the living motivation of a literature that has found itself quite at home within its purview. We may argue that at no time in the history of Western literature—if we are willing to omit the so-called "science" fiction of recent years—has scientific thought ever exercised so subtle and pervasive an influence as that of mythology—not even in the naturalistic novels of the nineteenth century.[4]

The student of literature will, however, gradually come to recognize that contrasts such as that mentioned above between science and mythology, while readily discernible in the thought of many writers, yield only a comparatively superficial insight into the great movements of ideas. Such contrasts hardly reveal the polarities that gradually become obvious as we set in opposition the dominant themes that characterize the great periods of thought and literature. These themes often constitute horizons within which ideas inherited from earlier periods take on a local aspect that they wholly lacked in former times. Thus we may recognize two dimensions in the study of ideas: the "vertical," as when we speak of *Platonism* in Shelley, and the "horizontal," as when we speak of *romantic* Platonism. When emphasizing the vertical axis, we recognize recurring ideas and recurring "isms." There is always danger that we will go too far toward identifying an idea as it appears in the context of one period with its manifestation in that of another. The result is a false sense of intellectual or spiritual community with historical figures who should not be treated as our "contemporaries." Platonism, we must admit, suffers sea-change as it passes from the Athens that had survived the Peloponnesian war to the England of the industrial revolution. This transformation is a challenge to the historian who must ask not "Did the romantics understand Plato?" but rather "How did they read or 'translate' him?" Consider the Platonism of Shelley, who was quite familiar with the text of his ancient master. Here it is the difference of treatment and of emphasis that most attracts our interest. To be sure, many isolated passages may be quoted to strengthen the impression that a genuine or Hellenic Platonism resides in Shelley's poems.

The One remains, the many change and pass;
Heaven's light forever shines, Earth's shadows fly;
Life, like a dome of many-colored glass,
Stains the white radiance of Eternity

This would seem to be a fairly orthodox Platonism derived from the central image of the sun in *The Republic*. But let us recall the wider context of Shelley's thought and our comment must be considerably qualified. After all, Shelley loved movement, transformation, and the flux of sensuous qualities. This world of change has also a reality and a beauty all its own. It is no mere appearance.

The everlasting universe of things
Flows through the mind, and rolls its rapid waves,
Now dark, now glittering, now reflecting gloom,
Now lending splendor, where from secret springs
The source of human thought its tribute brings
Of waters,—with a sound but half its own

This stanza from "Mont Blanc" is too modern to be genuine Platonism. So also is the "myth" of the "West Wind" far removed from that of the *Phaedrus*. Furthermore, a Platonism at home with a revolutionary liberalism, based on a belief in human perfectibility and progress, a Platonism colored by romantic notions of "free" (heterosexual) love and set into verse by a poet who had once been an enthusiastic amateur of modern chemistry is a Platonism almost sui generis.

We may mention in passing that Wordsworth's Platonism is quite as unorthodox as Shelley's. For example, Wordsworth's reinterpretation of the notion of Platonic reminiscence, so vividly presented in the "Intimations" Ode, is virtually an inversion of the ancient doctrine. Plato held that in certain privileged moments we may recall or reconstitute a vision of eternal truth, lost at birth, including the first principles or foundations of mathematical order, social justice, and of sensuous and intellectual beauty. These insights become more frequent and more comprehensive as our education progresses. For Wordsworth, we "recall" less and less frequently as we grow older the glorious wealth of the world of becoming, the "mighty waters" that support our existence and are so obvious to our childhood vision. This world, like Goethe's "golden tree of life," appears as a gray shadow of its true self to the practical man of affairs and to the scientific theorist. It can be wholly present only to that "wise passiveness" which the "noisy years of maturity make harder and harder to enjoy. Although Wordsworth's Ode is usually recognized as Platonic in spirit, it might seem to some that only the most general notion of "reminiscence" or recollection stands in common to both poet and philosopher. The details are almost wholly transformed.

These considerations call to our attention the profound contrasts existing between ancient and modern ways of looking at the world. If the reader desires another example, let him consider the ancient maxim "Know thyself," asking what it may have meant originally to the petitioners who called upon the Delphic oracle, what it meant to Socrates, and what, let us add, to Montaigne who found the Socratic use of the phrase so congenial. On the latter point Auerbach's fascinating chapter on Montaigne in *Mimesis* may be read with profit. Shelley, Wordsworth, and Montaigne recast Platonic themes but hardly because of any conscious intention to reconstruct his philosophy. We had better say that they transfer Platonism from one medium of thought and feeling to another and reshape its major concepts in doing so.

These discrepancies between ancient Platonism and its modern romantic counterpart call our attention to related ideas that are of especial significance for the historian. For the modern mind the immediate, the sensuous, the changing are more attractive and philosophically more significant than they ever were for Greek idealism. In the first place, the alignment of concepts that this contrast suggests constitutes an important area of historical study. But we may go further and insist that this contrast is highly pertinent to the historian's own attitude toward his subject matter. Before one can become a true historian of ideas one must learn to "take time seriously" and to recognize that time leaves its mark on ideas, as on things. Ideas can survive as cultural realities only by changing and readjusting themselves.

A sense of history and of the gradual transformation of human customs and ideas was hardly characteristic of ancient thinkers, for whom the ideal science was geometry and for whom the apparent cycles of the sun, moon, and the constellations, and the somewhat more complicated motions of the planets constituted the obvious framework of a geometric universe. From this standpoint, change is subordinate to form and to law and is essentially a matter of repetition within a permanent frame. Profound change of transformation toward essential novelty is unlikely.

Time, including human life, tends constantly to exemplify and reexemplify the same eternal principles. It is only within the last two centuries that we have become profoundly conscious of an historical mode of existence, and have recognized that we ourselves are "in" history or that in a sense we *are* a history that assumes new forms from age to age. There gradually emerges a sense of continuity with a past that is, quantitatively speaking, very distant from us and qualitatively very different. To be sure, we may "move about" in history by cultivating, as Collingwood among others would recommend, a sympathetic imagination that in some measure transcends the vast reaches of change. The past is still in a sense *our* past and as Hegel put it in his famous pun: "Wesen ist was gewesen ist." (Our essence is what we have been.)

This turn of thought is essentially a romantic one. Thus Wordsworth, who could speak with genuine pathos of the "unimaginable touch of time" and of "things silently gone out of mind" nonetheless in *The Prelude* described his enjoyment of the city of London and its historical monuments:

With strong Sensations, teeming as it did
Of past and present, such a place must needs
Have pleas'd me, in those times; I sought not then
Knowledge; but craved for power, and power I found
In all things; nothing had a circumscribed
And narrow influence; but all objects, being
Themselves capacious, also found in me
Capaciousness and amplitude of mind;
Such is the strength and glory of our Youth.
The Human nature unto which I felt
That I belong'd, and which I lov'd and reverenc'd,
Was not a punctual Presence, but a Spirit
Living in time and space, and far diffus'd.
In this my joy, in this my dignity
Consisted.

The love of the "far away and long ago," the pathos of "old, forgotten far off things" so characteristic of the romantics only reveals another aspect of this sense of history. We have often to admit that the past, although our own, is out of reach.

It is interesting to notice that this sense of time is first celebrated by the poets and men of letters before it exercises any profound or far reaching influence upon the work of the professional historian. The scholarly historian of the nineteenth century, especially in Germany, is clearly an offspring of romanticism, as are also the notions borrowed from Collingwood in the quotation introducing this chapter. Once this sense of history has been awakened in us, we often come to emphasize the distance between past and present even more than their continuity and their common life. There is even some danger that the modern student will, as his learning and his historical sensibility increase, despair of ever closing the gap between past and present and of offering, say, an adequate picture of the Athenian Plato or, for that matter, of the Elizabethan Hamlet. While such defeatism is extreme, a sober realization of historical distance should be encouraged. Certainly, it is indispensable to the scholar who must avoid reducing an idea to a recurring stereotype.

Let us briefly examine two or three examples of what we have for lack of a better term been describing as "historical distance." As Macaulay's learned schoolboy knows, Lord Nelson died at the battle of Trafalgar, shot down by marksmen perched in the rigging of enemy vessels. The admiral made a splendid target, for he stood his quarterdeck in brilliant full dress, wearing his many decorations despite the remonstrances of his officers. During the Napoleonic period and in the years that followed, Nelson's attitude was accepted as quite consistent with the character of a true hero, chivalrous and intrepid. It would not be generally so considered today, when soldiers are no longer paraded into battle in polychrome uniforms and when the ideal of personal combat has nearly faded from the scene. The modern civilian must make a real effort of imaginative reorientation to capture the sense of values that once presided over military life. Even the "citizen-soldier" of modern warfare is not readily equipped to do so. It is the task of the historian of ideas to illuminate these widely differing modes of thought.

The difference may be copiously illustrated by reference to literary texts. Consider, in passing, Douglas' ironical comment, in Shakespeare's *Henry IV*, on the ample wardrobe of the English king, who sent into battle a number of impersonators clad in royal armor and, on the other hand, the white plume of Henry of Navarre that was celebrated by Macaulay. Our present attitude as reflected in twentieth-century war poetry and war fiction is quite another thing. It is, however, more interesting to set it in contrast with the notions expressed by Shakespeare's Falstaff and Cervantes' Sancho Panza. Here the differences are harder to determine and are more significant although less spectacular. The twentieth-century poet, such as Pound, Owen, or Sassoon, who questions the dignity or glory of war casts a new light on Falstaff's reservations concerning military honor and on Sancho Panza's estimate of his master. In recent times such an attitude does not have to be presented as low comedy but can be taken quite seriously as a dignified and humane evaluation.

Some further illustrations of historical distance may be helpful. Let us choose a topic that illustrates the interrelationship of religion and the arts. In medieval and modern thought one finds it altogether fitting and proper to describe God as infinite or unlimited even though this may be taken to imply that finite man can never wholly comprehend the nature of deity. In earlier times, however, especially under the auspices of the Pythagorean philosophers, the notion of infinity carried a distinctly pejorative connotation. *Infinite* meant *indefinite, formless, unfinished,* as opposed to the self-contained and clearly defined structure of the finite, whose perfection lay in harmony, symmetry, and proportion. From this Pythagorean point of view, which is, in large measure, the point of view of classical art and literature, it would be little short of blasphemous nonsense to speak of an infinite God or even of an infinite good. To say that all things spring from the infinite and to introduce no supplementary principle of order such as justice or intelligence would bring one perilously close to Glycon's

> *All is laughter, all is dust, all is nothing.*
> *For all things are born of unreason.*

Here, we have what we may call the classical ideal of an organic unity, a one in many, wherein beginning, middle, and end [5] are manifest and wherein every part derives its vitality from the whole that is itself an organization of parts. This ideal is at once moral, religious, and aesthetic. And some students have boldly argued that it is reflected in the very structure of ancient, as opposed to modern, mathematics. This ideal may be described in the words that Quintilian used of the style of Pericles, *instans sibi* or *compact*. It is, in short, an apotheosis of finitude or "closure." Classical art and poetry of any period echo this ideal, if only faintly. To sense this, one has only to think of the facade of a Greek temple, as opposed to the interior of St. Sophia, or to study the periods of classical prose or the closed symmetry of a poem like William Browne's

> *Underneath this sable hearse*
> *Lies the subject of all verse.*
> *Sidney's sister, Pembroke's mother,*

Death, 'ere thou hast slain another,
Fair and learn'd and good as she,
Time shall throw a dart at thee!

Cosmos, meaning world-order, has, we may remember, the same root as the Greek verb *kosmeo,* meaning *I adorn.* Structure, especially symmetrical or periodic structure, stands for the true classicist at the heart of nature and is also the key to aesthetic value. The image of the sphere, that delighted ancient philosophers from Parmenides to Boethius, symbolizes the notion of finite symmetry and summarizes the ideas of order and of value. But the God of medieval and modern thought is not so to be presented. He is infinite and his being is unfathomable. Hence the cautious concern with which theologians and even philosophers of our own century consider the notion of a "finite God," so possessed have we become by the feeling that such a God would lack the awful majesty inseparable from deity. Indeed, in modern times many of us have quite lost the classical sense of finitude or closure. We are at home in vastness and enjoy open immensities both spatial and temporal. If we are disturbed by Pascal's "silence of infinite spaces," the sense of awe is not without a hint of exaltation; and further we rejoice in the notion of an indefinite future, a theater of progress and perfectibility. We still share Wordsworth's romantic sense that

Our destiny; our being's heart and home,
Is with infinitude, and only there;
With hope it is, hope that can never die,
Effort, and expectation, and desire
And something evermore about to be.

To be sure, among the ancients, the materialist Lucretius stands in awe of a boundless universe of which our little world is but a passing feature. But this enormous and self-sufficient "happenstance" of nature is, for all its fertility, indifferent to value, and human wisdom is founded on recognition of this truth which is incompatible with religion.

The medieval mind stands between the extreme positions that we have indicated. The medieval Christian rejoices in the infinite and mysterious majesty of God, whose fulness of being can only be adumbrated in human terms, thus inviting recourse to symbol and allegory. But he lacks our modern sense of the sublimity of the physical world and of endless time. His world is finite and the future that confronts him is fixed by providential disposition. *Non in tempore sed cum tempore finxit deus mundum.* There is, for the medieval thinker, something terrifying about an infinite world or system of nature. It is not until the dawn of modern thought that we find people arguing that the production of a finite world would be somehow beneath the dignity of an infinite God. Just so in later thought we hear that it would be beneath the dignity of an infinite creator not to produce *creative* creatures. And herein lies a theme that sets modern thought in sharp contrast with ancient and medieval.

According to the Biblical story, God created heaven and earth and all that they contain, and God created man in his own image. This distinguishes man from lesser creatures and secures him a privileged place in the universe. One might suppose that man, created in the image of God the Creator, would within the limits imposed by his finite or creaturely status, be himself a creator and that through exercise of his creative agency he would fulfill his destiny as a privileged creature, and further that through failure to exploit his special talents he would forfeit something of his divine birthright. A man from Mars considering the apparent implications of the Biblical story might well anticipate some such conclusion.

Nonetheless the "doctrine" that we have sketched describing man's unique status as a creative creature in God's world was very slow to take shape. In general, it is a modern view of things and it is only in a romantic consciousness that it first appears wholly reasonable. In earlier times, including the whole range of Christian thought, philosophers and theologians did not see in God's created image any suggestion of creative power. God was the only creator; indeed, for many, the only *maker* in any radical sense of the word. The divine image resident in man was recognized as human reason and the human capacity to love God and our fellowmen, but it possessed no counterpart of divine power.

Against such a background, the poet and the artist will appear primarily as imitators and, although imitation involves a measure of making or fashioning, they will look for their archetypes toward an order of things already firmly established by divine fiat or supported by the more permanent features of natural process. The romantic notion of the creative power of the artist, as expressed among others by William Blake, and popularized by Browning in "Abt Vogler," as well as the notion today entertained by existentialist philosophers, playwrights, and novelists, that man can somehow "make himself," would seem ridiculous and presumptuous, if not indeed sacrilegious, before comparatively recent times. We may summarize by pointing out that in the classical and medieval periods, by far the most widely accepted representations of human nature displayed a subordinate being obliged to accept his cosmic station and its duties, obeying imperatives or accepting values ultimately not of his own making. The few exceptions, such as the Greek Sophists, are interesting primarily because they stand in protest against dominant philosophies that can be at times embarrassed but not overcome.

The romantic notion is anticipated in the Renaissance by Scaliger who calls the poet "another God," and by Tasso, whom Shelley quotes to the effect that the poet is the only true creator other than God himself, and again by certain of the mystics, among them the protestant Jakob Böhme (died 1624), who insist that man participates with God in the everlasting process of creation. But the modern movement away from the traditional mode of thought has been a very slow one continually looking backward toward more conservative beliefs. Thus even Wordsworth's creative individualism, so enthusiastically expressed in *The Prelude*, is qualified in the "Ode to Duty" and retracted in later poems. Nonetheless the idea of man as creator is not lost and tends to accompany the development of modern humanism so that today we find a widespread popular respect for "creative thinking" and for "creative activity" in general.

This tendency reaches its extreme fruition in certain phases of recent existentialism, where human self-creation is described as subject to no norms or ideal archetypes. Here human nature, as opposed to its physical and biological substructures, is identified with creative freedom, whereby we project our own pattern of human nature and create a mode of life of our own choosing. This philosophy constitutes a bold denial of the notion that human freedom is ever subject to preestablished authority, historical necessity, or metaphysical limitations, although it may at times caricature itself by attributing to such nonentities a sort of pseudo reality. For the existentialist such imaginings constitute an effort to conceal our freedom from ourselves and to escape the responsibility that it entails. Human responsibility can come to free self-consciousness only within the horizon of a world view that admits no imperative authority imposing itself unconditionally upon human commitment and decision. Man comes to himself in a world where, as Nietzsche would put it, "God is dead." Thus Jean-Paul Sartre can hardly endorse Antigone's great speech in which she justifies her rebellion by appealing to an eternal law of justice that transcends her own situation.

> *I did not think your edicts strong enough*
> *To overrule the unwritten unalterable laws*
> *Of God and heaven, you being only a man.*
> *They are not of yesterday or to-day, but everlasting,*
> *Though where they came from, none of us can tell.*
> *Guilty of their transgression before God*
> *I cannot be.*

In contrast, we may cite the following from an existentialist novel: [6]

> Hélène leaned her chin on the palm of her hand. "Tell me, why do we live?"
>
> "I'm not one of the Evangelists," I said with slight embarrassment.
>
> "And yet you know why you live." She spread her fingers fanwise and studied them attentively. "I don't know why I do."
>
> "Surely there are things you like, things you want. . . ."
>
> She smiled. "I like chocolate and beautiful bicycles."
>
> "That's better than nothing."
>
> She looked at her fingers once again; of a sudden she seemed sad. "When I was small, I believed in God, and it was wonderful; at every moment of the day something was required of me; then it seemed to me that I *must* exist. It was an absolute necessity."
>
> I smiled sympathetically at her. "I think that where you go wrong is that you imagine that your reasons for living ought to fall on you ready-made from heaven, whereas we have to create them for ourselves."
>
> "But when we know that we've created them ourselves, we can't believe in them. It's only a way of deceiving ourselves."
>
> "We do not arbitrarily create these things out of nothing; we create them through the strength of our own love and our

own longing; and thus our creatures stand before us, solid and real."

The gap that separates the proto-Platonism of Sophocles from the creative humanism of the existentialist sets many problems for the student of the history of ideas. Again, the student when he distinguishes the existentialist position from that of the ancient Sophists, who declare the human individual the "measure of all things," faces a delicate and important task. The existentialist stands closer to Antigone than to the Sophist, as we usually picture him. The values and standards that the existentialist calls into being are not, as for the Sophist, evaluations imposed upon modes of conduct according to the interests of the individual who is at once agent and observer. It is something wholly different. The existentialist is not seeking to protect his interests or justify conduct already projected. He hopes rather through interpretation of his own situation to commit or engage himself in projects that will awaken and sustain interests powerful enough and enduring enough significantly to characterize his own existence. He seeks not to justify or to promote but to realize, even to create, his own existence.[7]

If the existentialism of today is of any lasting value, it is because its exponents have so clearly emphasized the central importance of the individual's consciousness of himself and of his situation. Despite the air of abrupt originality that surrounds existentialist thought, its contribution takes its place in a long tradition that has accompanied the development of art, literature, and philosophy in the West. The individual as a center of self-conscious decision has emerged slowly from a matrix of subpersonal group behavior such as that described by Lévy-Bruhl and by Bergson in his picture of a closed society.[8] Here conscience may be described as a sense of membership in a group from which the individual derives his human existence. Thus "we" and "our" precede "I" and "my." The singular pronouns only gradually acquire their full significance as we pass through ancient and medieval toward modern consciousness. Such development is often moral and religious in motivation and is manifest in the increasing prominence attached to the attitudes of conscience and of faith. Both of these include growing recognition of a selfhood whose very life springs from a sense of responsibility. The heroic figures of Prometheus and Antigone in the great tragedies and of Socrates as Plato presents him in the *Apology* and the *Crito* are assertions of a moral autonomy, essentially religious in significance, that is to be honored by both Stoics and Christians. Thereafter Christian emphasis upon the moral importance of an inner motivation, in our conduct, and Christian insistence upon the necessity of an absolute sincerity in matters of belief move gradually, despite institutional authoritarianism, toward the dominion of self-consciousness in the life of the individual, or perhaps one might say toward the emergence of self-conscious individuality. We might argue that the art and literature of many centuries reflect in one way or another a gradual and often vacillating progress toward the self-realization of the conscious and autonomous individual.

Many students have characterized the Renaissance as, par excellence, the period of individualism, suggesting a profound difference in kind between Renaissance and Middle Ages. Thus D. A. Traversi opens his study of Shakespeare [9] declaring that

> Medieval man was aware of a definite place in an established society, was firmly grounded in a universe whose nature and end were defined by Christian philosophy; the signs of breakdown which can be found in both Chaucer and Langland are still overshadowed in them by the effects of the mediaeval syn-

thesis. *Piers Plowman*, like the *Divine Comedy*, is not the expression of an isolated individual, but of a man whose individuality speaks within a determined social, philosophic, and religious context. The dominating facts of Shakespeare's age, seen from this point of view, were the destruction of this context and the discovery of the autonomous self which we associate with the Renaissance. The inevitable result was a vast extension of interests, and a corresponding lack of any spiritual or intellectual conception by which these interests might be disciplined. The literature of the Renaissance, being concerned with exploring this new conception of the self and its possibilities, could not hope for any adequate synthesis of its experience which should transcend the personal. Shakespeare's idiom and outlook are still largely mediaeval, but the harmony or pattern which we see gradually evolving out of his work is a purely *personal* pattern, the richest and greatest of its kind that has ever existed. Mr. Eliot once remarked that "Dante and Shakespeare divide the modern world equally between them: there is not a third." It is equally true that they divide what Mr. Eliot chose, for his own purposes, to call "the modern world" into two parts: the mediaeval part, dominated by the synthesis of faith and reason, and the strictly modern part, in which the enormous possibilities of the new discovery of the individual have been explored at the expense of that synthesis.

Nonetheless, we may argue in opposition to Traversi that the Renaissance "discovery" of the individual is but one of a series of such insights that extends from primitive stages of culture through the works of the Greek tragedians and the philosophers that followed them into the history of Christian Europe. Both scholars and creative writers are still concerned, as in all probability they will be for generations to come, with these "enormous possibilities," even when, with Eliot, they challenge a notion like that of romantic self-expression and emphasize an older form of individualism—that of self-fulfillment through sacrifice. The contrast, readily discernible between Sartre and Eliot, which is apparent through all their work, may be summarized in terms of their divergent interpretations of individuality. Eliot's individualism remains within the framework of Christian thought, while Sartre's theory repudiates any supernatural authority. For Sartre, all interpretation and evaluation spring from individual, human initiative. There is no superhuman commandment or gracious assistance directed toward mankind from above. Thus there is no single standard of value, no Platonic idea of the good, that presides over nature and human life. Strictly speaking, there is no established order demanding our recognition. We project our horizons and determine our own values.

We may observe parenthetically that, as they stand, neither the philosophy of Eliot nor that of Sartre is likely to dominate the movement of twentieth-century thought. Although characteristic of our time, they are both unstable and invite opposition. Appeal to a supernatural background grows constantly more difficult and on the other hand acceptance of the fully autonomous independence of the human individual can be a profoundly disturbing experience. To face the human situation, so understood, calls for a courage that most of us cannot long sustain. Existentialists readily admit that we often deceive ourselves into accepting a traditional view of things and a ready-made scheme of values, thus shrinking from the responsibility or self-determination that would render our human existence authentic. In his more pessimistic moments, Sartre himself has spoken of this human failure as virtually inevitable. Such thinking pervades much of recent literature, that dwells upon the futile absurdity of the human predicament. God is dead but we are unable to do without him. This recognition is often a source of tragic laughter rather than of sympathy or compassion.

Thus in recent thought and letters, a "black humor" and a certain relish of the absurd, even an enjoyment of human frustrations, characterize many works of fiction and drama. Here it is only through a scorn of life that we preserve our sanity. Yet we remain committed to seek in the shipwreck of our ideals the possibility of a certain honesty or freedom from self-deceit and we will continue to explore the "enormous possibilities" opened by our gradual discovery of the individual.

Let us conclude our discussion of the relation of literature to ideas by completing the ancient triad composed of the notions of God, man, and nature, the first two of which we have already considered. The idea of nature has undergone several transformations throughout its long and intricate development from the days of the early Greek cosmogonists. The ancient words *physis* and *natura* both indicate an original reference to procreation. Nature was seen to be a process not only of growth but of begetting and bearing. Thus in primitive modes of thought sexual imagery is employed freely to describe the origins of things that spring from the union of sky and earth. Here a primitive philosophy of opposites is apparent arising from the wealth of mythology concerning the beginning of all things: Chaos and Cosmos, Heaven and Earth, Day and Night, Hot and Cold, Moist and Dry, and later, Odd and Even. Justice or Fate, presiding over the boundless fertility of nature, holds the competing opposites in check so that there results a world of ordered, periodic process. This is manifest in the periodic motions of the heavenly bodies and in the regularity of the seasons where hot and cold, moist and dry are held within bounds, thus yielding a moderate climate that will support life. So conceived or imagined, the orderliness of nature on the one hand and the moral values of human self-discipline or self-imposed moderation on the other are seen as springing somehow from a common origin. Nature and man respond, both somewhat imperfectly and rather reluctantly, to the same cosmic influence.

This notion lingers on for centuries. Consider Milton's lines in "Arcades":

> *. . . then listen I*
> *To the celestial* Sirens *harmony,*
> *That sit upon the nine enfolded Sphears,*
> *And sing to those that hold the vital shears,*
> *And turn the* Adamantine *spindle round,*
> *On which the fate of gods and men is wound.*
> *Such sweet compulsion doth in musick ly,*
> *To lull the daughters of* Necessity,
> *And keep unsteddy Nature to her law,*
> *And the low world in measur'd motion draw*
> *After the heavenly tune*

and compare Wordsworth's personification of Duty who "preserve[s] the stars from wrong." In such a world, art may be said at once to imitate and perfect or complete nature. The artist may be thought to catch the tendency or direction latent in natural growth, to free it of accidental shortcomings, and so to reveal an ideal not to be envisaged otherwise. So is the human form transfigured in Greek sculpture but still presented in its natural perfection.

According to a variant interpretation, nature may appear as autonomous or as embodying in herself the harmony sometimes said to be imposed upon her. Nature then displays a wisdom or an efficiency surpassing the human. The universal fact of growth, the fitness of the organism for sustaining life in its proper environment, the healing power of nature, the accuracy of instinct, the "geometry of the spider's web," and the intricate beauty of many living forms are all recognized as revealing the wisdom and spirit or "plastic" power of living nature, celebrated by many writers including Shaftesbury and Wordsworth. Even human consciousness itself in its spontaneous and less deliberate moments may be thought to belong to nature so that for the romanticist and the Chinese Taoist the song of the poet and the song of the bird need not be contrasted too sharply, although the poet, unlike the bird, must "return" to nature, discarding the artificiality of his civilization.

For certain of the Stoic philosophers even human reason is recognized as "natural" so that nature absorbs human nature and includes the entire life of man in her purposes. Nature "intends" man to be a rational and reasonable animal. Of course, the word "unnatural" still refers to the human error whereby we sometimes, to our misfortune, try to separate ourselves from the course that nature assigned us, as in the case of an "unnatural" parent or child who smothers the affection that springs "naturally" in his breast or willfully ignores the "natural" order of things that includes family life. There is, however, a further step that may sometimes be taken as we interpret nature in this way. Montaigne in his essay "Of the Useful and the Honorable" writes as follows:

> Our structure, both public and private, is full of imperfection. But there is nothing useless in Nature, not even uselessness itself. Nothing has made its way into this universe that does not have a proper place in it. Our being is cemented with sickly qualities; ambition, jealousy, envy, revenge, superstition, and despair dwell in us with so natural a possession that their image is discerned also in beasts. And even cruelty, too, so unnatural a vice; for in the midst of compassion we feel within I know not what bittersweet sting of malicious pleasure in seeing others suffer; and children feel it . . .
>
> Whoever should remove from man the seeds of these qualities would destroy the fundamental conditions of our life. Likewise in all governments there are necessary offices which are

not only abject but vicious too; there vices find their place and are useful to the seaming together of our union, as poisons are useful for the preservation of our health.

Here the moral rigor implicit in the Stoic precepts is tempered by Montaigne to yield an ethic of tolerance based on a recognition of the infinite subtlety of nature's strategy.

Nonetheless, a distinction is generally maintained between nature and human nature or, most especially, between nature and the human consciousness that surveys nature and even judges her. Accordingly in ancient thought that has cleared itself of its mythological origins, we find *physis*, nature, set sharply in contrast with *nomos*, custom, and both with the aims and aspirations of the human individual. Human customs, considered by the Greek Sophists as matters of convention or agreement and including even the meanings attached to words, differ from the "natural" life of plants and animals. Thus the human individual faces two types of environment, the natural and the social, and two types of law. The Sophist delights in pointing out that the "laws" of nature are much firmer than those of human custom or convention. The latter may, indeed, be evaded with impunity by a clever and persuasive opportunist. But, as the farmer, mariner or physician will attest, the laws of nature are not to be thus scorned. Nature exacts her penalties relentlessly and commands a far greater respect on the part of the individual than the community or state, for all its pomp and air of authority, can succeed in doing. After all, man made the notions of right and wrong which are meaningless unless there is power to support them. As this line of thought continues, we find justice being defined as the interest of the stronger, that is, of the individual or party actually in power.

Here nature appears as a system of *fact* as opposed to

value or even to purpose. The word "nature" stands for the things that are and the way they behave. As such, nature tacitly rebukes the sentimentalism of those who would ignore causes in the name of ideals or purposes. The Sophists and the "realists," the advocates of power politics, often exploit these ideas for their own interests. But for a certain type of mind, this recognition of natural necessity takes on genuine dignity, an acquiescence almost comparable to Christian resignation. We may be reminded of the philosophy of Spinoza and of Keats' lines in *Hyperion* that equate personal freedom or sovereignty with our ability calmly to envisage circumstance.

Essentially different, however, is the Christian interpretation of nature. Here nature yields her authority and her finality to God who subordinates her to man. God has created nature as a suitable environment for human life and the features of the natural order of things may be described as God's gifts to man for whom he prepares a rich domain. Nature thus appears as an abundant pool of raw materials or even as a storehouse of useful objects awaiting human disposition. The danger lies only in that man may, being too fascinated by these gifts, forget their source and in thoughtless prosperity and ingratitude ignore his creaturely and dependent status. Thus the medieval thinker is often fearful of too great a concern with nature unless she may be interpreted as manifesting the glory of her maker. Otherwise, it is insisted, man will find no lasting satisfaction in such an interest. This attitude is by no means limited to the Middle Ages. Consider for instance Herbert's "The Pulley":

When God at first made man,
Having a glasse of blessings standing by;
Let us (said he) poure on him all we can:
Let the worlds riches, which dispersed lie,
Contract into a span.

So strength first made a way;
Then beautie flow'd, then wisdome, honour, pleasure:
Then almost all was out, God made a stay,
Perceiving that alone of all his treasure
Rest in the bottom lay.

For if I should (said he)
Bestow this jewell also on my creature,
He would adore my gifts instead of me,
And rest in Nature, not the God of Nature.
So both should losers be.

Yet let him keep the rest,
But keep them with repining restlessnesse:
Let him be rich and wearie, that at least,
If goodnesse leade him not, yet wearinesse
May tosse him to my breast.

In modern times, interest in nature takes on a new aspect. We are no longer content to enjoy the fruits of nature as we find them. We grow eager to subject nature to our will. Thus, with Bacon and Descartes, Europeans seek scientifically to direct natural process according to the maxim that we may control or transform nature by obeying her. Prediction of natural phenomena and control of causal sequences thus become the main business of the scientist who sees in the regularity of natural process the possibility of transforming our environment. Nor need he stop at this point. Human nature need no longer be treated as an exception. The systems of cause and effect that become apparent to the research student are finally interpreted as including not only nature in the older sense but human behavior as well, and man finds himself engulfed in the determinism that Descartes had recognized as characterizing only the physical world. Here we encounter a paradoxical turn of thought. The causal determinism, that has at its first appearance encouraged man to think of himself as the master of nature, shortly thereafter persuades him that he is himself but a part of nature and, as such, subject in thought and action to the law-abiding routine of causal sequences that he has not initiated.

There is something sublime about this all-encompassing system of causation before which the modern mind stood for generations in mingled fascination and dismay. Nature so conceived combines the orderliness of the ancient cosmos with the infinite expanse of a modern universe. The result carries a certain moral significance in that it inspires humility. Thus, for Meredith even Satan will stand abashed before the majesty of astronomical determinism, "the armies of unalterable law." Here necessity appears as mathematical or Newtonian in pattern. Nature displays the precision of an ideal chronometer. No longer the "homely nurse," no longer the unruly or awkward apprentice, nature appears as something much more impersonal: a system of law-abiding phenomena. All events of whatever sort "obey" the laws of nature.

At this point a singular crisis emerges that transforms once more the idea of nature. "Obedience" loses its original meaning since its opposite has been ruled out. No events ever "disobey" natural law. Thus the analogy is completely outworn. Nature is no more than a system of phenomena whose regularity, statistical or mechanical, exhausts its meaning. As such, nature becomes wholly inhuman, distant, and indifferent to our concerns. In Darwinian biology, "Mother Nature" yields to "natural selection," a metaphor to make clear the brute fact that in the struggle for survival weaker organisms and species are inevitably eliminated. The cold neutrality of natural process, even when "red in tooth and claw," is a stupefying rather than shocking revelation, from which many nineteenth-century writers like Tennyson tried desperately to escape.

Some of the efforts to escape this notion of nature's indifference land us in further difficulty. It may be suggested that natural selection is not a wholly mechanical matter. Perhaps in some way nature actually "favors" the strong, or, at any rate, justifies the notion that power is an end in itself. Here may be heard an echo of the Sophistic ethics. The survival of the strong sets a standard of value and *nomos* is once more absorbed by *physis*, albeit a *physis* in nineteenth-century dress. Here the Christian ethic of humility and brotherly love appears as "unnatural." The kingdom of heaven is surely not of this world, where life is first and foremost a matter of competition. At this juncture, one may adopt the strategy of a Nietzsche and celebrate the *Umwertung aller Werte*—the inversion of all values. Or one may take the attitude of the "naturalistic" novelist whose intention is to describe, perhaps to explain, but never to evaluate. Here the ideal of the naturalist is primarily an intellectual one. Nature challenges the artist along with the scientist to describe and explain. Evaluation is out of place. To undertake it is a mark of presumption.

There is still another possibility. Having repudiated the idea of nature as an exemplar of value, we may insist that values and evaluation reside not in nature but in human consciousness. Thus we come upon various efforts to establish some kind of humanism that will clearly distinguish human nature from its "natural" origin, environment, or substructure. We may recall the humanism of Irving Babbitt with its doctrine of conscience or "inner check" that seems to have exercised a real influence on modern letters, especially through Babbitt's student, T. S. Eliot. Or we may consider once more the philosophy of the existentialists, for whom human *subjectivity* is wholly distinct from the order of nature. In this view the individual's way of thinking of himself actually alters, even creates, his own mode of existence. Put very briefly, our subjectivity is not a part of nature in the sense just considered. To quote Sartre, a man is not a "piece of moss, a cabbage, or a paper knife." He is not, strictly speaking, a member of a species or a type. He is not cut to pattern. He is free, like the Adam of Pico della Mirandola to choose his own status, to classify himself, to accept a future and assume obligations. The individual *exists* in his decisions and commitments. Such existence is not a matter of habit or routine; it is not a matter of accepting ready-made alternatives; it is not a matter of obedience to law, human, natural, or divine. It cannot be observed from without and it follows no predetermined pattern and yet it fashions a pattern of its own. It is human subjectivity and as such it is like nothing else in the world. So oriented, existentialism stands as the absolute repudiation of the naturalism of the past century. We have noticed above that the existentialist concept of human subjectivity opens a line of thought that may present the individual with new difficulties. These may carry a threat to his sense of spiritual well-being quite as formidable as that springing from an out-and-out naturalism.

Perhaps the above examples, chosen almost at random, will suffice to indicate to the student a possible approach to literature, an approach from which he may discern a wealth of ideas present in every period and a certain complex or contrast of ideas characterizing each period. The student will find ideas of one kind or another relevant to every author that he studies. It should, of course, go without saying that the presence of an important idea in the work of an author does not, in itself, enhance the value of his contribution. On the other hand, without some reference to the ideas expressed in a poem or a novel we may hardly speak intelligently of its value. If we follow the Kantian tradition by describing aesthetic value as residing in a harmony of understanding and sensibility, we may consistently argue that familiarity with ideas embodied in or clearly relevant to a work of art is an important auxiliary of critical appreciation. Certainly many students have found this to be the case and no scholar or critic can afford wholly to ignore the ideas that have fascinated the imagination of the author that he studies. After all, such a study can hardly fail to expand our human sympathies and ultimately to support Walter Pater in his earnest belief that "nothing which has ever interested living men and women can wholly lose its vitality."

7

LITERATURE AND THE ARTS

MARY GAITHER

COMPARATIVE STUDIES of literature and the arts offer a touchy field of exploration. Not all those concerned are in agreement on the proper scope of such studies even if they are agreed that such studies are worthwhile. Terms of description which must be used as one moves from one art to another are frequently inadequate. Terms of identification, names of styles and movements, which are often common to two or more modes of artistic creation, do not always convey the same meaning. When we speak of the rhythm of a Shakespearean sonnet or of a Beethoven sonata are we speaking of the same thing? Can balance in a Van Gogh painting be described in the same terms as that in a drama of Lorca? When we speak of Expressionism in drama and painting are we speaking of the same mode? When we describe Impressionism in painting can we apply the same description of style and idea to Impressionism in music and literature?

For the student of literature and the arts the problem of making oneself understood while using the terms at his disposal is a difficult one. Many critics, especially in literature, have attempted to find precise terms appropriate for elucidating a particular form. For example, John Crowe Ransom in poetry and Francis Fergusson in drama have sought to provide definitive terms when they analyze and interpret these forms of literature.[1]

Assuming that studies of literature and its relation to the other arts are desirable, and being forewarned of the complications of communication, the investigation of certain problems of comparison can be both stimulating and satisfying. The student must keep always in mind his immediate goal and not be diverted by charming but unproductive will-o-the-wisps; he must not create comparisons where they are not valid or force them just for the sake of the comparison.

The area of investigation offers countless subjects, limited indeed only by man's knowledge and time itself. However, the approaches to comparative studies of the arts and literature seem to be of three primary kinds: relationship of form and content, influence, and synthesis.[2] There may, of course, be overlapping, but the emphasis will identify the approach. In the following I should like to illustrate some of these approaches by examining some outstanding studies.

Of the three major kinds of study, only the first need be defined. Form and content is at best an inadequate description of problems which embrace the wide range of style, technique, narrative, and idea. Undoubtedly the majority of studies fall within the vast range of form and all that compounds it. Even relationships between two forms of art existing generations apart and seen only as a way of sharpening our appreciation of either may justifiably be considered in this category. I am thinking here of Stephen Spender's provocative preface to *The Novices of Sais*[3] by Novalis, published together with sixty of Paul Klee's nature drawings, not as illustrations but as parallels. Juxtaposed as they are, we are made to feel more about both Novalis and Klee than we might have otherwise. Spender describes the work of both the eighteenth-century poet and the twentieth-century artist as "a curiously interior world; a world of pure art and pure contemplation, of imagist poems, and an intense, glowing yet humorous and meticulous imagination. The drawings here are meant as . . . a kind of reflection of the world of Novalis within the world of Paul Klee." Another illustration of how the juxtaposition of a poem with a painting may illuminate meaning can be seen in W. H. Auden's poem "Musée des Beaux Arts" in which he spans human suffering by calling attention to the composition of Breughel's "Icarus." Both these illustrations of a relationship between poetry and painting are highly subjective but no less effective for their subjectivity. They demonstrate the facile relationships between the arts which lie close to the surface needing only a perceptive mind to bring them into full view. But there are other, more formal and systematic approaches with which the student should be acquainted.

A classic study of the relationship between literature and the arts is an essay by the eighteenth-century German critic, Gotthold Ephraim Lessing. When Lessing sought to define the respective limits of poetry and the plastic arts in *Laocoön,* he contended that certain subjects were more suitable for painting, others more suitable for poetry. His point of departure is the group sculpture, the Laocoön, unearthed at Rome in 1506. In comparing the sculptor's presentation of Laocoön and his sons in the coils of the two sea monsters with Vergil's account of the same incident in *The Aeneid,* Lessing was concerned with the question of whether it was aesthetically desirable only to suggest the pain as the sculptor had done or to depict it graphically as Vergil had done. Few will deny the vividness of Vergil's account: "He strains his hands to tear their knots apart, his fillets spattered with foul black venom; at once to heaven raises awful cries; as when, bellowing, a bull shakes the wavering axe from his neck and rushes wounded from the altar." [4]

Lessing accepts what each artist in his interpretation

of the subject has done as being within the limits of his respective art. While the sculptor has done well in not allowing Laocoön to shriek, the poet has done equally well in allowing him to do so. Lessing's basis for this conclusion is that the natural limitations of the plastic arts (of which, for the ancients, beauty was the highest law) [5] and the natural flexibility of poetry supported such interpretations. The poet is not compelled to compress his "picture" into the space of a single moment, nor to observe any of the other limits of plastic imitation. Once he has succeeded in conveying to the reader all his hero's nobler qualities (which obviously the sculptor cannot do), the reader will give little thought to bodily form or physical action. On the other hand, the Greek sculptors have in portraying the torture felt by Laocoön reduced it to such a degree that it is compatible with beauty. Contorting the face or throwing the body into a forced position would have robbed the statue of the "beautiful lines . . . which define it in a quieter condition" (p. 12). Had either the artist or the poet failed to recognize the laws by which his respective art governs itself, he would have failed to create an aesthetically pleasing art form.

Lessing's effort to separate the mode of poetry from that of the plastic arts is based upon two considerations: the art forms and our own modes of perception. Lessing observes that time is the element of poetry and space the element of the plastic arts (p. 55). When we look at a canvas we apprehend the whole by seeing the relation of its objects in space. When we read a poem our grasp of it depends upon a sequence of effects in time. A greater responsibility for the right choice of subject devolves upon the painter than on the poet if his end result is to convey a meaningful whole. He should therefore choose the "most pregnant moment" of action to portray. He will be able to suggest a subsequent action, but that is all he can do–

suggest. The spatial form within which he must work limits him to portraying "physical beauty." Physical beauty is that which "arises from the harmonious effect of manifold parts that can be taken in at one view" (p. 74).

While the artist is limited in what he may depict by the spatial relationship, the poet is freer in his choice of material but is limited in his means. That which the painter expresses with color and line in space is more difficult to render with words in time. The poet, rather than describing a thing or person, often depends upon describing the effect which it makes (e.g., Homer describes the effects of Helen's beauty rather than the beauty itself). This the poet can do quite easily, since he does not have to restrain himself within the limits of the painter. He can move from moment to moment, idea to idea, depicting motion and action in time, all of which is beyond the limit of the painter. For Lessing, the realm of the plastic arts is limited to objects in space, while that of poetry includes movement in time.

In most modern writing and painting the principles of aesthetic perception which Lessing notes are still operative, but some modern writers, who use the stream-of-consciousness technique, have recognized the principle of spatial perception in creating a new narrative form. Spatial form is as common in literature today as it is in the plastic arts. Joseph Frank in a study of spatial form in modern literature states: "Modern literature exemplified by such writers as T. S. Eliot, Ezra Pound, Marcel Proust, and James Joyce is moving in the direction of the spatial form. This means the reader is intended to apprehend their work spatially in a moment of time, rather than as a sequence."[6] The method of perception is the same as that described by Lessing in the plastic arts, but the object of the perception is different.

Mr. Frank points out that the reader receives the

whole impression of the complete works of writers such as he has mentioned, not page by page, nor action by action, but by means of "reflexive reference" whereby the reader fits together reference after reference and gains at the conclusion of his reading a complete picture of what the poet or novelist has accomplished through spatial form. Modern poetry in particular "is based upon a space-logic which demands a complete reorientation in the reader's attitude towards language." The reader must relate and organize apparently isolated fragments and word clusters to an implied and focused situation within the poem itself. The principle of reflexive reference is a basic conception of modern poetry and establishes the link between modern poetry and similar experiments in the modern novel. From Flaubert to Joyce and Proust, Mr. Frank demonstrates this principle which produces spatial form and reaches its culmination in a relatively unknown novel, *Nightwood* by Djuna Barnes.[7]

Mr. Frank feels that "just as modern artists have abandoned any attempt at naturalistic representation" so has Miss Barnes abandoned "any pretensions to . . . verisimilitude," and the result in the latter case is "a world as strange to the reader at first sight, as the world of abstract art was to its first spectators." In his detailed analysis of this novel Mr. Frank sees that what holds the chapters together is not progressive action of any kind, either physical action or thinking, but rather the use of images and symbols which have to be constantly referred and cross-referred to one another "throughout the time-act of reading." He concludes that since the unit of meaning in *Nightwood* is usually a phrase or sequence of phrases "it carries the evolution of spatial form in the novel forward to a point where it is practically undistinguishable from modern poetry."

Applied to a novel less obscure and esoteric in idea

but equally spatial in form, Virginia Woolf's *Mrs. Dalloway*, Mr. Frank's theory can be given further proof of validity. The time covered in *Mrs. Dalloway* is one day in June 1923. In this day we move though certain sections of London taking in the sights; smelling the odors of a big city; hearing the noises of buses, an aeroplane, the voices of beggars; meeting shoppers, saunterers in the park, the crowds that move to and fro in the streets. We also move in and out of a few selected homes, a doctor's office, stores and shops. Within these two physical bounds of particular time and place, Virginia Woolf presents Clarissa Dalloway and the handful of other characters who are necessary to an understanding of the main figure and the complexity of themes expressed. As the doctor in Miss Barnes's *Nightwood* serves as the unifying factor for what seem to be unrelated parts, a unifying factor, but not progressive action or thinking, holds together Mrs. Woolf's novel: the use of certain symbols and images which occur and recur throughout the space of the novel—the party which Mrs. Dalloway is giving and which provides the culminating point of the piece, the striking of Big Ben and other motifs of time and sound, the sun images, the seemingly disconnected lines from *Cymbeline* and *The Winter's Tale*, the flower symbols, unidentified personages—all add up to the total effect. We must make note of them, relate them to the major characters, else the intended identity of the two figures of Clarissa and Septimus remains lost and the whole work meaningless. We must almost literally stand still in space and move back and forth in time, not only with the characters but by ourselves, in order to fit together by "reflexive reference" the parts of the whole and apprehend the work "spatially in a moment of time rather than as a sequence."

The interrelation of the arts may often help the critic toward a deeper understanding of the work that he studies. But we may go further: the artist himself may profit by recognizing such an analogy. T. S. Eliot in his essay on "The Music of Poetry" [8] states explicitly what the study of music may contribute to poetry.

I think that a poet may gain much from the study of music. . . . I believe that the properties in which music concerns the poet most nearly, are the sense of rhythm and the sense of structure. . . . The use of recurrent themes is as natural to poetry as to music. There are possibilities for verse which bear some analogy to the development of a theme by different groups of instruments; there are possibilities of transitions in a poem comparable to the different movements of a symphony or a quartet; there are possibilities of a contrapuntal arrangement of subject-matter.

Upon reading this we think of Eliot's *Four Quartets* and try to find a comparison between the form of the poems and the analogous musical form. Miss Helen Gardner [9] has carried out this comparison and found it fruitful. Her careful analysis deepens our appreciation of the poems themselves; it also verifies the poet's own theory as stated above.

Four Quartets is composed of four poems, each named for a place related to a time in the total experience of men. Burnt Norton, East Coker, and Little Gidding are English villages, the Dry Salvages a group of rocks off the New England coast. Each poem is divided into five parts which Miss Gardner sees as "five movements each with its own inner structure." The first movement "contains statement and counter-statement" similar to the "first and second subject of a movement in a strict sonata form." The second movement treats a single subject in two different ways, the effect of which Miss Gardner says is "like hearing the same melody played on a different group of instruments, or differently harmonized, or hearing it syncopated, or elaborated in variations." The third movement presents less of a musical analogy; the fourth is seen as a "brief lyrical movement" after which the fifth "recapitulates the themes of the poem with personal and topical applications and makes a resolution of the contradictions of the first."

Besides calling our attention to the apparent composition of the poems along principles of musical form, Miss Gardner indicates the recurrence of images, symbols, and certain words which thus take on a deepened and expanded meaning. Eliot himself describes this "music of meaning" but without specific reference to *Four Quartets*. He writes:

> The music of a word is, so to speak, at a point of intersection: it arises from its relation first to the words immediately preceding and following it, and indefinitely to the rest of its content; and from another relation, that of its immediate meaning in that context to all the other meanings which it has had in other contexts, to its greater or less wealth of association. . . . My purpose here is to insist that a "musical poem" is a poem which has a musical pattern of sound and a musical pattern of the secondary meaning of the words which compose it, and that these two patterns are indissoluble and one.[10]

Miss Gardner in going beyond the musical composition and treatment of thematic materials in *Four Quartets* finds another musical reminder in Eliot's treatment of images "which recur with constant modifications, from their context, or from their combination with other recurring images, as a phrase recurs with modifications in music." The images and symbols are common, obvious and familiar when we first meet them but "as they recur they alter as a phrase does when we hear it on a different instrument, or in another key, or when it is blended and combined with another phrase, or in some way turned round, or inverted." By the method hinted at by Eliot himself Miss Gardner's analysis does much to enhance the poet's work by showing us ways of "listening" to it that might not have occurred to us.[11] Such an effort, satisfying as it is, suggests a way to approach the work of other poets who have also become aware of this "music of meaning." It should go without saying that such studies as Miss Gardner's can be done only by those with knowledge of musical forms sufficient to point the way.

In passing we may point to another illustration of what light the knowledge of another art, in this case a particular mode of painting, can shed on the understanding of a poem. This may be seen in Sir Herbert Read's tracing the parallel between dream-formation and poem-formation in one of his own poems.[12] In doing so, Read makes quite clear the relation between surrealism in art and surrealism in literature and the source of both in the psychology which gave surrealism its impetus. The consideration of the rhyme employed and the examination of the images lead him to describe such a poem, i.e., a surrealist poem, "as the manifest content of a dream whose latent thoughts have been turned into sensory images or visual scenes; the abstract, that is to say, is merged again in the concrete form from which it sprang."

Up to this point we have been concerned with relationships without reference to a common denominator of time or cultural influence. It has been pointed out that the knowledge of principles of one medium may suggest new approaches to a totally different medium of artistic expression. We turn now to parallels that are found to exist between art and literature as a result of their contemporaneity. It is difficult here to steer clear of the problem of influence. It is also difficult to avoid the implication that different art forms of the same period developed under the same influences.

An enterprising study that tries to allow for the possibilities of such influence is Helmut Hatzfeld's *Literature*

Through Art which the author subtitles "a new approach to French literature." The restriction of the study to the literature and art of one nation has obvious advantages not the least of which is the consideration of two art forms conditioned by the same factors and thus more likely to reveal a community of reflection. The theory underlying Hatzfeld's examination of literature and art is simply that a consideration, side by side, of different art forms within the same cultural epoch must increase the possibilities for interpretation. Placing a poem or novel beside a painting or piece of sculpture may very well reveal a new meaning of the literary text, may illustrate the different expression of the same motif or theme "according to the separate domain and medium of poet and painter," may prove mutual influences and inspirations. The emphasis of this comparative study, however, is the "cultural pattern of the epoch."

The author, in considering texts and art works from the same periods, has brought to bear on his comparisons "the common spiritual root behind the related examples." The conclusion drawn from this extensive study of the interrelations of culture and artistic expression is that the literature and art of any given historical epoch may be approached from seven categories: 1] details of a literary text elucidated by a picture, 2] details of a picture clarified by a literary text, 3] concepts and motifs of literature clarified by the arts of design, 4] motifs of pictures elucidated through literature, 5] and 6] literary-linguistic forms and literary-stylistic expressions in literature and art, and 7] borderlines between literature and art.[13]

Hatzfeld's method does provide illuminations of both literature and art and deepens our insights into the character of the artistic expression. Comparison of the landscapes of Claude Lorrain and the dialogue of Racine's dramas underscores the concept of formal beauty and idealized arrangement of nature held by the seventeenth-century poets and painters. The full description, poetic language, the melancholy air to be found in the writing of Chateaubriand are exemplified in paintings of Girodet-Tricson, Delaroche, David, and Gérard, all contributing to certain aspects of the romantic spirit that dwelt on the exotic and foreign, the "soulless physical beauty." The key to the "dark, cryptic, and the ununderstandable" in Rimbaud's "Mystique," from *Les Illuminations,* may be found in Gauguin's painting "Jacob Wrestling With the Angel," and the psychic conflict in Van Gogh is paralleled in the poems of Émile Verhaeren. An equally convincing parallel both in form and content is to be seen in the comparison of Courbet's "Funeral at Ornans" and Flaubert's description of Emma's burial in *Madame Bovary*. In both, exactness of detail conveys an objective picture of a given moment in life. Hatzfeld's study may be criticized for its definitions and choice of illustration, perhaps even for the theory upon which it is based, forcing at times comparisons which are artificial. But it does give insights into the meaning of the literature and art of a given period and it does suggest the potential of the philological approach.

A different approach to a study of the relationship of literature to the arts is Calvin Brown's *Music and Literature.*[14] Instead of being concerned with parallelisms from a cultural and philological point of view, Brown considers the relationship of literature and music based upon the elements they have in common, upon the instances of collaboration between the two (from the folk epic to opera), and upon the cases of influence of a writer upon a musician, a musician upon a writer. Brown provides so many specific examples of relationships between literature and music that it is hard to demonstrate his method. However, the chapters on Whitman and Aiken serve to show two different kinds of analysis of the same literary form. Whitman's "When Lilacs Last in the Dooryard Bloom'd" is analyzed for its musical development of symbols, an unconscious and inspired musical treatment by a "musical illiterate." Brown sees the poem not as one "about" the death of Lincoln but as "the complex and beautiful interrelationship in the poet's mind by which a number of hitherto insignificant things have come to symbolize a complex experience" (p. 194). The chapter on Aiken offers a contrast in subject, for the poet here is consciously and deliberately creating poetry based upon musical principles. Using his knowledge of Aiken's intention Brown illustrates copiously from Aiken's poetry the formal musical arrangement which the poet uses, concluding that Aiken, more than any one else who has tried, has succeeded by means of musical symbols and techniques to "let us hear whole concerts of this fleeting, elusive music of the mind" (p. 207). Brown is not concerned with historical development or the reflection of any common cultural background—he takes all music and all literature as his province in this study. Although not so interesting as Hatzfeld's *Music and Literature*, Brown's work offers less to argue with and undoubtedly gives the student more concrete suggestions for problems of comparison and methods of research.

One of the areas to exert an influence upon comparative studies of literature and art has been that of art history. Heinrich Wölfflin's *Principles of Art History* (1915) formulated the theory of artistic creation on the basis of the way things are seen and felt. Occupied with the contrast of Renaissance and Baroque, Wölfflin described their respective features as they reflected different levels of perception and contended that Baroque is a natural development from Renaissance and not a decline, that the change can be demonstrated by looking at the art work in five different aspects: the image itself (linear-painterly), the arrangement in space (flat-deep), the way the parts of the whole are combined (distinct parts-unified whole), the structure (closed-open), and the view of the whole (clear-blurred). The importance here of Wölfflin's principles is the effect they have had upon literary historians in providing them with similar means of interpreting literary styles. Oskar Walzel [15] in Germany and Fritz Strich [16] in Switzerland applied Wölfflin's method to English (Shakespeare) and German literature with partial success.

The significance of these attempts to apply the principles of art history to literary history lies in the discovery that one cannot simply borrow the basic concepts of one art medium and apply them to another even of the same period, though one may find both art forms containing common elements. Since there is not a parallel development in form and style, the principles for interpreting a given art form must derive from the nature of the work itself. Attention to one art of the same period will undoubtedly suggest concepts for interpreting another, but they cannot merely be transferred. Hatzfeld's study does not attempt to establish basic concepts for interpreting both literature and art of the same period, but rather gives seven ways by which a study of literature through art may increase our understanding of both without insisting upon a parallel development.

A more recent attempt to describe and interpret literature through art styles and art criticism is Wylie Sypher's *Four Stages of Renaissance Style.*[17] The author is prompted by what others after Wölfflin and Walzel discovered—that working with contrasts like Renaissance and Baroque tends to oversimplify the matter, improperly makes art fit a pattern, and does not take into account all the varieties and movements that cannot fit into either of the two opposites. Sypher's approach is based entirely upon style. Rather than talk about parallels in styles between the arts, he prefers to use the term "analogy" between styles to describe the various ways in which the arts reflect social changes, each style with "its own evolution, transformation and eventual disappearance" (p. 7). In the emergence of these styles there are frequently "exchanges" of techniques between arts when the technique of one penetrates another as sculpture in painting, narrative in music, water color in oil painting. When there are combinations or interpenetrations of several techniques there are what Sypher calls "transformations" of style: "the tone poem in music uses techniques that are pictorial and narrative, generating at the intersection of three opposing techniques an equivocal order of art with inherently nonmusical values of color and anecdote" (p. 9). And as there are analogies of style so may there be analogies of form—the way in which the artist arranges his material—and Sypher contends that "if we can find analogies of form within the various arts of the renaissance, we possibly can define for literature as well as for painting, sculpture, and architecture the mechanisms of a changing renaissance style that emerges, transforms itself, re-emerges, and at last plays itself out in a severe equation" (p. 10).

It is thus that Sypher examines the literature, painting, sculpture, architecture of three centuries and shows how their corresponding changes in style reflect various factors that give identity to the styles—sometimes pure, sometimes transitions—and how these styles form a sequence of four stages: renaissance, mannerist, baroque, and late-baroque. These styles, however, do not arise and develop simultaneously in each country. There are "lags" from one country to the next, from one art to the next. And the work of one artist may even reflect at different times different styles.

At present one may distinguish different trends in this field of studies. Extreme skepticism against past accomplishments and present endeavors is authoritatively represented by Wellek and Warren's *Theory of Literature.*[18] Mr. Wellek's chapter eleven, "Literature and Other Arts," forms the end and, in a way, the climax of "the extrinsic" (and therefore the undesirable) approach to the study of literature. After an excellent and swift survey of both practice and theory from Horace to Walzel the chapter concludes with a grave warning not to attempt a synthesis too soon. "Only when we have evolved a successful system of terms for the analysis of literary works of art can we delimit literary periods, not as metaphysical entities dominated by a 'time spirit.' Having established such outlines of strictly literary evolution, we then can ask the question whether this evolution is, in some way, similar to the similarly established evolution of the other arts. The answer will be, as we can see, not a flat 'yes' or 'no.' It will take the form of an intricate pattern of coincidences and divergences rather than parallel lines" (p. 135).

However, the wary attitude of the pure theorist is not shared by the majority of researchers in the field. The center of their activity is to be found in the *Journal of Aesthetics and Art Criticism,* founded in 1941. The journal is full of lively controversies, but the group represented by it, the American Society for Aesthetics, is constantly striving for synthesis, no matter how tentative and how temporary. In a presidential address (1956) before the society, H. Hungerland pointed to both conflict and compromise: "The scientific investigation of aesthetic phenomena has been hampered by a pseudo-conflict between 'relativistic' and 'universalistic.' . . . I should like to suggest that probably 'the aesthetic response' in general can best be defined in terms of the core of a number of overlapping areas. The areas seen as overlapping would be the aesthetic-response-to-literature, the aesthetic-response-to-music, etc., and one should not expect the general definition to be applicable in all respects to all the areas." [19] Again and again one finds in the pages of the journal calls to carry on the work in spite of conflicting theories: "I do not share the view of many aestheticians . . . that the adequacy of evaluation depends primarily on a satisfactory critical theory." Or, "we should cease to expect to supplant emotionalist theories by formalist theories or vice versa. There is no choice to be made between these, and if it is offered, something of value is in danger of being ignored." [20] But the most substantial documentation of the widespread activity in the theory of the arts and their relations is found in the journal's annual "Selective Current Bibliography for Aesthetics and Related Fields" compiled by H. Hungerland.

Still less concerned with theory and dedicated to the literary point of view is a discussion group of the Modern Language Association, Literature and the Other Arts. The papers before this discussion group frequently treat the relation of a particular author to the sister arts. Here, too, an important by-product has been an annual bibliography, all numbers since 1952 reprinted in 1968.[21]

With all art and literature for its province, their study offers countless possibilities from chance associations between single works of art to highly complex patterns of interpenetration of the literary and art work of entire cultural epochs. Nor is this approach to the study of the arts an artificial one. The serious artist and critic are ever-conscious of the "natural affinities" that exist between art and literature, and almost without exception allow these affinities themselves to suggest the parallels, the influences, the borrowings that become the basis for comparative analysis. At times the artist himself is consciously aware of themes, techniques of composition, formal arrangement, and development of ideas that come from another work of art. This awareness may provide only an inspiration or it may be more obvious in an actual expression. Lessing, Baudelaire, T. S. Eliot, for example, provide convincing illustration of this consciousness and its fruits. For the comparatist, the point has this significance: the relevance of literature to the arts is not an invention of the critics; it is an actual fact acknowledged by the artists themselves.

8

LITERATURE FOR THE UNLETTERED

STITH THOMPSON

THOUGH THE TITLE of this chapter may seem paradoxical, it was not made so deliberately to pique curiosity. It is actually about as accurate a statement of the topic as possible. Of course, a narrow definition of literature would always imply writing and reading and would utterly exclude those old tales, songs, myths, legends, rituals, and orations which are directed toward those who do not habitually read. Though it may take some indulgence on the part of the reader, the term literature is here applied to such manifestations of the human spirit as those, since they serve the same purpose for the unlettered as written literature does for readers and writers.

Unlettered has been chosen rather than illiterate to describe the beneficiaries of such literature. For "illiterate" has in these days taken on a bad odor. We are apt to think of a person surrounded by public schools but failing to take advantage of opportunities—in a word, shiftless, unambitious, perhaps low in intellectual powers. But we must remember that the lack of ability to read and write has not always had this connotation even in our own culture. Few of our seventeenth- and eighteenth-century grandmothers went far beyond signing their names—if they did not actually content themselves with making a cross at the bottom of a deed or mortgage.

If by literate persons we mean those who are in the

habit of getting their information from writing or print instead of from the spoken word, we must realize how restricted this group is. Outside of a relatively few countries of Europe and lands that they have influenced, the vast majority still remain unlettered, and as we go back across the centuries the readers become an ever smaller and more select class. Even in the great days of Egypt, of Greece and Rome, most of the writing was for a small elite, and only when the oral medium was employed, as in the orations or the dramas or the recited poems, did the great mass benefit by literature.

This general lack of the art of reading and writing among a people, whether Chinese, Melanesians or ancient Greeks, means that the attitude now commonly held toward the illiterates among us must be abandoned when we broaden and deepen our outlook. It is a fair guess that there are proportionately as many talented people in an unlettered group as among readers. These peoples have their leaders and their led. They have taletellers and listeners, epic poets and rhapsodes and spellbound audiences, musicians, dancers, orators, statesmen, warriors—as well as men and women sages. The high intelligence of those who went to the theater in Athens has often been remarked, but the great mass of them observed and heard and talked, but could not read. And if this was true in Athens, how much more so in Sparta or Macedonia!

The expanding of the capacities of the human spirit which has accompanied the use of writing accounts for the most remarkable difference between the gifted men of today and those of five thousand years ago or of far-flung primitive peoples. Short as the time span since the first hieroglyphics, and few as the lettered have been, it is through writing that the carefully considered thoughts of man have been handed down to become a part of the intellectual and artistic world of those who can read. Philosophy, science, law—all become permanent and are expanded by each lettered generation. And, above all, the finely wrought turn of phrase, or the exactly patterned poem, or the tale told with superb artistry is fixed for all time—no longer fluid, no longer uncertain, no longer dependent on the fluctuations of memory and forgetfulness. The world of those who read is, or at least can be, of infinitely greater richness than that of the unlettered.

But the very extent of unlettered humanity in all past ages, and even now, makes the study of its artistic and literary endeavors a challenge not only for the ethnologist but also for the student of letters. The tales told and the songs sung by the cave dwellers in Spain two hundred centuries ago, by those who tended the flocks of Abraham, by the subjects of the great Inca, by the present-day Eskimo, by the Yugoslav peasant or American backwoodsman—have these anything in common, anything which contrasts with the products of the writer's pen?

Of course, some of these people we shall never learn about, for they are beyond our reach. We can see the paintings of the cave men, but can never hear their tales. But though there are large areas which we may not explore, more than enough remain to occupy us if we would examine the literature meant for those who do not read. In the separate endeavors of all of these peoples to learn to tell tales or sing songs which others would enjoy and keep on telling and singing, did the unlettered storyteller or poet find that certain devices were successful and certain others were not successful? In other words, did he hit upon some of what we would call laws of composition? Or is this oral literature characterized merely by certain deficiencies, lacks which only writing can supply? As we look at the oral literature over the world and in all time, can we perceive any evolution, any development—for example, from simple to complex, from crude to artistic?

Perhaps it may be well to come at once to this question of evolution of oral literature. In the early years of this century, it was still the fashion to speak of the evolution of culture. Respectable ethnologists were still arranging people into strata, saying that a particular tribe belonged to the very lowest culture, and another somewhat higher, and that it was possible to arrange all the peoples of the globe according to a hierarchy, beginning at simple and going to the most complex. It was also assumed that all of the separate elements of culture would evolve within this framework, and that one tribe would certainly be like another, even though in the opposite part of the world, if they belonged on the same step of the evolutionary ladder.

But little by little ethnologists have given up such naïve ideas. While the geologist may recognize his strata and always be confident that a particular formation lies above another, no matter where found, the student of culture must realize that every people has developed in its own way, that changes and movements have proceeded unevenly. It is not possible to say that because a tribe in Central Asia manifests a certain kind of oral literature, another tribe in another part of the world roughly its equal in general complexity will have the same kind of oral literature. The bold scheme of a comprehensive study of the evolution of literature based upon the tales and songs of all of the peoples of the world arranged in order, let us say from one to twenty, and filling in all the gaps in the evolutionary scheme—that we have had to give up entirely. Too many elements enter into a particular culture, some coming from local environment, some from the influence of neighboring tribes, and some from unexpected drives in particular directions. The narrative art of a tribe in the South Pacific or central Africa may have little relation to the material culture of that people.

If the evolution of literature must be abandoned as a pleasant delusion, the study of literature of the unlettered populations of the world is not thereby made less important or less valid. On the contrary, with a growing awareness of all the complexities which enter into the literary tradition of such peoples, this investigation becomes more and more challenging. What seemed to an earlier generation to be the working of a very simple law of development now appears as the result of a complex of many forces.

One will look in vain for any sharp line of demarcation between the oral literature of so-called primitive peoples and that of the unlettered who are surrounded by a civilized society. There are, however, some general differences, and we ordinarily find ourselves dealing with the literature of primitive peoples separately. This is largely a matter of convenience. For though we may be thinking only of primitive peoples on certain days of the week, even on these days some consideration of modern peasants will always be creeping in. With this understanding, we may observe something of the range of the oral literature of peoples whom we now call primitives.

In the world of the preliterates, of the natives of Australia and New Zealand, and of Oceania, of the Indians of North and South America, of the Africans south of the Sahara, and of many scattered peoples in Southeast Asia, we find much in common in spite of large individual differences. In every one there will certainly be found some types of literary expression, usually myths and legends, and songs which we can only call lyric. But there is one form which is almost entirely absent from groups like this —narrative song.

The ballad students of an earlier generation were always looking for the ballads of primitive peoples to show something of the evolution of the great epics. I recall one of my old professors whose skepticism about this theory I did not then suspect. I suggested to him a certain study which would involve looking into the narrative songs of the American Indians; and he consented—I think now with a certain dry amusement. But I had to come back to him after some weeks of search and confess failure because I could find no such songs among the American Indians. Then he suggested that I try the Africans. My luck was no better there. It simply turned out that there were no narrative songs among the American Indians or the Africans—nothing, certainly, which would foreshadow anything like the epics as Europeans know them.

Though short lyric songs of many peoples have been collected and are worthy of study, the best of all subjects for the comparative study of literature in its full range is prose narrative. Tales, legends, or myths are to be found everywhere and are known also among our peasant groups and in our own literary tradition. People with so simple a culture as the Central Australians have legends and myths, some of them dealing with the world of long ago and some with their own contemporary life. And through all the range of primitive peoples, according to their temperaments and their environment and their tribal associations, myths have developed in some places, legends in others, and in still others artistic fictional tales—all according to the vital interests of the particular people. For the literary expression of a simple group must be functional: it must play a real part in the life of the tribe. The very fact that it persists as a part of the activity of the people shows that it has served a purpose and continues to do so. But this does not mean that it is necessarily serving any utilitarian end, that it has any practical economic value. For even in the Trobriand Islands, where Bronislaw Malinowski has so well studied the process of mythmaking and where myths contribute to the magic which these folk use for their coral gardens, even there life is more than food and raiment.

Perhaps the most potent force making for the production of all literary forms among primitive peoples as well as in our own culture is the great need for relief from boredom. The long hours of the night around the tribal campfire in war as well as in peace, the tedious days or weeks of voyages or journeys by foot or caravan, and the festive hours of relaxation in taverns and bazaars or at the banquets of chiefs and kings—all of these occupy a large part in the life of simple peoples, as well as in our own. For these occasions nothing has been more satisfactory than the telling of stories—amusing or informative or edifying.

All peoples enjoy tales which make them laugh. Of these stories, when we consider them the world over, there is a great variety. Very often—and not alone among the simplest peoples—the humorous tale is merely one of discomfiture, showing a kind of sadistic delight in seeing someone, preferably a person or being of great dignity or even divinity, brought down to the level of ordinary mortals and properly cudgeled or disgraced. The great culture hero of our northern Indians appears now as the dignified Hiawatha and now as the fool taking pity on the creaking limbs of the tree and getting caught between them. Or the amusing tale may concern the cleverness which overcomes stupidity or malice. Hence the whole cycle of anecdotes the world over of the clever fox or rabbit or jackal and his tricks on the stupid bear.

And it is not civilized man who first invented the risqué tale. People everywhere have been interested in grossly exaggerated stories of bodily members and their functioning, of stupendous sexual prowess, of the breach of the tribal sexual tabus, and of clever and sometimes brutal seductions; but such stories are ubiquitous and of course have not ceased with the invention of writing.

For more serious moments, whether informally or as a part of ritual observance, men everywhere and presumably at all times have had a great interest in hearing about the past, in learning of the world about them and speculating on the mysterious powers that seem to govern the life of nature, of man, and of brutes. Stories, therefore, of spirits and demons and often, on a higher plane, of gods and demigods, both in some vast historic past or now in their relation with men, have always interested primitive man—not to speak of the kings who listened to Homer's poems or the Sunday-school child of today—or at least of yesterday. The world which encompasses us, the sun, moon and stars, the animals, the trees and plants—how did all of these come to be? In response to his natural curiosity, primitive man has told tales of the creation of the universe and of the arrangement of all things as they now are. Almost all peoples have their first chapter of Genesis and their Metamorphoses, and doubtless had them thousands of years before Moses or Ovid. History, science, theology, philosophy, or at least the rudiments of these, have always interested men in their leisure time and have contributed incidentally to their education.

Stories of heroes and their incredible success in the face of monstrous adversaries—dragons, gigantic evil spirits, or overwhelming human opposition—have exercised the inventive imagination of primitive taletellers and held their audiences. Every group has made up its own heroes, and though the possible details of the hero's birth, his youth, and his adventures are definitely limited by the very nature of life, there is no necessary common pattern to them all. Maui, the semidivine hero of the Polynesians, is engaged in unbelievable supernatural adventures, tossing islands about over three thousand miles of ocean. The Iroquois heroes spend their time escaping from or overcoming the evil plots of malignant human beings; and other heroes before and after Hercules have journeyed through hell and brought home Cerberus. Or like Orpheus they have sought to regain some primitive Eurydice.

But the fictional tales of primitive man are not confined to the exploits of heroes. When we remember that in our present-day folktales the supernatural is taken for granted, we need not wonder that the stories of simpler peoples should be filled with magic wonders, with journeys to other worlds—above, below, or across—and with transformations from man to beast, with werewolves, and witches and fairies. And there is always the absorbing interest in luck of all kinds, in the finding of buried treasure, in the unexpected reunion of separated friends or loved ones, of the help, often undeserving, which comes to those in trouble and of strange adventures that may happen from some insignificant accident—these are some of the elements out of which primitive fiction is composed, and which we still see in the fairy tales of today.

Sometimes these fictional narratives become quite as complex and well constructed as any European fairy tale. I happen, for example, to have worked for some years on a single North American Indian tale—one which seems to be purely native and which has spread over a good part of the North American continent. Certainly this tale indicates an interest in storytelling and considerable invention on the part of the man who made it up, perhaps centuries ago. I cite it because it will illustrate something of the capacities of primitive peoples in constructing tales: Two girls are sleeping out one night and see two stars. Each of them wishes that she may be married to one of the stars. The next morning they find themselves in the upper world, one of them married to a young man, and one to an old one. The girls live there for some time, but they are forbidden ever to dig in the ground. One day, merely out of disobedience or sometimes because they have been egged on to do so, they dig in the ground and see below their old home and their tribe. They are seized with a longing to return and sometimes with supernatural help or with the aid of some animal, they make a long rope and descend upon it.

From that point the story is handled in several different ways, and each of these handlings constitutes a complex and continuous tradition. Sometimes the girls are lodged in a top of a tree and various animals pass below trying to induce the girls to come down. Finally they promise one of the animals that they will marry him and so they are allowed to descend. Later they deceive this animal and reach their home. Other whole sections of the country have put a different introduction to this story, so that there is only one girl who ascends to the upper world, and in that case she has a son by the upper-world husband and this son becomes the great hero after they descend and reach their home. The adventures of this hero, then, may extend to hours of taletelling.

For us the telling of such a tale, extending, as I have suggested, into hours, may seem tedious; but we must remember that primitive man and indeed most men everywhere have infinite leisure and patience. It is not unusual to hear of taletelling that lasts with due interruption for many days. And just as there seemed to be a premium on length for the medieval romances, there is often a feeling among the unlettered that a story is good in proportion to how long it lasts. Some tribes consider a story successful only when it succeeds eventually in putting everyone in the audience to sleep. The bedtime story is no modern invention.

Though the tale is a way of making primitive man's leisure more pleasant and amusing, it is often told under very strict rules. Some peoples find their lives very much ordered by seasons of the year and by the succession of day and night. Sometimes among such groups stories of a certain kind must not be told in the summer, sometimes not in the winter. There are stories suitable for daytime and for night; stories that only men can tell or women; finally, stories that belong definitely to the ceremonial life of the people. These may be told only as a part of the long rituals that accompany religious observances.

If one wishes to see the way in which stories are worked into rituals, he could not do better than to examine the ceremonials of the Navaho or the rites of the Grand Medicine Lodge of the Ojibwa. In the latter we have stories that tell the sacred legend which is illustrated by the activities performed in the ritual. Hiawatha, or Nanibozho as his real name is, has a brother who, while skating over the lake, is pulled under by the evil spirits and dies. After the mourning of the hero in his tipi, there appears at the door the spirit of his brother with a live coal. This is handed to Hiawatha and he is told that it is a symbol of eternal life and that he should form the Grand Medicine Lodge in order to keep the spark alive. This tale is now a central part of the lodge ceremonial.

One of the great moot questions among folklorists today is: which of these came first? Was there first a ritual and then a myth to support the ritual, or was the ritual invented in order to illustrate the story? It seems to me that such speculations as this are useless. It may well be shown that among such historic peoples as the Greeks and the peoples of the ancient Orient stories were sometimes invented to illustrate preexisting rituals. And yet we cannot conclude that this is a universal experience or that it is even typical of primitive man. Was the Easter celebration first or the story which that celebration illustrates? Those who worry overmuch about the mutual relations of ritual and myth also concern themselves with trying to make a sharp line between myth and tale. I am sure that no such line can be drawn, and that certainly none that we might draw would be recognized by any primitive group. For practical purposes we may well think of myth as a story of the gods and heroes and the beginnings of things; but all the tales of preliterate groups are filled with the supernatural and heroic, and it is quite impossible to say where this heroic world leaves off and the world of everyday begins.

Some of the materials and some of the functions of the tales of primitive peoples, and, in many respects, the tales of all unlettered peoples, have now been suggested. Do these oral tales possess any common characteristics as distinct from the written fiction which has overshadowed them in our own civilization?

When we begin to examine large bodies of literature meant for hearers rather than for readers, we perceive certain traits dictated by the circumstances of all oral literature. This is as true of the narrative poems which perhaps underlie our great epics as it is of the tales, because the same type of composition and preservation is present in both. It must be remembered that all of this literature is told by someone, and that the teller has learned what he is telling from someone else. He knows that faithfulness to the tradition is the most valued of all qualities in the tale-teller or the singer of the epic song. He must, if possible, transmit it as he has heard it. This sometimes requires a prodigious memory. One has only to consider the long rituals of the Navaho, extending sometimes when they are taken down to hundreds of pages of print. These rituals are delivered from memory and they are ineffective unless they are remembered exactly. It is said that the Homeric poems were thus carried on by bards for two or three centuries at least, and we know of present Yugoslav epic poems which are as long as the *Iliad* or the *Odyssey* and which are given entirely from memory. I have listened to hour-long tales in the west of Ireland and have been assured by those who have tested the recordings of these tales over long periods that they are remembered precisely as they are told.

For this kind of memory it is natural that the literature of oral peoples should have taken on a form that would assist the narrator. Thus we find in all tales and poems a large amount of repetition. Similar situations bring forth similar descriptions. Tales open and close with formulas. Huge sections are repeated verbatim. Those of us who studied Greek in school will remember the joy we used to have in coming across whole pages in Homer which repeated something we had already worked up some days before. The parts of primitive and folk narrative which are purely formulistic have never been thoroughly studied, but we know now from the efforts of Professor Lord of Harvard that, in the Yugoslav epics and in the Homeric poems at least, the formulistic and formulaic constitute much the larger part of the poems. So it is with all folk tales: always repetition and formulas. And these formulas extend beyond the merely verbal, because the characters themselves become stereotyped. Only sharp contrasts, blacks and whites, appear in such tales. Actual characterization is almost missing. Realism seldom appears in any of the stories, but rather absurd exaggerations, supernatural happenings of all kinds, often with no motivation. Even in such semisophisticated stories as those of the Arabian Nights practically all of these qualities are still present. I think it might be easy to find exceptions to some of the things I have said about the style of oral literature: one could point out the remarkable, and sometimes tedious, explanation of motives in the tales of the Kota of India. But by and large, primitive tales lack adequate motivation.

As for the songs of primitive peoples, they contain little text and are nearly all music, and are of most interest to the musician. Aside from the songs of love, war, or magic, there are some beautiful productions which we can only call chants. Such are the prayer-songs of the Papago and the long chants already mentioned in the Navaho rituals. These have much in common with such poems as those in the Egyptian Book of the Dead, with their repetition, their saying the same phrase over and over and over again, the kind of repetition which Jesus condemned in Israel and which is still a part of the ritual of the Russian Orthodox Church.

What happens to such primitive forms as the oral folk tale and the oral poem when they are in the hands of the unlettered within a civilization of readers and writers? Is there a difference, really, between the literary productions of primitive peoples and the peasantry of Asia and Europe? Many differences of course exist, but none of these are really profound. The folk tales of European peasants have the same formal characteristics as those of primitive peoples, but in general they are more tightly knit, are better motivated, and have the kind of beginning, middle, and end of which Aristotle approves. On the other hand, the peasant stories of many of the sophisticated Oriental peoples are extremely hard to outline. Unless they have been borrowed directly from Europeans they are likely to ramble interminably and apparently without reason. A story told in India seems to be almost without form, but when the same one is found in Europe it is well constructed. Do we have a case of a chaotic Indian tale coming to Europe and taking on form, or do we merely see the disintegration of a good European story which has found its way to India? Perhaps the best folk tales nowadays in our Western culture are to be found in Ireland, where they are still preserved by professional folk-tale tellers who learned them years ago from a master who had learned them from a previous master. As they come into our own continent, both north and south, these European folk tales have a tendency to degenerate. The very conditions of a peasantry, illiterate but often endowed with abilities, are lacking in the United States as well as in most of the rest of America. Such tales are definitely relics, and one has to go into remote corners to find them. They are often very interesting when found, but they are interesting as relics, and not as a vital part of our culture.

In talking about literature for the unlettered, I hope I have not given the impression that there is any sharp boundary line between the unlettered and the lettered world. The differences are smoothed over by many transitions. Some literary forms act as bridges for this gap. Perhaps the most interesting of all these is the epic, the so-called folk epic—especially the *Iliad* and the *Odyssey*. The Homeric poems were first of all oral and they remained so for several centuries before they were written down in Athens. After the remarkable analytical work recently done on the Yugoslav epics which are still being sung in Serbia and Macedonia, the oral devices in the Homeric poems cannot be denied. Were there heroic poems before Homer, telling of the Trojan war or possibly of the adventures of a hero like Odysseus? In spite of the present emphasis upon the creative ability of the poet who brought these epics together, it seems to me that there is every evidence of a society in which oral heroic songs were sung and that the time and place were only waiting for the great master to appear and to compose them into enduring epics. In Finland, also, there were and are many hundreds of heroic songs. These were gathered together more than a century ago and deliberately put into an epic called the *Kalevala*. These oral songs which lie back of the *Kalevala* can be studied, but they are no longer being composed. They are written down, and the epic is written, and though it reflects much of the oral phraseology, it is no longer a poem that would be learned and transmitted from singer to hearer.

In Russia there survives a live tradition of epic songs. These are based upon events in Russian history, many of them a thousand years old. The singers, however, are usually illiterate and they compose in a purely formulistic style. Much like them, but also different in many respects, are the already mentioned epic songs of Macedonia. As these become written down, will they also become like the Finnish epic songs and the *Kalevala,* fixed and stereotyped? It seems quite likely that with the advance of literacy this will happen. There is an accelerated tendency toward writing, and as we record more and more of the oral tales and put them into our libraries, the live tradition of oral taletelling in our own culture has a tendency to dry up.

For two thousand years now, folk literature has been affected by written literature. Tales heard from the folk may be taken over, as by Apuleius in the case of Cupid and Psyche during the second century of our era, and then they may again become oral, or the written form may be merely one of hundreds of different versions. It is certain that the great printed collections of Basile or Perrault or Grimm have affected the tradition of our tales in Europe in a way that is permanent. Today, in a great many parts of the Western world, such folk literature is merely a survival and as such is interesting to the scholar who goes to recover it before it is entirely lost. Or its preservation may become merely a matter of romanticism, merely an enthusiasm over a simple form which is different from what we meet everyday. All folklorists have at least a partly antiquarian point of view, so that they look around in holes and corners to see if they cannot rescue some remnant of a dying tradition.

But it will not do to be nostalgic about these things, for centuries of experience and association have habituated us to the written or printed page and to a different world of thought and literary style. After the Greeks had shown the fine nuances of expression which their remarkable language permitted them and had left their works fixed for all time on skins or papyri, the intellectuals of our Western world would never revert to the old, eternally changing, eternally fluid literature of their unlettered ancestors or neighbors. In spite of cultural setbacks, of stupidity and villainy, we are the inheritors of three thousand years.

If we would understand our literature well, however, we should know the soil from which it grew—the long hundreds and thousands of years when men spoke or sang and listened and kept what they had heard in memory. Person to person, generation to generation, the clever to the stupid or the stupid to the clever—so the spoken word of two thousand years before survives, is lost, or changes. Such literature never subjects itself to a final text. It produces many beautiful products, beautiful in their own way, but not in ours. For the great advance toward artistic perfection in literature came only with the written word.

Who is responsible for composing unwritten literature? In most cases we do not know at all. Outstanding men have certainly always existed. Who were the poets who preceded Homer by a thousand years? Were they priests? vagabonds? or mere local geniuses? One of these days, perhaps, we shall know more about the history of the poet, about the artist and his place in the culture of the world. And much of such history will deal with literature for the unlettered.

BIBLIOGRAPHICAL NOTE

Cf. E. B. Tyler, *Primitive Culture*, 2 vols. (London, 1871, and New York, 1958); A. S. Mackenzie, *The Evolution of Literature* (New York, 1911); Francis B. Gummere, *The Beginnings of Poetry* (New York, 1901); Bronislaw Malinowski, *Coral Gardens and their Magic* (New York, 1935) and *Myth in Primitive Psychology* (New York, 1926); Stith Thompson, *Tales of the North American Indians* (Cambridge, Massachusetts, 1929) and *Motif-Index of Folk-Literature*, 6 vols. (Copenhagen and Bloomington, 1955–58).

9

TWO TYPES OF CLASSICAL TRAGEDY

The Senecan Revolution

NORMAN T. PRATT

THIS STUDY offers two comparisons of basic importance for the interpretation of Western drama. The first will indicate some differences of orientation between the two major types of tragic drama surviving from antiquity, by differentiating the dramas written on the theme Phaedra-Hippolytus by Euripides and Seneca. Our purpose is to throw some light upon a major transition in the course of European tragedy, at the point where the classical Greek tradition ends, and the trends of the "modern" period, including Shakespeare, begin to emerge. The second section will move from *Oedipus the King* to *King Lear,* and then return to Seneca. Thus the contrast between Greek and Senecan drama will be deepened, but also extended to indicate what the "Senecan revolution" meant for the course of future drama. In both comparisons, a basis of differentiation is presented, not a study of the plays in full detail.[1]

A while ago it was the literary fashion to emphasize the ritual origin of Greek tragedy and, often, to analyze its form and to interpret the meaning in ritualistic terms. It is, to be sure, one of the few things which we can come close to knowing about the origin of Greek tragic drama that one of its sources was ritual song performed in worship of Dionysus. Dionysus, whom we often think of as the god of wine (Roman Bacchus), was actually a fertility divinity linked with nature's reproductive power and with the cycle of life and death among living things, and conceived of in male terms. Most specifically, he was associated with the life cycle of the vine: its production of harvest, the deathlike pruning of its vegetation after harvest, and its reproduction at the advent of the new season.

There is very much that we do not know about all this; the skein of available evidence is scanty and tangled. But it seems clear enough from data concerning such fertility rites and from the evidence of the plays themselves that Greek tragic drama received from ritual—like the ritual of Dionysus—a conception of nature: nature as a complex of forces which bring health or disease to plants and animals. One purpose of such ritual was to effect a reconciliation between individual living things or social organisms and the powers of nature: to avert the destructive impurities, to achieve life-nourishing purity.

The approach to these dramatic creations as founded on and conditioned by ritual has contributed considerable illumination—and much distortion when carried to extremes. For example, Francis Fergusson's influential analysis of *Oedipus the King*[2] is built upon the following ideas: "The Cambridge School of Classical Anthropologists has shown in great detail that the form of Greek tragedy follows the form of a very ancient ritual, that of the *Enniautos-Daimon* [*sic*], or seasonal god." "It is this tragic rhythm of action which is the substance or spiritual content of the play, and the clue to its extraordinarily comprehensive form."

It would be unjust to be captious about this method, for it has succeeded in revealing implications and dimensions which are fresh discoveries, and in reminding readers that we are dealing not only with a great literary tradition, but also with dramas rooted in communal ritual. However —to give a very familiar and generally discredited example—serious distortion results from viewing Oedipus as a ritual scapegoat through whom the impurities of the city are exorcised. It is one dimension of the drama that impurity and abnormality in the family of Laius have brought upon Thebes a taint which must be removed—this must be recognized if we are to understand the role of Apollo the purifier in the drama—but at the end of the tragedy we are left, not with a purified Thebes, but with a suffering tragic hero and the mystery of his experience. The point must be made that there is a great difference in level of intellectual maturity between the plays themselves and the ritualistic concepts by which the "Cambridge anthropologists" and their followers analyze the texts. The fifth-century dramatist shows himself far more sophisticated than this kind of analysis represents him to have been. Another major danger is that the imprint of ritual thus tends to become a kind of mechanistic factor which presses the drama into a formal mold. The creative function of the dramatist is seriously slighted.

Even so, a strong ritualistic motivation is apparent in the texts. A ritualistic concept is found in the orientation of these tragedies toward the issues involved in the relations between man and the powers controlling the universe. Further, the human situation vis-à-vis these powers characteristically involves impurity or abnormality or injustice which calls for some kind of purification. There are many guises of purification in the texts.

A second general point is also essential for the understanding of Euripides' *Hippolytus* and, for that matter, most of the Greek plays. The Greek conception of divinity is radically different from the Judaeo-Christian ideas familiar to Western readers of Greek literature, and is often a source of serious misunderstanding. For example, modern readers of Homer are often mystified by the action in the first book of the *Iliad* when Achilles is about to draw his sword in the quarrel with Agamemnon, but Athena suddenly appears to check him; or in the *Odyssey* by the repeated appearances of Athena to help Telemachus who is struggling to make decisions and to achieve maturity in a difficult personal situation. What is the significance of Athena's appearances? Does Homer expect us to believe that Athena appears physically, or is this simply a metaphorical way of saying that Achilles' better judgment prevailed, or that Telemachus is approaching adult intelligence?

The answer seems to be that Homer does ask the reader to accept her appearance as a physical action *and* that a kind of metaphor is involved. Athena is a divine person, she has a personal identity which can be described and recognized; her emotional and intellectual makeup is well defined. But it is equally important to observe that Athena characteristically appears in situations which involve the application of mind to practical situations; on this basis we can understand how her functions as goddess of warfare and mistress of handicraft could be absorbed into the fully developed conception of her nature. In these Homeric passages she exemplifies the Greek way of saying that active intelligence is more than the thinking mechanism of an individual creature; it is a significant and pervasive aspect of experience. It is bigger than human. It is "divine."

This conception of divinity has a number of important implications for the understanding of the Euripidean *Hippolytus*. For one thing, in Greek literature of the classical period generally, the gods are not pure symbols. One has to reckon with them as personalities and as symbols. For another, one has to be very careful in analyzing the relationship between divine powers and human actions.

Much that has been written about Greek tragedy as "tragedy of fate and determinism" founders on the false assumption that all aspects of divinity in these strongly religious dramas involve forces which are external to human affairs and directly determine human actions. Analysis based on this assumption often produces the conclusion, or the strong tendency toward it, that the freedom of the human being is severely restricted by divine control. Bothersome questions arise. Why does the dramatist devote so much attention to the delineation of human character if the role and significance of character are so restricted? If men are close to being puppets manipulated by external forces, does the human scene have enough status, can it be taken seriously enough to be "tragic" at all? Or do we have simply pessimism – or optimism?

It is true that the Greeks were intensely aware of the constant impact of outside elements upon man's experience. This recognition is fundamental in their earliest literary document which has survived, the *Iliad*. But the idea of absolute predeterminism is *not* characteristically Greek. These people keenly felt the instability of human fortune under the impact of bigger-than-human forces, but they were also strongly individualistic and insistent upon human prerogatives, whether the context be political or intellectual; this is perhaps one reason why the role of "fate" is a matter for such intense concern. In any event, on this whole matter there is a wide range of positions taken by individual poets, as well as other thinkers, and these views must be analyzed in terms of the individual poem or drama. There was no orthodoxy on such issues comparable to that found in the Christian tradition.

One point of consequence is the way in which the individual artist uses this conception of the gods. Are his gods more significant as active personalities? Or as symbols? Even though exact answers may elude us, at least rough distinctions are possible, as between the gods of Aeschylus' *Oresteia* and of the *Hippolytus*. The appropriate answer will matter greatly. When, as in the *Hippolytus*, the gods function primarily as symbols of the phenomena which are manifested by the human figures in their characters and actions, the artist is not saying that human action is determined by the gods in any absolute sense, but is universalizing the factors present in the human situation. The notion "tragedy of fate" is dangerous and intricate.

The prologue of the *Hippolytus* confronts us with these issues immediately. Aphrodite (Cypris), claiming the honor due to her as an Olympian, announces that she will punish Hippolytus' scorn by death at his father's hands, and that the process of revenge requires Phaedra's death also. The goddess is heartlessly protecting her own interests. At the end of the drama, Artemis' attitude is comparable; she says to Hippolytus: [3]

> *Cypris shall find the angry shafts she hurled*
> *against you for your piety and innocence*
> *shall cost her dear.*
> *I'll wait until she loves a mortal next time,*
> *and with this hand—with these unerring arrows*
> *I'll punish him.*

It is very difficult to state Euripides' religious views clearly, probably because he did not resolve some issues himself. His views are the product of an uneasy, sophisticated, critical mind moved by the rational tendencies of his time. But it seems possible to approach somewhere near the center of his position in this drama, by using the notion of symbolic personalities sketched above. The symbolic aspect of Aphrodite and Artemis is of the utmost importance in the drama. In this aspect the goddesses are, in fact, the whole context of the tragedy. However, *as per-*

sonal deities they raise grave doubts for the dramatist. Artemis describes the relationship among the gods as a matter of mechanical protocol:

> *For it was Cypris managed the thing this way*
> *to gratify her anger against Hippolytus.*
> *This is the settled custom of the Gods:*
> *No one may fly in the face of another's wish:*
> *we remain aloof and neutral.*

The human reaction to this thought is elsewhere expressed sensitively by the Chorus:

> *The care of God for us is a great thing,*
> *if a man believe it at heart:*
> *it plucks the burden of sorrow from him.*
> *So I have a secret hope*
> *of someone, a God, who is wise and plans;*
> *but my hopes grow dim when I see*
> *the deeds of men and their destinies.*

Professor Kitto interprets Artemis' words this way: "She paints Olympus as a place of moral chaos—which can indicate only that what these deities represent, instinctive passions, is independent of reason and morality." [4] The whole point appears to be somewhat sharper, because Euripides seems also to mean: "If you look to these gods as personalities for comfort and rational concern, you are probably deluded; they seem to be indifferent and irresponsible."

At any rate the main function of the goddesses is to represent sexual passion and ascetic purity as "divine" phenomena, that is, as motive forces which are pervasive and persistent. Passion is the force that moves the dramatic action, but the motive of purity is essential for the impasse which produces tragedy. In other words, the phenomena represented by the goddesses are in destructive collision. The Greek way of saying this is found in some more words of Artemis:

> *For that most hated Goddess,*
> *hated by all of us whose joy is virginity,*
> *drove her with love's sharp prickings to desire*
> *your son.*

Hippolytus and Phaedra are then victims of the force of sexual love. But victims in what sense? The drama has often been interpreted to mean that they are victims of their own extremes. Throughout the text such notions as "moderation" and "excess" are reiterated. But are the characters and actions of Hippolytus and Phaedra (and Theseus) extreme in such a way that their excesses could be resolved by some principle of control?

Essentially the two main characters express humanly the full force of the phenomena figured by Aphrodite and Artemis. Phaedra takes her own life and causes, through Theseus' curse, the death of Hippolytus not because she is weak or irrational, but simply because she is overpowered by love. Every reasonable demand that she try to achieve control is satisfied by her own description of her strong and self-conscious struggle to conquer love with discretion and good sense. She makes the point herself:

> *I think that our lives are worse than the mind's quality*
> *would warrant. There are many who know virtue.*
> *We know the good, we apprehend it clearly.*
> *But we can't bring it to achievement.*

Honesty and loyalty are her natural characteristics. The evil which comes from her: the false accusation of Hippolytus and her vindictiveness toward him—these are the products of shame and the desperate attempt to secure her children's future, as the results of being overpowered.

In some respects Hippolytus is one of the most disagreeable figures found in the Greek plays. The Greeks of the fifth-century audience must have felt even more strongly than we do that he is disastrously contemptuous of a fundamental law of human experience. Very obtrusive indeed are his pride, self-love, and violence. However, these faults come essentially from his extreme dedication to the purity of forest and meadow, to the chastity of uncivilized nature figured by the Maiden Goddess of Wild Things, Artemis. It is a barren and unnatural commitment, as Euripides clearly feels, but it makes a legitimate claim for attention and respect. Incidentally, these values associated with Artemis would of course be recognized immediately by Euripides' Greek audience; the modern reader has to re-create the original context in this respect.

And Hippolytus is good. This is acknowledged—not only by himself!—by the Messenger (whose statements are factual), Artemis and Theseus. His quality is also demonstrated in the final stages of the action where he is compassionate toward Theseus and frees him of guilt. His death is caused in part by refusal to break his oath of silence. It is typical of Euripides' wry-faced manner to create this disagreeable fanatic whose moral purity is nevertheless authentic.

It is impossible, then, to find in the drama, as the dramatist has shaped it, any means of control or moderation which could be realized. Phaedra has struggled for rational solution, but is overwhelmed by "Aphrodite." Any kind of adjustment by Hippolytus is unthinkable. The *Hippolytus* is not primarily a "tragedy of character" but of the conditions of human existence. Everything points in this direction: the prominent roles of Aphrodite and Artemis, and of what they stand for; the characters of Phaedra and of Hippolytus. Further, in the form of the drama, the power of "Aphrodite" is represented as a "storm from the sea" (along with related ideas) in a substantial pattern of figurative language throughout the text. For example, Aphrodite's first word in the Greek text of the prologue calls herself "mighty"; by a simple verbal repetition the Nurse later refers to her as coming to men like a "mighty wave" (443). Phaedra is tossed by a storm (315) and struggles to swim out (470). The traditional epithet of Aphrodite as the "sea-born queen" is used with special point (415, 522). In the first stasimon (525–64) Eros and Aphrodite are linked with stormy elements (530, 559, 563). The sound of the conversation of the Nurse and Hippolytus overheard by Phaedra is the sound "of rushing water" (576).

The second stasimon contains a brilliant development of this figurative theme. The Chorus has just learned that Phaedra intends to die. In the first half of their beautiful, anguished song (732–51), they pray to become birds and fly over the sea to western fabled lands: via the Adriatic place where the tears of the sisters mourning the death of Phaethon become radiant drops of amber and are fixed in beauty, far on to the limit of the world marked by the Pillars of Heracles where the marriage bower of Zeus and Hera is secure and rich in the bounty of Earth.

This flight from the painful here-and-now, over the muted grief of the Phaethontiades to the bliss of the gods, is matched in the second half (752–75) by the return-journey to reality. The white-winged boat that brought Phaedra from Crete over the boisterous sea to a joyless marriage was under bad omens from start to landfall. By a switch of language, the ship is identified with Phaedra herself. "She" lands at Athens, and the mooring ropes are fastened. Phaedra, broken up by the power of Aphrodite and "foundering under bitter misfortune" (769), will fit the noose to her white neck.

Later, Theseus looks upon a sea of disaster (822–24). The final catastrophe is caused by the sea monster sent by Poseidon. Thus Euripides clearly communicates his conception that the tragedy of *Hippolytus* comes from evil which is organic in the natural order of the conditions in which humans live. It is essentially this "natural" evil that accounts for the extremes found in the characters and actions of Phaedra, Hippolytus and Theseus.

Turning to the *Phaedra* of the Roman Seneca takes us over a wide gap—in time, kind and quality. His plays, of the first century A.D., are usually thought of as conscious imitations of various Greek tragedies (apparently Seneca was particularly attracted to the themes dramatized by Euripides), although we suffer from having little substantial knowledge of Latin tragic drama before Seneca. In any event we are here interested not so much in the point-to-point relationship between the Euripidean and Senecan dramas as in some explanation of the differences between them as types of drama.

Senecan drama is not directly related to communal ritual like the Greek. It is the product of the study and presumably was written to be recited to literary groups rather than staged. Condemnations of Seneca the dramatist are commonplace. His works are, in comparison to the Greek, second-rate melodrama loaded with rhetoric, mythological and other lore, and violent action (sometimes, as in the *Phaedra*, horribly violent). They are excessively intense in matter and form.

However, these plays challenge analysis for several important reasons. The striking disparity between the Greek and Roman products in the same dramatic tradition calls for explanation. Also, the ubiquitous historical influence of Seneca upon English and European drama of the sixteenth and seventeenth centuries makes it essential to understand the nature of the source. Further, it must be remembered that Senecan influence was not merely a regrettable fact, but in a number of ways had a positive salutary effect. For example, the fully developed structure and language of the Senecan play disciplined the drama written under its influence; or again, the device of introspective monologue, which was shaped by rhetorical and Stoic elements in Seneca, became a powerful tool for later dramatists. Finally, most critics appear to take it as a personal insult that Seneca undertook to write drama, and there has been relatively little effort to understand what made the plays what they are—for good *and* bad.

The writer has suggested elsewhere that Stoicism formed Senecan drama much more fundamentally than has been realized.[5] It is obvious, of course, that Stoic themes, along with others, appear in the texts. More latently, conceptions from this source seem to have directed the very premises underlying Senecan drama. We are on sure ground in one essential respect, namely that Seneca was formally a Stoic and wrote many philosophical essays and epistles which can be brought into revealing relationship with the plays.

A very brief sketch of Stoicism is necessary. It is a very comprehensive, and somewhat paradoxical, system based on the equation "virtue = reason = nature." Virtue is the greatest good for man and is achieved by the exercise of reason, the highest human capacity. But the force of reason is not merely human. It permeates all of nature, producing harmony, system, and direction toward the good. This power in nature is also described in religious terms; it is equated with god, it is divine. (It is also, paradoxically, associated with the material fire.) Thus the potential rationality in man stems from his participation in the divine. The human being and the universe are, then, parallel organisms constructed in the best possible way for the realization of good through reason.

One familiar, but crucial, point should be stressed.

Tragic drama is, of course, concerned with various forms of evil as they touch humans. A system like Stoicism which is essentially optimistic is hard put to explain imperfections in a world where reason is believed to be the dominant force. The prose writings of Seneca, like all Stoic literature, present a whole battery of arguments attempting to meet the issue: evil only seems to be evil, and must be part of nature's rational plan; imperfection tests and develops man's mettle; what seems to be evil can be neutralized by man's understanding of "what is in his control" and what is not; evil can be converted to good by endurance, etc. For our purpose the most interesting question is: how does a dramatist with Stoic ideas—or at least this Stoic dramatist—account for catastrophe in tragic drama?

The Stoic philosopher deals with imperfection primarily in terms of the moral condition of the human being. Men's behavior is a battleground of reason vs. passion. The most frequent theme in Stoic writings is that error and evil result when passion overcomes reason. For example, rage, the most common emotion in the Senecan plays, is considered temporary insanity in the first book of Seneca's essay *On Anger:* it is "the most hideous and frenzied of all the emotions," [6] contrary to nature and principal enemy of reason. On the other hand, practice of the virtues of wisdom, courage, moderation and endurance not only eliminates weakness within man, but also negates the effect of catastrophe coming from without.

The parallel to what is found in the *Phaedra* is very close. Seneca has written a dramatization of criminal psychology, charged with extreme abnormality and irrationality; indeed, this is the main source of the intensity and horror which are Seneca's failings. A few illustrations will show that the formulation of these elements is Stoic.

Phaedra recognizes in herself the curse of unnatural love received from her mother (this is only mentioned in Euripides). She introspectively states the moral conflict: *Quid ratio possit? Vicit ac regnat furor.* "What can reason do? Passion has conquered and now rules supreme."[7] Theseus is a mad adulterer. Hippolytus can hardly be anything else than a rather colorless victim, for destruction comes wholly from Phaedra, and there is no significant impasse between the two as in Euripides; he speaks as a Stoic when he praises life in the woods and identifies it with the Golden Age.[8] The Nurse both preaches Stoic virtue to Phaedra and urges Epicurean indulgence upon Hippolytus. Perhaps most significant of all is the thought of the Nurse that "base and sin-mad lust . . . has made love into a god and, to enjoy more liberty, has given passion [*furori*] the title of an unreal divinity."[9] Love and passion are moral conditions in men, not conditions of existence. The contrast with Euripides is radical.

Similar features can be found in all the Senecan plays. Also, there are instances where the opposite side of Stoic morality is seen, i.e., where reason prevails and Stoic virtues overcome catastrophe. For example, in the *Troades,* Astyanax and Polyxena face death with such equanimity that they are victors. It seems apparent that Stoicism led Seneca the dramatist to a completely moralistic view of error and catastrophe: evil is either externalized as the workings of fate or fortune which can be nullified by reason, or is thought to be caused by the deterioration of character which results when passion destroys reason. This is a far cry from the characteristic Greek view that evil is organic in the natural order of things and cannot be eliminated by mere rationality, as in the case of Euripides' Phaedra.

In fact, it is very doubtful that the effect of tragedy can be achieved in drama written on these Stoic premises.

Such an explanation of human experience is too simple and shallow; it eliminates the possibility of a significant relationship between, on the one hand, what men do and suffer and, on the other, the sources of this experience both within and outside of man. The mystery essential to tragedy is gone.

Other important factors, of course, contributed to making Senecan drama what it is. But Seneca's Stoicism was a source of basic limitations. Composing tragic drama under these limitations and on these premises—whether consciously or unconsciously—the dramatist was restricted in what he could achieve. He chose to intensify, to portray the psychology of behavior, particularly irrational behavior, powerfully and vividly. The center of dramatic attention was turned inward. This new orientation made Senecan drama a landmark in the development of psychological drama, and was carried by Senecan influence wherever it went.

There is a remarkable parallelism between *Oedipus the King* and *King Lear*. In language and action the theme of seeing and not-seeing fills both plays from beginning to end.[10] Recognition of this theme carries us to the very heart of each tragedy.

Sophocles bases his whole tale of Oedipus upon an involved visual pattern. The magnificent movement from *Oedipus the King* through *Oedipus at Colonus* takes us on a course from one mystery to another, and in both mysteries the functions of seeing and not-seeing are interlocked. What the blind Teiresias sees, Oedipus sees only at the point where he blinds himself, and at Colonus the blinded Oedipus achieves spiritual vision and guides the way to the spot of his mysterious glorification. But we confine our attention here to Oedipus at Thebes and to the significance of his successful, and disastrous, search for the truth. When Oedipus sees the truth, what is it that Sophocles leads *us* to see?

In Bernard Knox's fine analysis, the final vision is of a paradox. He puts the case of Oedipus this way: "The *Oedipus Tyrannus* of Sophocles combines two apparently irreconcilable themes, the greatness of the gods and the greatness of man, and the combination of these themes is inevitably tragic, for the greatness of the gods is most clearly and powerfully demonstrated by man's defeat. . . . Sophocles' tragedy presents us with a terrible affirmation of man's subordinate position in the universe, and at the same time with a heroic vision of man's victory in defeat." [11] The two sides of the paradox are laid against each other, strong, stark, incapable of any real resolution.

Such logical conflict, such "irrationality" is disturbing enough under any circumstances. But the paradox has unique power in this drama because of the shock produced by the relationship between divine power and human power. In one terrible sense this relationship is compatible. It is finally revealed that the gods and Oedipus are not in conflict at all. Rather, they are working together for the revelation of the truth. The superiority of the gods is demonstrated by allowing the hero's status to be crushed under the weight of pollution brought down upon himself by his own supreme effort.

In another way, the relationship between divine and human greatness is discordant and rasping. Our sense of irrationality is greatly intensified by the very rationality of Oedipus' search for the polluted one: investigating, remembering, tracking, cross-questioning, applying all his energy and intelligence.[12] Sophocles' art engrosses us in the king's rational search. Our attention is concentrated upon the unfolding of evidence and the exercise of logic. And what does all this searching intelligence finally reveal?

The ignorance of man and the unfathomable order of the gods. Our own shock parallels the anguish of the self-blinding, and we want to close *our* eyes to the unreasonableness of the catastrophe. We can keep them open only because the gods cannot be challenged and because Oedipus continues to be Oedipus in his spirited reaction to misery.

The hostility of the world where Oedipus' experience takes place may be spoken of in another way, in terms of ritual. Although, as we have said above, Sophocles' Oedipus is no mere scapegoat sacrificed to cleanse the pollution of his family and city, the elements of ritual are still to be felt in the dramatist's intelligent and subtle creation. The laws governing nature and society, the purity of the family and the sanctity of blood relationship, have been violated. Apollo the purifier must reveal this corruption, and in one dimension the self-blinding is a sacrifice performed by the king both as the source of the taint and as the responsible agent of the community. These conditions carry the imprint of a ritual view of man's environment: that is, the world is potentially ever a hostile place where the uneasy relationship between man and nature may develop impurity, and the only recourse is some kind of sacrificial purification.

In any case, this is the world revealed to us by Sophocles in the intensity of Oedipus' suffering. It is a radically dualistic world. It contains the great rational Oedipus. But it is also a mad world of accident and coincidence: where a Corinthian shepherd takes an infant from a Theban shepherd, where Oedipus consults the oracle because of a drunken insult by some Corinthian, where the paths of father and son converge at a crossroad, where the lone survivor of Laius' band is the same Theban shepherd, where the son arrives in Thebes at a time of great crisis, where the Queen is the marriage-prize for the one who solves the crisis, where the messenger from Corinth is the same Corinthian shepherd, where the same two old shepherds survive, the only two men who can connect the foundling with the house of Laius and with Corinth. Only in a bad comedy would credibility be stretched so far! These happenings are the marks of an arbitrary world where things just happen and where a rational man places himself on the tracks in the path of the onrushing Divine Limited. Oedipus, and we with him, are in a divinely ordered system where the rational purpose of a spirited good king is disastrously turned against him by the force of capricious circumstance. The divine order brings disorder to human experience.

If in this fashion we can say that *Oedipus the King* transmits the picture of disorder in nature, recent Shakespearean criticism is in substantial agreement that *King Lear* expresses nature in disorder. These terms, disorder in nature for Sophocles, and nature in disorder for Shakespeare, are only catch phrases, but they point to a contrast between two types of tragedy, radically different in their conceptions of evil. In this Greek play, and in others in varying degrees, it is the very nature of nature that wounds human experience. Suffering is constituently built into the makeup of how things are, above and beyond man's influence upon what happens. The unique power of Greek drama lies in its intense and bare concentration upon the imperfection of the world, or rather its imperfectibility: the *hamartia* of nature, we might call it. In *Lear* it is not nature itself that is defective, but only part of it, that is, the human dimension. Nature is flawed through man who has the "ability to achieve salvation" and the "liability to damnation," in Robert Heilman's language.[13] Shakespeare's world is *theoretically* perfectible, and suffering is caused by a falling-off from what might have been, from what presumably could be. No such thing is possible in Oedipus' experience.

The tragedy *Lear* does not have the concentrated

power achieved by Sophocles—this was gone forever with the end of Greek tragedy—but it is unmatched in poetic richness and range of insight. These qualities come from a mighty moral struggle between two groups of characters ranged about Lear and Gloucester, in fact two groups of six each: the essentially evil Goneril, Regan, Burgundy, Cornwall, Oswald, and Edmund; and the essentially good Cordelia, France, Albany, Kent, the Fool and Edgar.[14] These characters live by two different sets of values belonging to two kinds of "nature."

It is a commonplace of current Shakespearean interpretation to recognize that "nature" is the dominant idea and metaphor of the drama.[15] The feature is important not only for the understanding of Shakespeare, but also as perhaps the most significant link between the Elizabethan tradition and the Senecan. Later we will indicate that the relationship between Senecan melodrama and Shakespearean tragedy is not to be found through conventional source-hunting but is to be seen truly in their related conceptions of nature and in their comparable dramatic uses of these conceptions.

Shakespearean critics analyze the moral struggle of *King Lear* in various terms. In reading some of the more influential views, one feels uncomfortably that the bard is represented to be a master of philosophy rather than of drama, but he does seem to have been remarkably keen in absorbing the ideas and issues of his day. John F. Danby finds the key in the interlocking of two doctrines current in Elizabethan times, associated with Hooker and with Hobbes.[16] In the one, the traditional view of sixteenth-century Christianity, nature is benignant, "an ordered and beautiful arrangement, to which we must adjust ourselves." In Hobbes, man is bedeviled, torn in the conflict between the irreconcilable forces of reason and the passions. It is characteristic of religious and philosophical thought in the Elizabethan period that the views of both Hooker and Hobbes can be squared with Christianity and with Stoicism, for these two traditions were fused inseparably. Danby goes on to show the dramatic consequences of these ideas; for example, "Cordelia embodies the [ordered and beautiful] Nature which Edmund denies to exist, and which Lear—although he believes in it—cannot recognize when it is before him." [17]

Hiram Haydn, regarding *Lear* as "a Stoic play," finds a similar opposition between the ordered harmony of Stoicism and Edmund's egocentric, Epicurean view of nature, and concludes: "The divergent points of view toward nature and the gods are sharply drawn, with the proponents of 'Nature' and of Stoicism radically differing. On the one hand, blind nature, controlled only by fortune and chance; on the other, a nature governed by gods who represent a law of retributive justice. . . . In the end, it is a true Stoic world, and justice has been dispensed." [18]

Other interpretations are less philosophical, but show the dramatic and poetic workings of the same kind of conflict. Heilman's *This Great Stage* is a landmark in analyzing the themes and patterns of figurative language used to express destructive force and spiritual illumination. In various forms, Nature is a giant metaphor for both moral order and the falling away from moral order. Harold C. Goddard is one of a number who find that the drama is centered around the religious theme of the acquisition of spiritual vision: the storm buffeting Lear on the heath conveys at once both the blackness, the blindness of passion that has come upon the king, and the flashes of the vision emerging in him.[19] Another dimension impresses Kenneth Muir. He emphasizes that Shakespeare has used the setting of Lear's pre-Christian world to examine the moral and religious ideas under attack from the rationalism of his day, and to show, without the authority of revealed religion, that the values of patience, fortitude, love and charity can emerge from within the nature of man himself: Shakespeare "shows us his pagan characters groping their way towards a recognition of the values traditional in his society." [20]

Particularly impressive is the analysis by Oscar J. Campbell.[21] He considers *Lear* a morality play taken outside the strictly Christian tradition and transformed into the magnificent tragedy of "a completely unstoical man" who finally achieves spiritual vision compounded of "Stoic insight and Christian humility." What is more, this illumination comes about through a sequence of experiences recognized as the path to wisdom in the Stoic thought of Cicero, Seneca, Plutarch, Epictetus, Marcus Aurelius, whose moral philosophy was a major influence upon thought in the England of Shakespeare's time. Therefore Stoic ideas loom large in what Lear comes to understand: the values of resignation to the will above man, of humility in human relationships, and of willing obedience to destiny. The thought of *King Lear* is thus a product of grafting Renaissance Stoicism upon traditional Christian piety.

Such an interpretation works exceedingly well in giving account of the play dramatically. As Campbell goes on to show, the king initially breaks the cardinal Stoic principles of right behavior. The kingship is important to him for its external trappings: he must have his proper retinue. Right from the beginning in rejecting Cordelia and banishing Kent he violates all reason and is addicted to anger—temporary insanity in Stoic terms. Self-knowledge and self-control are quite beyond him.

So the search for sanity and truth begins. Lear is helped partly along the way by his companions, Kent and the Fool, both of whom Campbell connects with the

Cynic-Stoic tradition brought to the Elizabethans by Roman satire. The plain-speaking Kent and the wise Fool by their blunt and searching comments stimulate the king to strip off superficiality and to see more deeply into the fundamental human needs of protection and compassion (3.4.32–6):

> *O! I have ta'en*
> *Too little care of this. Take physic, Pomp;*
> *Expose thyself to feel what wretches feel,*
> *That thou mayst shake the superflux to them,*
> *And show the Heavens more just.*

However, Stoicism is not adequate to answer the questions raised by the dramatist. The tragedy does not end in a mere victory over passion nor, certainly, in tranquillity and imperturbability. Perhaps Shakespeare instinctively saw the psychological naïveté of Stoicism. For him, passion is overcome not by reason, but by the greater and finer passion of "utter devotion to the eternal blessings of the spirit," as Campbell puts it. The suffering of Lear in the storm has Stoic meaning: from being subjected to the storm of unreason within himself and the storm of discord in the elements of nature, he is chastened and led to recognize the humanity shared with his fellows. But the experience is purgatorial also in a Christian sense and reaches the level of salvation, for having passed through the storm he is ready to receive Cordelia's love fully and to return it. The final result is not the negative indifference of Stoicism but the active healing force of unselfish love. In the final scene where Lear enters with Cordelia dead in his arms, the agony of loss yields to the ecstasy of redemption, and Lear's heart bursts in the joy of it (5.3.257–63, 265–67, 305–11).

For our contrast between *Lear* and *Oedipus* it is essential to note one common feature of all these Shakespearean interpretations: namely, that the keen sense of loss and waste left to us at the end is linked with the incongruous notion that a moral and religious order has emerged from all the destruction. At least in *King Lear,* if not more generally in Shakespeare, our feeling of the tragic comes essentially from the paradox of a moral order containing elements so destructive, conflicts within men and between them so disruptive, that order can be restored only at the price of prodigious suffering and ravage. If we recognize that Christian ideas loom large behind the pagan scene of *Lear,* the explanation of the paradox is not far to seek. It fits rather comfortably into the frame of traditional Christian beliefs in the dualism of God and the Fiend, uncontrolled human choices of good and evil, the purgatorial effect of suffering, and the saving power of love.

However, the point about *Lear* to be stressed is that it ends, as the most powerful tragedies do, in affirmation, in this case the affirmation of a continuing, self-asserting moral order, no matter how desperately high the price. This statement cannot be made about *Oedipus,* at least in my reading of it. For Sophocles, the divine order involves moral values, to be sure, but it is basically an order of nature rather than of morality, and we cannot find any meaningful, decisive relationship between moral values, or the lack of them, and the downfall of Oedipus. For that matter, "downfall" is a false term, for in Sophocles the affirmation is not of a moral order, but of a great human spirit who remains on his feet and goes on. The change in the treatment of moral matter is a great difference between Greek and most modern tragedy. But it began in Seneca.

At the present time the place of Seneca in the scholarship about Elizabethan drama is rather curious and unstable. Stoic influences upon the Elizabethans are more keenly recognized than ever before, as shown in the selection of views about *Lear* just presented, and the particular importance of Seneca in the *philosophical* tradition is widely acknowledged. For example, Lily B. Campbell [22] sets out "to find what was known and thought about passion in the sixteenth century," to illuminate the fact that "Shakespeare in all his tragedies was primarily concerned with passion rather than with action." She shows in figures like Chaucer, Boccaccio, and Lydgate the persistent medieval view of tragedies as *exempla*, as demonstrations of the destructive effect of Fortune and sin. In the Renaissance, as Christian ideas become more sophisticated, the role of Fortune is reconciled with the moral justice of God, and the misfortunes of men are traced not to chance but to sinful action resulting from the passions. The wheel of Fortune turns as part of the moral mechanism bringing down upon men the consequences of their errors and follies. Consequently Renaissance tragedy is oriented toward the conflict between reason and unreason, temperance and passion, in close relationship to the moral philosophy of the day compounded of Christianity, ancient medicine, classical philosophy (particularly Peripatetic and Stoic), and medieval modifications of classical philosophy. It is unnecessary to dwell further on the widespread influence of Senecan Stoicism on sixteenth-century English drama. But what of the impact of the Senecan dramas themselves? Earlier scholarship has shown beyond question the popularity of the Senecan plays in England and Europe, the wide extent of their melodramatic influence on pre-Shakespearean drama, and the echoes of Senecan themes in Shakespeare himself. Current work on Shakespeare pays rather little attention to this historical scholarship, for several reasons. For one thing, current criticism tends to be apathetic or hostile to historical research. For another, we may agree with the antihistorical critic that source-hunting of Senecan elements in Shakespeare has not produced many important findings. Since we know, however, that both the prose writings and the dramas of the Roman were ubiquitous in the complex context that nurtured the genius of Shakespeare, it is natural to assume that the *dramas* of Seneca were an influential medium in conveying Senecan and Stoic material to the *dramatists* of the day, and to look for relationships more fundamental than those revealed by conventional source-hunting.

In assessing Seneca and his place in the dramatic tradition, there is another difficulty, on the Senecan side. Despite the long tradition of classical scholarship, we have not gained a critical understanding of these melodramas; consequently, investigation of their influence has had a weak foundation. Understandably enough, the obvious weaknesses of this second-rate dramatist have been analyzed and castigated by critics. But we are still left with the important question: From what elements do the strengths and weaknesses of these plays result? If we can answer this question more adequately, we will be on the way toward a sounder appraisal both of the texts and of their role in the tradition.

In recent years, a more objective and sympathetic criticism of Senecan drama has been emerging. It recognizes the heavy hand of tradition upon the plays, but regards them as something new in classical drama, as a unique product essentially of rhetoric and Stoicism. It finds a close relationship between Seneca's prose writings and the dramas. As the essays and letters apply the Stoic ideal of rational control to everyday concerns and insecurities, so the plays are *exempla* of the destructiveness of irrationality.

Most of the premises and conditions controlling Seneca in his composition are obvious. He was fully conscious of writing in a long-established dramatic tradition and felt bound by the traditional themes. To his versions of the inherited themes he brought the extreme virtuosity of a rhetorician trained in all the tricks of the trade—and then some. But one aspect of his approach to composition is particularly important and not so obvious. He had to make a decision—whether consciously or subconsciously—about the motivation of the catastrophes in his versions of the traditional themes. From what sources were the catastrophes to come about? From imperfections in the makeup of the world? From chance? From the unfathomable purposes of the gods? From conflicts within human nature?

His Stoicism dictated certain answers to this question. If one subscribes to the optimistic Stoic view of the universe as an orderly, harmonious and purposeful structure, it is simply impossible to attribute violence and suffering to the workings of nature or to chance or to mysterious divine purpose. Men may *think* that evil exists in superhuman terms, but this is only because they do not understand the great rational scheme of things—as the Stoic says interminably. What is more, the great scheme is identical with how things are fated to be and with how divine providence wills things to be. No, in a rational macrocosm the only source of disruption in human life is lack of reason or perversion of reason in man the microcosm. Nor in human nature, as the Stoics understand it, can there be a continuing conflict or mixed motives, for reason and unreason, the two sources of all emotions, are mutually exclusive, and the irrationality of passion is a progressive condition. In fact, in the pessimistic neo-Stoicism of Seneca unreason is an incurable disease with no effective possibility of recuperation or renewal.

So Stoicism restricts the dramatist's conception. He is forced into creating essentially two types of characters, as unlike as day and night: the rational ones, like Polyxena and Astyanax in the *Troades,* young Tantalus in the *Thyestes,* and Hercules in the *Hercules on Oeta,* unperturbed by the grossest kind of violence and pain; and the utterly irrational ones, like Medea, Phaedra, Clytemnestra, Atreus, who are the major source of destruction in every Senecan play, consumed with insecurity and violence. Although Seneca often makes a rhetorical show of conflict between reason and unreason, in these cases unreason always prevails.

Looking at the Senecan characters in this way makes one realize that not even the genius of Shakespeare could have rescued Seneca from melodrama. In Stoic terms catastrophe can come only from the mechanism of human character. It cannot arise from dualistic conflict between two realms of existence or two systems of value. There is no possibility that the good purposes of an Oedipus can result in catastrophe, or of Lear-like progression from blindness to vision. Order and disorder cannot be mixed.

The saturation of the Senecan texts with the ideas of order and disorder is revealed by the study of the figurative language in all the plays.[23] It is difficult to wade through the indiscriminate welter of figures typical of Senecan style, but clear patterns do emerge, and they greatly illuminate the dramatic themes.

Most of the patterns can be ranked in two categories: they have to do either with rationality as a feature of the universe and an ideal of human behavior, or with the chaos and destructiveness of human irrationality. As a result, the figures have a double structure, with each pattern having two opposing aspects. There are massive systems of language expressing abstract ideas: the notion of "control" is contrasted with "unrestraint," "security" with "insecurity," "bright" with "dark," "clean" with "foul." There are two major metaphors, "sea-storm" and "fire."

The latter is particularly significant because of the role of the element fire in Stoicism. The Stoics distinguished between two types of fire: the creative kind which composes spirit and is identical with reason; and the all-consuming kind known to men on earth. Quite consistently with this distinction, the dramatist uses the metaphor "fire" contrastively, both to suggest the rational order of nature manifested in the sun and stars, and to figure passion and insanity. As a whole, the plays contain a fused mass of figurative language depicting irrationality as destructive, chaotic, dark, foul, and deathly, the negation of order, security, brightness, and life. Clearly all this is Stoic in purpose.

One example of the metaphor "sea-storm" will bring us back to *Lear*. Seneca's *Agamemnon* treats the familiar subject of Agamemnon's return and murder, but the prevailing theme is the sense of insecurity shared by every speaking character and group. To show the obliteration of any hope of security, the dramatist skillfully fuses the abstract idea "security-insecurity" with the personification Fortune and the metaphor "sea-storm." The shifting movement connected with Fortune is expressed by language of wavelike motion. This language leads naturally to the figure "sea-storm," developed in close relationship with Fortune. In the very first choral passage Seneca writes that Fortune allows kingship no peace, but buffets it with repeated storms. Agamemnon is puffed up by the wind blast of Fortune. Clytemnestra tosses in tides of conflicting emotions. And so forth. Thus the metaphor "sea-storm" becomes a major device expressing the emotional and intellectual chaos of the play, much in the manner of Lear on the stormy heath.

This parallel is pointed out not to show a specific connection between Seneca and Shakespeare, but to indicate that the great change from the orientation of *Oedipus* to the orientation of *Lear* had already largely taken place in Seneca. Such generalizations are dangerous, but important to try. To go from Sophocles to Seneca is to move from one type of serious drama to a fundamentally different type, in the sense of passing from one conception of the human condition to a radically different conception. The catastrophe in *Oedipus* comes not from a moral conflict, but from a confronting of two statuses, human and divine. The conflict could not be reconciled, the dualism could not be removed, by any change of moral state.

In Seneca, the stage is set for a different kind of drama, tragedy of moral order. Although the rhetorical fireworks obscure the ideas, his plays are based upon the Stoic conception of a rational moral order. The catastrophes are caused by characters who deviate from the moral standard. Such a system is much too simple and rigid to give a tragic effect, of course, because Seneca can give us no grounds for sympathizing with these characters as participants in normal human experience, no grounds for regarding their behavior as anything but revolting aberration. They have broken all the rules and fallen into progressive degradation with no possibility of reversing their steps.

Shakespeare was able to avoid such moralistic melodrama for a number of reasons. One important reason is that his mind was fed by the wider range of ideas found in Stoicized Christianity of his day. He was able to think of existence in terms of a genuine dualism of good and evil, to portray a world where redemption is possible and the moral order arises from suffering. Yet he was also able to use strong Senecan elements.

The Chorus in Seneca's *Phaedra* observes (959–88): [24]

O Nature, mighty mother of the gods, and you, fire-bearing Olympus' lord, who through the swift firmament whirl the scattered stars, and the wandering courses of the planets, who make the heavens turn on swift axis, why do you take such care to keep perpetual the pathways of the lofty sky, that now the white frosts of winter may strip the woods, now to the plantations their leafage come again, that now in summer the Lion's fervent heat may ripen the grain and the year regulate its powers? But why, again, do you, who hold so wide sway, and by whose hands the ponderous masses of the vast universe are poised and wheel their appointed courses —why do you dwell afar, all too indifferent to men, not anxious to bring blessing to the good, and to the evil, bane?

Fate without order rules the affairs of men, scatters her gifts with unseeing hand, fostering the worse; dire lust prevails against pure men, and crime sits ruling in the lofty palace. The rabble rejoice to give government to the vile, paying high honors even where they hate. Warped are the rewards of uprightness sad virtue gains; wretched poverty dogs the pure, and the adulterer, strong in wickedness, reigns supreme. O decency, honor, how empty and how false!

The order of supernal nature *versus* the chaos of men's actions: this is near the world of *Lear*.

10

THE STUDY OF LITERARY GENRES

ULRICH WEISSTEIN

THE STUDENT who considers literature from a comparative point of view will find that the concept of genre, like that of period, current, and movement, opens an extremely fruitful field of investigation.[1] In cultivating this area of literary theory, the scholar must proceed historically as well as critically if he is to discover principles that make possible a systematic arrangement of his material. At the same time, he must endeavor to operate descriptively rather than prescriptively; for due to the inherent relativity of all things historical a clear and unambiguous delimitation of genres is practically unattainable, so that no true atomic model will ever emerge. Yet such a model has been envisaged by genologists throughout the ages.

In classical antiquity, Cicero was one of the first writers to stress the segregation of literary genres in his prefatory essay *De optimo genere oratorum* (52 B.C.), and Quintilian followed the example in the *Institutio Oratoria*, his famous handbook of rhetoric.[2] Horace's letter to the brothers Piso (*Ad Pisones*, commonly known as *De arte poetica*) contains what may be regarded as the classic formulation of this view in the admonitions "denique sit quodvis, simplex dumtaxat et unum" (No matter what the subject, let it be simple and uniform) and "singula quaeque locum teneant sortita decentem" (Each particular genre should keep the place allotted to it).[3] Such demands for generic purity are, as a rule, characteristic of the classical or neoclassical frame of mind, which is inured to tradition and wishes to preserve the established order. Thus Schiller writes to Goethe, alluding to their joint attempt to ascertain the nature of the drama and the epic:

> Your present business of separating and purifying the two kinds is surely of the greatest significance. But, like myself, you will be convinced that, in order to exclude from a work of art everything that is foreign to its kind, one would have to include everything that is germane to it. Precisely that we cannot do, however, at present. And since we are unable to assemble all the conditions proper to each of the two kinds, we are forced to mix them.[4]

This fusion (or confusion), which Schiller regarded as a necessary evil, is often exalted in periods inimical to tradition (as in the case of synesthesia and the Romantic *Gesamtkunstwerk*).

So far in the course of the history of our discipline, comparatists have, unfortunately, been remiss in their duty toward the history and theory of genres. Especially since the failure of Ferdinand Brunetière's biologistic attempt to establish a fixed pattern for the evolution of certain literary forms hardly anyone dared, for a generation or two, to till this furrow.[5] Even the third International Congress of Literary History, held in Lyon in late spring of 1939, did little to improve the situation, although the problem of literary types was its principal topic of discussion.[6] There was simply too much diversity in the views presented to allow for the necessary synthesis on a universal scale.

Until recently, *Comparative Literature* was the only specialized journal in the West to show an interest in genology, although (in all fairness) it must be admitted that few relevant contributions have appeared in the first twenty years of its existence. Neither *Comparative Literature Studies* nor the *Revue de littérature comparée* or *Arcadia* stress the subject, and the Proceedings of the triennial meetings of the ICLA make no amends. In Eastern Europe, on the other hand, the Polish periodical *Zagadnienia Rodzajów Literackich*—published, since 1958, at the University of Lodz—constitutes an important outlet. All the more welcome was the founding of *Genre,* a quarterly edited by members of the English Department faculty at the University of Illinois in Chicago. The second issue of this journal contains the text of three papers read at a forum held during the 1967 meeting of the Modern Language Association in Chicago, together with brief evaluative comments by three discussants.[7] Of the three participants, Eliseo Vivas shows by far the soundest understanding of the logical and historical problems involved, whereas Sheldon Sacks' essay is psychologically oriented and Germaine Brée's suffers from a certain lack of consistency in the use of such key terms as *theme, motif, mode,* and *genre.*[8]

In most of the available handbooks and surveys, too, the theory of genres is either totally ignored or treated with more or less disdain. Wellek and Warren's *Theory of Literature* (chap. 17) is a notable exception. Especially the German scholars often fail to do the topic justice, as will be shown in the course of our argument. The most radical position regarding this matter was, not unexpectedly, taken by Benedetto Croce who considered generic classification a waste of time.[9] As for the French comparatists of the old school, they could never properly focus on the issue, largely because they treated genology under the dual aspect of littérature comparée and littérature générale. To the latter sphere Van Tieghem assigned the study of classical tragedy, romantic drama, the sonnet, and the rustic novel (*La Littérature comparée,* p. 176) and, elsewhere, that of pastoral poetry and the sentimental novel.[10] Yet *genres et styles* are also treated at length in the second chapter of the main part of his manual (pp. 70–86), where the major kinds are listed and discussed in the mechanical sequence *genres en prose, genres poétiques,* and *le théâtre.* The superficiality of this treatment can be explained—though hardly excused—by the fact that, following the then current practice of Comparative Literature at the Sorbonne, Van Tieghem restricted his survey to modern literature, thereby avoiding the tricky question of the survival of ancient genres.

In his brief eclectic guide, M.-F. Guyard devotes a scant five pages (*La Littérature comparée,* pp. 44–48) to our subject. Like his master (though in different order), he deals with drama, poetry, and fiction respectively. Pichois and Rousseau reduce the scope even further, and half of the limited space they grant to genology (*La Littérature comparée,* pp. 96–99) is taken up by an attempted explanation of the difference between monogenesis (*vide* Walter Scott and the historical novel) and polygenesis (*vide* the rustic novels of George Sand, George Eliot, and Jeremias Gotthelf). A reversal of this trend is noticeable in the latest French manual, Simon Jeune's *Littérature générale et Littérature comparée,* where an entire chapter (pp. 72–82) is devoted to the study of literary genres, albeit under the heading of general literature.[11]

Given this state of affairs, one can hardly exaggerate the importance attaching to the place of genre studies within the general framework of Comparative Literature. For in this branch of our discipline—perhaps even more so than in the case of thematology and the study of movements, periods, and currents—a confrontation of literary history and theory occurs on a broad, international basis. In the present context we may, naturally, ignore such forms as have developed exclusively within a national or regional literature, without significantly penetrating beyond its confines: such as the many complex metrical and strophic patterns of Provençal poetry, the Alpine *Schnadahüpfl*, and—in spite of some brave efforts at imitation in the German tongue—the English limerick. Hundreds of such provincial genres from the literatures of all five continents are catalogued and described in dictionaries like the *Encyclopedia of Poetry and Poetics*.[12] Equally beside the point are the historical surveys of specific universal genres evidenced within a national literature, since they are bound to remain fragmentary and disjointed. It is sad that barely any monographic studies of such universal forms have, so far, been undertaken. They are, accordingly, an urgent desideratum of comparative scholarship. Of the major kinds it is undoubtedly the drama which has been most adequately treated in this respect, whereas neither the novel (or fiction as a whole) nor lyric poetry have as yet been surveyed *in toto*.

We have mentioned the problems facing the scholar interested in studying the survival of ancient Greek or Roman genres or their revival in the modern age. These are often caused by the lack of firsthand evidence; for while it is sometimes erroneous to assume that genres flourishing since the Renaissance have no antecedents in antiquity, the existence of such models is, at times, hypothetical, the only proof being that furnished by references or quotations in ancient literary criticism. A good case in point would be the dithyramb, especially since, even in antiquity, it underwent repeated changes.

One must also consider the possibility that a genre known and practiced in antiquity has actually vanished, but that its name persists and serves to designate a modern genre that may, or may not, be its exact equivalent. In such a case, the comparative literary historian is charged with the task of investigating and analyzing the changing conditions responsible for this survival and the process by means of which the label was separated from the original content. The reverse is true in cases where a genre passes from one national literature to another without retaining its name. A special study could and should be made of what happens when such changes occur and how adequately the generic terms are translated from one language into another; for, etymologically, a change of name usually implies an, often imperceptible, change of meaning. One need only think of the somewhat fluid relationship between *cento* and *pastiche* or of the English version of Boileau's *Art Poétique* by Sir William Soame and John Dryden, where *rondeau* appears as *round, ballade* as *ballad,* and *vaudeville* as *lampoon.*

Equally significant for the student of comparative genology is the phenomenon known as contamination, i.e., a historical situation in which the essential difference between two genres, or even kinds, of literature is obscured by the presence of terms with a similar sound or spelling. A classic example is that of satire; for although Quintilian (*Institutio Oratoria,* bk. 10, chap. 1, sec. 93) proudly asserts "satira quidem tota nostra est" (satire is altogether our own), Horace wavers between *satira* and *satura* and speaks of the Old Comedy as a model of the genre.[13] With a little ingenuity, then, the roots of Roman verse satire could be assumed to lie in the Greek satyr play, which the Greeks themselves did not regard as a separate genre. As in so many other instances, it was Isidore of Seville, the Webster of the early Middle Ages, who incurs much of the blame for this confusion, which it took many centuries to dispel. For he and his emulators enshrined the error by designating the masters of Roman satire (Horace, Persius, Juvenal, etc.) as comic playwrights.

While this contamination, fraught with serious consequences for the medieval theory of literature (whatever its worth), was primarily the result of a linguistic parallelism, the confusion surrounding the major kinds has other and, generally, more complex causes. We need only call to mind Dante's discussion of tragedy and comedy in his letter to Can Grande della Scala of Verona. In order to understand the poet's argument, one must realize that in the Middle Ages drama was not necessarily understood to be meant for stage performance. On the contrary, it was often taken to be fit for recitation, i.e., a *genus narrationum*—probably in the wake of Seneca's attitude toward his own closet dramas. In his epistle, Dante states the following reasons for calling his work a comedy:

For if we consider the subject-matter, at the beginning it is horrible and foul, as being Hell; but at the close it is happy, desirable, and pleasing, as being Paradise. As regards the style of language, it is unstudied and lowly, being in the vulgar tongue, in which even women hold their talk. And hence it is evident why the work is called a comedy.[14]

At this point, we should like to call attention to still another quirk in the history of literary genres. In the *Theory of Literature* we are told that "genre in the nineteenth century and in our own time suffers from the same difficulty as 'period': we are conscious of the quick changes in literary fashion—a new literary generation every ten years, rather than every fifty: in American poetry, the age of *vers libre*, the age of Eliot, the age of Auden." [15] Pondering the significance and relevance of this assertion we conclude, with Guyard, that this state of affairs is attributable not so much to a constantly accelerated generic "change of the guard" as to the rapid perfection of novel literary techniques and modes of presentation:

La notion de genre, autrefois si importante, s'efface devant celle de *technique*. Romancier, poète ou dramaturge, l'écrivain ne se soucie plus tellement d'être fidèle aux conventions d'une forme bien définie, que de prendre un certain point de vue sur les événements. Que ce point de vue soit celui de la durée ou de la psychanalyse, il faut pour le garder s'astreindre à certaines règles et l'on découvre que le problème des genres est transposé, non aboli.[16]

That such collisions between genres and techniques are fairly common is, once again, shown by the changing views on satire. For in spite of several recent attempts (such as Alvin Kernan's book) to salvage satire as a genre, the label is now ordinarily understood to refer to a technique pressed into the service of didacticism and applicable to numerous literary genres.[17] *Mutatis mutandis*, the same is true of parody, travesty, the burlesque and the grotesque. Especially the last two phenomena deserve close scrutiny on the part of those scholars who wish to retain the distinction between genres and techniques or modes (*die Groteske* and *die Burleske* as opposed to *das Groteske* and *das Burleske*).[18]

Much work in this area of specialization remains to be done by the comparatist; and it is hoped that the International Dictionary of Literary Terms, now in the making under the auspices of the ICLA, will furnish the clarifications needed in so many cases. Such elucidations, however, should not be restricted to our Western culture but ought to include comparisons involving different civilizations.

As for actual genological *rapports de fait* between East and West, for instance, it cannot be denied that, notably since the middle of the nineteenth century, European and American writers (as well as painters and composers) have been increasingly impressed and influenced by Oriental models. Thus the prototype of the Japanese haiku has fired the imagination of the Imagists, as well as that of Paul Claudel and numerous avant-garde poets of our own day. And the formal properties of the No play (less frequently their content) have found admirers in such playwrights as Yeats, Claudel, and Brecht. Their imitations prod the question to what extent such re-creations can be regarded as being compatible with their models and whether the pressure exerted by the Western tradition has caused a distortion of the original forms. In search of an answer, René Etiemble shrewdly observes:

Claudel publia de prétendus *dodoitsu*, et les *haikais* foisonnèrent en Europe. Savoir si les poèmes publiés ici sous ce nomme-là méritent encore une *appelation* que les marchands de fromage ou de vin diraient *contrôlée*, une *marque* que les fabricants de chaussettes ou de soutien-gorge diraient *déposée*. Lisent-ils ceux de nos prétendus *haikais* qui s'efforcent à la concision de l'original, les Japonais de ma connaissance n'y retrouvent rien des leurs. Cette déception depend-elle des conditions économiques ou politiques? Des superstructures philosophiques ou religieuses? Des images traditionelles? De la phonétique, de la grammaire des langues? [19]

Etiemble has no ready answer but suggests that it is impossible to transplant a genre that is firmly anchored in a specific historicogeographical context from one culture to another. On the other hand, the study of such unsuccessful experiments may demonstrate the wide gap which separates East and West and suggest some of the reasons for its existence. Pure analogy studies in comparative genology may fulfill a similar function and are likely to benefit Oriental scholars even more than their Occidental colleagues. For until very recently no systematic classification of literary phenomena according to their generic qualities was attempted in the Far Eastern countries, although the theory of genres has long been a basic element of Indian esthetics.

In his inaugural lecture at St. Petersburg University, Alexander Veselovsky championed the theory of a compulsory step-by-step progression of the three major literary kinds. In his opinion, the successive development of epic poetry (Homer), lyric poetry (Pindar), and drama (Aeschylus), which characterizes Greek literary history up to the classical age, was the necessary correlate of a historical progression from objectivity to subjectivity, and from there to a fusion of the two in a state perhaps most aptly described as that of reflection. Thus, in the Russian scholar's view, "what we might call the epic, lyric and dramatic world view actually had to occur in the particular succession indicated, determined by the ever greater development of individualism." [20] This is a theory not unparalleled in the age of positivism; for it finds its more strictly sociological analogue in H. M. Posnett's book *Comparative Literature* (1886) and—with greater literary sophistication—in the writings of Ferdinand Brunetière. However, contemporary scholarship emphatically rejects such simplistic—evolutionary or teleological—schemes of historical progression.

If, continuing to treat our problem historically, we consult the Greeks, we find that, for them, a tripartite division of the major kinds was theoretically possible but practically unattainable. For Aristotle, the epic and the drama were still the only two kinds identifiable as such, while—for reasons still to be spelled out in detail—lyrical poetry remained amorphous and, therefore, hard to classify. When the Stagirite poses the question as to the superiority of one kind over the other, the choice is only between tragedy and the epic. He finally opts for tragedy by arguing:

> And superior it is because it has all the epic elements . . . with the music and scenic effects as important accessories; and these afford the most vivid combination of pleasures. Further, it has vividness of impression in reading as well as in representation. Moreover, the art attains its end within nar-

rower limits; for the concentrated effect is more pleasurable than one which is spread over a long time and so diluted.[21]

In modern times, the epic has lost its glamor (just as lyrical poetry has won esteem) because the *poème héroïque* is as extinct as the Romance, its subspecies which, although conceptually differentiated and ultimately transformed into a prose genre, is historically related to it. It is all the more regrettable that today there does not seem to exist a universally valid name for the literary kind which embraces all narrative genres, whether couched in poetry or prose; for even the English *fiction* applies only to prose forms such as the novel, the novella, the short story, etc. On the other hand, a division of imaginative literature into prose and poetry is no longer feasible, since, in the meantime, numerous intermediate genres—such as the verse novel, the Lyrical Novel,[22] the *poème en prose*—as well as mixed forms—such as Dante's *Vita nuova,* Boccaccio's *Decamerone,* Goethe's *Faust,* and Strindberg's *Dream Play*—have been constituted.

Even a quadripartite division of literature into epic poetry, lyric poetry, drama, and didactic writings has been attempted from time to time, without ever catching on. This failure most likely results from the fact that the didactic is a mode rather than a kind or genre and relates primarily to an author's intentions and the effect which his work achieves. As a mode, however, it is at home in many genres, although some of these—the verse satire, the fable, the parable, the Morality, and perhaps even the legend and the fairy tale—show a marked preponderance for this approach. On the other hand, such patently didactic works as the lost poems of Empedocles, Lucretius' *De rerum natura,* and Brecht's unfinished versification of the Communist Manifesto belong to belles lettres partly for formal (metrical) reasons and partly—as in the case of Brecht—because they were authored by a poet.

Aristotle vehemently objected to the *ars metrica* cultivated in his time.

> Even if a treatise on medicine or natural philosophy be brought out in verse, the name of poet is by custom given to the author; and yet Homer and Empedocles have nothing in common except the meter: the former, therefore, is properly styled poet, the latter physicist rather than poet.[23]

In addition to defining the, often tenuous, relationship between didactic and nondidactic elements in a given class or species, the theory of literary genres is also charged with circumscribing and defining such marginal forms as are often excluded from the realm of belles lettres proper. We think, first of all, of the essay, the biography, and the autobiography and, among the miniature forms, the maxim, the aperçu, the aphorism, the Character (*caractère*) and the fragment—many of which are barely beginning to gain a measure of scholarly recognition.[24] To these we must add those phenomena which Baldensperger and Friederich somewhat loosely group under the heading of semiliterary genres and which are keys to our understanding of the mutual illumination of the arts: the libretto, the film script, the radio play and, last but not least, the emblem.[25]

A manner of classification particularly congenial to the student of the arts and their interrelationship is the division according to what Aristotle calls the means of imitation. This criterion is used in the opening passage of the *Poetics*, where literature is confronted with those other arts with which it shares one or several of these means. Indeed, no genological study would be complete without a reference to music—not because language, too, makes use of sounds, but primarily because music (the art inspired by the Muses) was originally wedded to the verbal arts. The reference is not to epic poetry, in spite of the fact that the bards or minstrels recited the lines to their own musical accompaniment; for even in antiquity this practice had a bearing only on the actual presentation, insofar as no music was specifically composed to go with the poetry. For this reason Aristotle justly includes the Epic among the strictly literary kinds, since it is one of the arts which "imitate by means of language alone, and that either in prose or verse—which verse, again, may either combine different meters or consist of but one kind."[26]

Curiously enough, Aristotle concludes by stating that this art "has hitherto been without a name." This statement is essential for the understanding of his (and the Greek) approach to the theory of genres; for it shows, as O. B. Hardison, Jr., has demonstrated,[27] that the ancients did not have a collective term for the major kind of non-dramatic literature that was not symbiotically fused with music. Among the genres which use several means of expression (meaning, in our context, words as well as music), Aristotle differentiates between those in which these means are employed simultaneously (the dithyramb and the nome) and those in which they figure alternately (tragedy and comedy). Unfortunately, it is no longer generally known that Greek tragedy was, in every way, a *Gesamtkunstwerk,* meaning that the standard texts handed down to us are merely the librettos of multidimensional plays akin to operas. This fact is underscored by the survival of two lines from Euripides' *Orestes,* together with their musical notation.[28]

The problems of generic classification looming for the student of lyrical poetry—now generally regarded as the third major kind of literature—are particularly excruciating, since its ties with music are etymologically fixed; for lyric means "accompanied by the lyre." Similarly, several ancient and modern lyrical genres, such as the ode (*ode* =

song), the song (*Lied, chanson*), and the sonnet presuppose an intimate relationship in degrees varying from age to age and from literature to literature. Greek literary criticism—at least in the classical and postclassical ages—was not yet prepared to assign a collective name to the lyric kind. The reasons are succinctly stated in the following entry, signed G. L., from the *Lexikon der alten Welt:*

What today, in contradistinction to the epic and the drama, we call lyric poetry was not uniformly conceived in antiquity. For one, the ancient drama contained lyrical passages as well, and ancient literary theory distinguished between lyrical and elegiac poetry. This is due partly to the closer ties which existed between language, music and the dance in ancient times.[29]

The Greeks themselves, using the manner of production as a yardstick, separated choric from monodic poetry, which latter carried the label "melic." It was only in Hellenistic times that a clearcut, pedantic division was created, which prevailed well into the Middle Ages. This feat was accomplished with the help of a canon of nine classic poets (Alcaeus, Alcman, Anacreon, Bacchylides, Ibycus, Pindar, Sappho, Simonides, and Stesichorus), upon whom the honorific title lyricists was bestowed. From that point on, the epithet *melic* was primarily used to designate noncanonic poetry. Attempts to increase the number of the classics were, on the whole, unsuccessful, except in some cases where major poets of subsequent ages continued to use the traditional forms. The term "lyrical poetry" (*lyrike*) first appears in the *techne grammatike* of Dionysius Thrax (ca. 170–90 B.C.) as a label for the major kind.

Horace, too, was unable to overcome these terminological difficulties; for in the *Ars Poetica* he alternately calls himself *lyricus* and *fidicen* (from *fides* = lyre); and well into the eighteenth (Germany) and nineteenth (France) centuries the term *ode* was widely used as a synonym for "lyrical poem." However, it applied only to consciously and individually created art (*Kunstdichtung*) and excluded the popular (folksong) elements. A critic as perceptive as Herder still wavered in his usage and called the ode the "vein of the drama and the epic, the only three kinds (*Arten*) of true poetry." [30] It was only in the writings of the German Romantic poets and critics (Novalis, the brothers Schlegel, and Schelling) that the tripartite scheme of the major kinds became universally accepted.

Not to be forgotten in our survey of the various approaches to the theory of genres is the questionable use of lyric, dramatic, and epic in their adjectival rather than nominal guise—a practice which still enjoys considerable favor, especially in the German-speaking countries. The purpose underlying this usage is to show that literary genres are improper groupings and that the best one can do in the way of drawing generic distinctions is to extract certain basic qualities, moods or states of mind—which brings the theory of genres dangerously close to being a psychological puzzle game, quite apart from the fact that the practitioners of this method sin, like Croce, by deliberately cutting themselves off from the historical context in which genres develop.

In his "Noten und Abhandlungen zum *West-Östlichen Divan*," Goethe observes that there are too many different points of view from which to consider the various kinds. The solution he offers is based on the assumption that there are three *Naturformen* of literature, namely the lucidly narrative, the enthusiastically excited, and the personally active (*die klar erzählende, die enthusiastisch aufgeregte und die persönlich handelnde*), in other words, attitudes relevant to the epic, lyric poetry, and the drama. Goethe goes on to say that these *Naturformen* may exist by themselves or in conjunction with each other, and that they are often found together even in the shortest poem. In particular, he seemed to regard the ballad as a kind of literary protozoon in which all three natural forms exist *in nuce*.

In order to arrange the individual genres in relation to each other and the natural forms (*Urformen*), Goethe proposed to arrange them schematically in such a way as to produce a circular pattern in which their proximity to one, two, or all of the *Urformen* is visually demonstrated. Models for each species were to be found until the circle containing all possible genres was completed. Goethe himself never played this pedantic game; but the German scholar Julius Petersen subsequently executed the manoeuver in his book *Die Wissenschaft von der Dichtung*.[31]

The notion that this approach is more fruitful for literary criticism than the historical study of the genres is most persistently advanced by the Swiss Germanist Emil Staiger. Like Goethe, Staiger believes "that every genuine literary work partakes of all genres, though in different degrees and manners, and that it is this proportionate difference which accounts for the abundance of the historically evolved genres."[32] He defended his censure of the usual poetics of genres by protesting that in modern times the number of form-content configurations has so rapidly increased that it has gotten out of hand. According to Staiger, however, a theory of genres is meaningful only if each species looks up to an acknowledged model.

> Since antiquity, however, the models have increased a thousandfold . . . (and) if the theory of genres wishes to remain fair to all individual examples, it must—to speak only of poetry—compare ballads, songs, hymns, odes, sonnets and epigrams with each other, trace the history of each of these genres through one or two thousand years and find a common

denominator qualifying them as lyrical poetry. But what is common to all such poems can only be something indifferent. Moreover, it ceases to be valid as soon as a new poet appears and presents an as yet unfamiliar model.[33]

We have already indicated that Staiger's view is shared by several of his German contemporaries, notably by the late Wolfgang Kayser, whose influential and widely used handbook *Das sprachliche Kunstwerk* also concerns itself with the structure (*Gefüge*) of genres. When screening the appropriate chapter (the tenth), one notes with dismay that the individual genres are hardly touched upon since "what they add to our understanding of a work has been discussed in earlier chapters, especially the ones concerned with techniques (*Darstellungsweisen*)."[34] If one consults these chapters, one discovers that, in them, the major kinds are summarily, and rather unsystematically, dealt with in a total of twenty-five pages (of which only four concern themselves with lyrical poetry and five with the drama), whereas chapter 10 extends to nearly sixty pages.

Let us call attention to a book written by the Dutch scholar André Jolles and published in German under the title *Einfache Formen* [Simple forms], 1930.[35] The forms in question are what we might call preliterary genres best considered as "specific kinds of mental activity constituted by the changing attitudes which man, creating form by means of language, adopts towards the objects he encounters."[36] Jolles lists nine such basic types, which he takes to be building blocks for the more demanding genres: *Legende* (legend in the sense of saint's biography), *Sage* ("a story popularly taken as historical but not verifiable"), *Mythe, Rätsel* (riddle), *Spruch* (proverb), *Kasus* (case, as in "court case"), *Memorabile* (a personal record of noteworthy events and experiences), *Märchen* (fairy tale), and *Witz* (joke). He did not regard the series as complete but thought, for example, of including the fable.

We have stated that the common feature of Jolles' simple forms is their preliterary or extraliterary character; for a case becomes literary only as a salient anecdote (Goethe's "unerhörte Begebenheit") or by expansion into the theme of a longer narrative or dramatic work, the *Memorabile* by its insertion into a diary or autobiography, the *Mythe* by its transformation into a plot (= *mythos*), etc. As far as their subject matter is concerned, these simple forms have relatively little in common, whereas structurally they tend to be rather less than more complex than most literary genres. However, among themselves, they considerably vary in scope extending, as they do, from the microcosm of the joke or riddle to the rich articulation of some fairy tales and legends.

Having, so far, primarily concerned ourselves with the literary kinds, we now turn to the actual genres and the various ways of arranging them in an aesthetic cosmos. For it is understood that some such systematic arrangement must be attempted, since a mere cataloguing of the diverse phenomena, whose number is legion, would yield no genological insight and would acquiesce in chaos. The need for clarification is underscored by the lists furnished by Goethe and Wolfgang Kayser respectively. In the above-mentioned notes to *Der West-Östliche Divan*, the Weimar sage alphabetically enumerates "allegory, ballad, cantata, drama, elegy, epigram, epistle, epic, novella (*Erzählung*), fable, heroid, idyl, didactic poem (*Lehrgedicht*), ode, parody, novel (*Roman*), romance, satire,"[37] whereas Kayser arranges his entries in the more hierarchic order "novel, epistolary novel, *Dialogroman*, picaresque novel, historical novel; ode, elegy, sonnet, *alba* (dawn song); auto, vaudeville, tragedy, comedy, Greek tragedy, melodrama."[38]

While Goethe indiscriminately catalogues literary

genres belonging to different classes and representing different orders of magnitude, Kayser clearly orients himself toward the major kinds. However, instead of listing the novel, the novella, the short story, the epic, the romance, etc., he singles out the novel together with certain of its subspecies and moves from a higher to a lower level of genological discourse. Goethe attaches the following comments to his random list.

If we scan the above list carefully, we notice that the types are sometimes named after their formal appearance and sometimes after their subject matter, but rarely according to their essential form. Moreover, one quickly realizes that some of them can be grouped together while others may be subordinated to each other.[39]

Goethe attempted a more expedient grouping—with methodologically questionable results—in the section "Naturformen der Poesie." From E.-M. Voigt's discussion of Greek lyrical poetry in one of his contributions to the *Lexikon der alten Welt* we learn that, in effect, Goethe's problem was not, as Staiger maintains, a specifically modern one; for in Hellenic practice

the terms themselves denote the poems according to different criteria: according to the refrain (paean, hymeneus), the action they accompany (hyporcheme, prosodion), the content or the occasion (encomium, epinicion), the chorus (partheneion), the meter (iambus) or simply as song (hymnus, melos).[40]

Let us now discuss the various principles of classification and, in doing so, seek to establish their value for the historical-critical study of genres from a comparative point of view. From the very beginning, it should be clear, however, that it is naturally impossible to arrange all regional, national, and international forms in an encompassing scheme. Since every survey of this field is bound to be more or less stringently selective, the quest for completeness is futile and must be abandoned in favor of an attempt to clarify the reasons why, in their poetics, Aristotle, Horace, and Boileau refer to certain genres but leave others untouched. It seems to us that such an inquiry would throw new light on the historical circumstances surrounding their survival or disappearance.

It seems fairly obvious that generic classifications based on psychological criteria are ordinarily to be taken with a grain of salt, no matter whether it is a question of the psychology of the author or that of his public (reader, spectator, or listener); for here, in spite of archetypal patterns, the subjective is bound to hold sway. A good case in point is Schiller's discrimination of the naïve and the sentimental (better, the reflexive), and his reference to the various genres reflecting these polar attitudes, in his famous essay "Über naive und sentimentalische Dichtung" (1795). The naïve, according to Schiller, is "nothing but the voluntary being, the existence of things by themselves and in accordance with innate and immutable laws," whereas the sentimental results from the fact that "in modern times man has lost touch with nature and nature, in its full truth, is to be found only outside of society in the inanimate world." [41] The further mankind departs from the naïve condition (and we know that it does so with ever increasing speed), the greater will be the preponderance of sentimental over naïve genres. If only for this pragmatic reason, a modern poetics of genres based on Schiller's dichotomy would be decidedly lopsided and fall short of its purpose.

More familiar and far more serious in its consequences is the division of literary genres by their intended effect. Embracing this perspective, Aristotle defines tragedy as the imitation of a serious action "through pity and fear effecting the proper purgation of these emotions." Two things should be noted in this connection. First of all, the author of the *Poetics* apparently does not assign the same aesthetic significance to the effects produced by the work of art as he does to the means, the subject matter, and the mode of expression; for fear and pity enter our field of vision only in chapter 6 of his treatise, whereas the other elements are scrutinized in chapters 1–3.

Secondly, we should remember that pity and fear are *feelings* most strongly evoked in public performance and, hence, of less immediate significance in the composition and consumption—to use a sociological term—of fiction or poetry which, at least in the modern era, impinge upon us in the privacy of our homes.[42] Indeed, it can be shown that, traditionally, generic designations derived from the intended effect of the literary product are more frequently encountered in the drama (*Lustspiel, Trauerspiel, Rührstück*) than in fiction (sentimental novel, *Schauerroman*) or poetry.

For the student of comparative literature this approach is especially unproductive, since twentieth-century man is fully aware that the same event or object is judged differently, and produces diverse effects, not only in different cultures but also at different times—and in different places—within the same culture. What the Australian bushman calls beautiful or touching may seem ugly and repulsive to the Watussi, and the Aztec's heroic deed may seem cowardly to the Dutchman. In a passage from *Stephen Hero*, Joyce articulates this view by stating

> No esthetic theory . . . is of any value which investigates with the aid of the lantern of tradition. What we symbolise in black the Chinaman may symbolise in yellow; each has his own tradition. Greek beauty laughs at Coptic beauty and the American Indian derides them both. It is almost impossible to reconcile all tradition.[43]

It is ironic that, this anthropological insight notwithstanding, young Dedalus continues to build his theory of art around the Aquinatic dictum *pulcra sunt quae visa placent*, which he interprets to mean "that, though the same object may not seem beautiful to all people, all people who admire a beautiful object find in it certain relations which satisfy and coincide with the stages themselves of all esthetic apprehension."[44] In other words: Joyce operates with psychological constants.

The oldest and most venerable way of classifying genres is found in Plato's *Republic* (392b–394d), where emphasis is placed on what we now tend to call "point of view." Socrates, speaking to Adeimantus, observes:

> I suppose that all mythology and poetry is a narration of events, either past, present or to come. . . . And narration may be either simple narration or imitation, or a union of the two. . . . [Thus] poetry and mythology are, in some cases, wholly imitative, instances of this being supplied by tragedy and comedy. There is also the opposite style, in which the poet is the only speaker—of this the dithyramb affords the best example. And the combination of both is found in the epic and in several other types of literature.[45]

The value of this method is appreciably reduced by the underlying pedagogical intention; for Plato regards mimesis as dangerous for the state since, in the mimetic genres, the poet propounds his own ideas through the mouths of his characters, thereby presenting as objective fact what is actually his personal opinion. If one disregards the didactic aspect of Plato's theory, on the other hand, the distinctions made by Socrates merely relate to technical or stylistic devices which are also mentioned in the *Poetics* (1448a), where no major genological significance is attached to them, however. Their full meaning emerged only in the second half of the nineteenth century, first with Flaubert and then with Henry James. Following Guyard's suggestions, a latter-day Plato would have to record all the refinements of fictional perspective which have occurred in the last fifty years, adding references to the stream of consciousness, the *style indirect libre* (*erlebte Rede*, narrated monologue), etc.[46]

Perhaps the most frequently used methods of classification are, naturally, those oriented toward form or content. The more's the pity that these cannot always be clearly separated. Hence the following recipe offered in the *Theory of Literature:*

Genre should be conceived . . . as a grouping of literary works based, theoretically, upon both outer form (specific meter or structure) and also upon inner form (attitude, tone, purpose—more crudely, subject and audience). The ostensible basis may be one or the other (e.g., the "pastoral" or "satire" for the inner form; dipodic verse and Pindaric ode for the outer); but the critical problem will then be to find the other dimension to complete the diagram.[47]

In the light of the dialectic embraced by Wellek and Warren, it is instructive to look, once more, at Horace's epistolary treatise where, both in the case of lyrical poetry and the epic, the genre is identified by its preferred subject matter rather than its formal trappings; for the bard is said to have described *res gestae regumque ducumque et tristia bella* (the actions of kings and rulers and sad wars) and the poet is charged with celebrating *divos puerosque deorum/et pugilem victorem et equum certamine primum /et iuvenum curas et libera vina* (gods and the sons of gods and boxing champions and derby winners, the desires of young people and the liberating wine).[48]

Particularly instructive for the comparatist is the example of gradual fusion of formal and conceptual qualities offered by the elegy and the iamb which, in the peripatetic aesthetic subscribed to by Horace, were distinguished from lyrical poetry because they lacked the musical element. In the fourth chapter of the *Poetics*, we are told that the iamb was originally regarded as the meter most suitable for satirical poetry but that, since it closely approximates the rhythm of colloquial speech, it was later used in the dialogue passages of the drama, thereby becoming neutralized and losing its validity as a generic label. Today, the genological attrition is complete, and the iamb leads a shadow existence as the most common of all poetic meters.

Polemicizing against the *ars metrica*, Aristotle states, in the first chapter of his treatise (1447[b]), that "people do indeed commonly connect the idea of poetry or 'making' with that of verse and speak of elegiac poets or of epic (that is, hexameter) poets; implying that it is not imitation that makes them poets but the meter that entitles them to the common name." Formally speaking, the elegy is a poem couched in elegiac distichs, i.e., one dactylic hexameter followed by one dactylic pentameter. As for its content, it was originally used as a vehicle expressing sorrow over the loss of a beloved person, although subsequently the elegiac poets were increasingly concerned with amatory matters as Ovid had treated them in his *Amores*. The combination of love and death seems later to have become a hallmark of this tradition, as witnessed by Rilke's *Duino Elegies*. In the course of this development, however, the genre lost its innate formal properties and was no longer written in distichs. Wellek and Warren note that in England "Gray's *Elegy (on a Country Churchyard)*, written in the heroic quatrain, not in couplets, effectually destroys any continuation in English of elegy as any tender personal poem written in end-stopped couplets." [49]

As for the classification of genres according to their subject matter, the strict application of this criterion is likely to produce a proliferation of subspecies without distinct physiognomies. Wolfgang Kayser's list of types of novels, quoted above, could easily be enlarged to include such forms as the *Bildungsroman*, the pastoral novel, the political novel,[50] the courtly novel of the German Baroque, the utopian novel, etc. It is obvious that, given such a large body of works constituting a major literary kind, some sort of breakdown is mandatory; but how is one to square this circle?

Kayser's list is by no means restricted to matters of content; for in the case of the epistolary novel, for example, the manner of presentation is already more or less clearly implied. Even the *Bildungsroman*—with its patently didactic overtones, which become more pronounced as we proceed from the *Lehrjahre* to the *Wanderjahre*—presupposes a basic pattern in so far as the growth and education of the hero progress in a definite, irreversible biological and pedagogical order. Conversely, the picaresque novel requires a loose structure and a frequent change of scene.[51] In the case of the murder mystery and the detective thriller, the structure is less rigidly predetermined, except that, suspense being used as a chief device, the identity of the criminal is rarely revealed before the end. The Gothic novel, finally, comes much closer to constituting a literary genre; for here the setting and many of the props are prescribed by a closely knit convention established by a generally acknowledged model, Horace Walpole's *The Castle of Otranto*.

The *Bildungsroman*, the picaresque novel, the Gothic novel, the epistolary novel, etc., may perhaps be regarded as genres for still another reason: they have no direct counterparts in the other major kinds of literature (lyric poetry, the drama, and the epic), whereas the whodunit and the historical novel have their exact dramatic equivalents. With the utopian and the rustic novel we come closer to the realm of sociological classification, a realm which would also have to include the (often satirically barbed) novel of school life, the proletarian novel et al. In this kind of narrative, the setting is usually the determining factor, and a rather superficial one at that. In the case of the historical novel—to which Georg Lukács and Lion Feuchtwanger have devoted critical-historical monographs [52]—Wellek and Warren would like to make an exception, "not merely because its subject is less restricted . . . but primarily because of the ties of the historical novel to the Romantic movement and to nationalism—because of the new feeling about, attitude toward, that past which it implies." [53] Pichois and Rousseau would probably agree, in so far as the historical novel, in their opinion, is essentially monogenetic, i.e., derived from a single prototype or author.

One should think that purely formal criteria of genre classification speak for themselves, since they seem to be inherently quantitative. Thus there is no problem in grouping plays according to the number of acts into which they are divided (but where would we place Greek tragedy?) and in arranging various kinds of narrative according to their length (such as, 50,000 words constitute a minimum for the novel, 10,000 words a maximum for the novella, with the short novel, the novelette, and the long novella falling in between, and the anecdote and short story occupying the lowest rung of the ladder). Although such divisions would seem to be altogether mechanical, quantitative criteria may sometimes acquire a qualitative coloring—in analogy to the annalistic labels attached to period styles. This is certainly true of several lyric genres, such as the sonnet in general and the Petrarchan sonnet in particular, and although we tend to repudiate the *ars metrica* with Aristotle, we readily admit that at least the specialist is likely to associate distinct generic properties with metrical patterns, as in the case of the *endecasillabo*, the *terza rima*, the *Alexandrine* and the *Schüttelreim* (poetic spoonerism). The same applies, with even greater force, to the poets themselves, as Paul Valéry demonstrates in his persuasive essay "Concerning *Le Cimetière marin*."[54]

We started out by saying that, given the enormous range and complexity of the literary phenomena known variously as kinds, types, genres, and classes, the historically oriented student of genology as a branch of Comparative Literature will find it next to impossible to fashion a frame of reference in which a distinct place is assigned to each of these. The best he can hope to do is to disentangle some of the knottiest problems, reveal anachronisms and shed light on some of the many confusions perpetrated in the course of literary history. In addition to handling the various approaches to genre definition in as deft and flexible a manner as the circumstances may require, he must also see to it that, methodologically, generic qualities are separated from those relating primarily to technique (as in satire) and from those infringing on thematic categories (as in Northrop Frye's *modes*). Thus, while in our post-Romantic age it would be vain to insist, with Horace, that "each particular genre should keep the place allotted to it," we should nevertheless endeavor to draw lines of demarcation where conditions are ripe and make sure that our terminology is as consistent as is humanly possible and defensible in the light of the historical context.

11

WEST EUROPEAN ROMANTICISM

Definition and Scope

HENRY H. H. REMAK

THE STUDENT of literature cannot, like his colleague in the sciences, rely on the availability of basic terms with clearcut and universally accepted meanings. Even within the realms of scholarship restricted to one national literature, connotations like Baroque, Enlightenment, Realism, Impressionism, etc., give rise to extremely variegated if not contradictory evaluations. Further difficulties arise when scholars blithely use a term arrived at by their interpretation of a national development without qualifying it as to national origin and applicability. Van Tieghem's *Le Romantisme dans la littérature européenne,* for example, places Romanticism [1] in sharp contrast to Classicism. This may be true for *French* Romanticism and *French* Classicism, but certainly not for the attitude of *German* Romanticism toward *German* Classicism, or of English, Italian, and Spanish Romanticism toward their national brands of Classicism, for that matter. Morse Peckham's sprightly "Toward a theory of Romanticism" should have been entitled "Toward a theory of *English* Romanticism," since the reader will look in vain for a consideration of Romanticism outside England.[2] Examples of this kind can be multiplied at will.

In the following pages, we shall pass in review some

definitions and reasons for nondefinition of Romanticism, and pick out and compare a number of strands held to be romantic in an attempt to find out whether or not and to what, if any, extent we may legitimately speak of Romanticism as a *European* phenomenon. The conclusions reached must be regarded as distinctly approximate. Romanticism has been chosen because it combines the elements of momentousness and controversy more than any other period connotation. For our present purposes, it does no more than to serve as an illustration of the kinds of difficulties and painful decisions encountered by the student of comparative literature when examining the usefulness and essential composition of literary labels employed in more than one country. The same could be done for such coinages as Renaissance, Baroque, Classicism, Realism, Symbolism, Expressionism, etc.

The first quandary facing us is that of limitation. Ideally, our analysis should include literatures anywhere in the world. Our knowledge, time, and space do not permit us to do that. We shall restrict ourselves to the five important West European literatures (English, French, German, Italian, and Spanish). For the same reasons, we shall have to forego, largely, consideration of the other arts. It stands to reason that a full-fledged examination of European Romanticism—as of other literary currents or movements—would gain immeasurably if we admitted as evidence insights gained from the fine arts and the music of the respective periods (as well as from philosophy, politics, sociology, and economics, in appropriate cases). In both these neglected categories, off-the-beaten-path literatures and spheres related to literature, comparative studies have barely made a beginning.

Another decision has to be reached: Should a difference be made—and if so, how strict a difference—between Romanticism as an alleged historical movement and romanticism as a forever recurring emotional condition? Peckham (somewhat rashly, we think) doubts any connections between both; Baldensperger affirms them. Connections or not, Barrère, Berr, and Van Tieghem favor a separation; Kluckhohn and Praz propose to reserve the term exclusively for historical Romanticism. Babbitt, Croce, Grierson, Lucas, de Meeüs, and Peyre, however, seem to consider the two as one. Recent Italian scholarship appears to seek to combine both views. Siciliano calls Romanticism a unique spiritual phenomenon manifesting itself in all activities of art and thought from the early 1700's to our own days. Marcazzan wonders whether contemporary Decadentism is still part of the Romantic movement or whether it represents a new stage of development. Mittner connects German Romanticism as a historic movement with German romanticism as an eternal tendency of the German spirit.[3]

While there are, in our own judgment, undoubtedly affinities between both categories of "romanticism," we must, for our purposes, focus on the alleged historical phenomenon, or else any attempt to delineate "romanticism" as a period movement collapses a priori.[4]

A large and respectable body of critics[5] maintains that Romanticism cannot be compressed into a formula at all. Individualism and fluctuation, as primordial constituents of Romanticism, do not admit, they say, of a generally definable doctrine. There are as many definitions of Romanticism as there are authors chosen to represent it.[6] At any rate, the divergences between the Romanticism of a particular country and that of another overshadow whatever resemblances may exist. There are, to be sure, romantic writers and features; there may be a romantic period; perhaps there are Romanticisms, but there is no Romanticis*m*. These critics are apt to remind us that the romantic writers themselves seldom used the controversial term and cast doubt on its usefulness. The effect of the skeptical attitude taken by these scholars can be measured by the increasing abandonment of "Romantic *school*" in favor of less definite terms ("movement," "current," "temper," or even "foci of friendship"). But these "nominalists" have been challenged by such articulate and incisive observers as Praz, Wellek, and Peckham, who assert that the task of defining Romanticism as an international movement is far from hopeless. Wellek and Peckham have actually come forward with specific solutions and definitions. We shall very briefly list a few of the skeptical as well as of the affirmative views.

Perhaps the most formidable exponent of the "negative" camp is the eminent historian of ideas, Arthur Lovejoy. His thesis that we should think of Romanticism*s*, not of Romanticis*m*, was first stated in a 1924 *PMLA* article (reprinted in the *Essays in the History of Ideas*, 1948), and amplified or modified in the last chapters of the *Great Chain of Being* (1936) as well as in his 1941 article in the *Journal of the History of Ideas*.[7] It must be remembered that Lovejoy's negative attitude toward *one* type of Romanticism prevailing in Western Europe is only part of the intended proof of his general conviction that scholarship has laid too much stress on the systematic and consistent elements in writers, and has tended to ignore, belittle, or explain away divergences, inconsistencies, contradictions, and struggles which are the trademark of outstanding authors (uniformity being more characteristic of smaller minds).[8]

Henri Peyre has undertaken to weaken the chronological unity of West European Romanticism by pulling France from under it. The great French Romantic poets, Peyre holds,[9] are Baudelaire, Rimbaud, and Lautréamont, whose works appeared decades and up to a half century after those composed by authors hitherto taken for granted as representing the Romantic generation: Hugo, Lamartine, Vigny, and Musset. If, Peyre says, we insist on locating genuine French Romantics in the first decades of the nineteenth century, we must either resort to lesser celebrities like Gérard de Nerval, or to such figures as Balzac (commonly classed as a realist), Michelet (a historian), Delacroix (a painter), and Berlioz (a composer)! [10] This apparently paradoxical view is much less so when it is seen that, like Lovejoy's position, Peyre's attitude is a spoke strengthening a wheel, part of a more general theory. In Peyre's case, his attack on Western European Romanticism as a fairly homogeneous movement fits into his overall belief that the notion of literary generations should be substituted for that of movements and schools. It is not surprising to find that Wellek, the champion of the concept of a pan-European Romanticism, happens to be a notable proponent of the belief that literary movements are reliable tools in the literary carpenter shop. Again and again, we find upon closer scrutiny that the arguments for or against the existence of a West European literary movement called "Romanticism" are only a skirmish or, at best, a battle in a crucial war of literary history.

This observation applies with equal or greater strength to Benedetto Croce, whose spirit seems to hover over the battlefield as the patron saint of the "negative" contingents. Croce has attacked the idea and the practice of literary history, claiming that it may be history, but has little to do with literature. Much, indeed most that has gone on by the name of literary history belongs, according to him, to other realms of knowledge: biography, sociology, ideology, philosophy, politics, religion, etc. To Croce, the study of literature ought to mean the analysis of rare, isolated masterpieces of rare, isolated great men and women of letters. Each work must be viewed as a separate entity, as something unique, without reference to other phenomena, authors, or even other works by the same author.[11] Croce's aesthetics have undoubtedly proved to be a boon to contemporary literary criticism; at the same time, his theories, if fully accepted, would wreak havoc with the realm of literary history and with it spell the end of such period concepts as "Romanticism." In its place, there would be lone masterpieces dotting an otherwise blank map, without lifelines between them: literary anarchy, in short.[12]

The authors of the two papers on English Romanticism in the *PMLA* symposium (1940), Elizabeth Nitchie and Hoxie Fairchild, also align themselves with the skeptics. Miss Nitchie does not even believe that there is *an* English Romanticism.[13] Fairchild, by stressing the insularity of English Romanticism, saps the argument for a European Romanticism. His accentuation of the evolutionary (rather than revolutionary) aspects of Romanticism, which he relates, as does Van Tieghem, to eighteenth-century literature, points in the same direction; the advocates of a coherent European Romantic movement are bound to underline the original contributions of Romanticism (Wellek, Peckham). More recently, Friederich remarks that "the use of any one [common denominator for Romanticism] usually requires a twisting of the interpretation of a considerable portion of romantic literature in order to make it a product of the common denominator." [14]

It is clear that the advocates of an essentially identical European Romanticism are under much greater pressure than their adversaries to come through with definitions of Romanticism. Attempts at such definitions are legion.[15] Very generally speaking, there seem to be two main types of definition, with a transitional area in between.

In the first kind of definition, one or two alleged traits of Romanticism are singled out and made to stand for Romanticism as a whole. Madame de Staël tells us that Romanticism refers to chivalry. For Hugo, Romanticism is Liberalism in literature. Hedge sees in it mystery and aspiration, Lanson a lyrical expansion of individualism, Lucas an intoxicating dream, Immerwahr an imaginative literary process. Ker and Geoffrey Scott underscore its cult of the past, Picon its dedication to originality, Deutschbein its concern with synthesis, Milch its nationalism.

Frequently, a sharper definition of Romanticism is sought by contrasting it with other movements, especially Classicism. Romanticism is essentially a reaction against the excesses of intellectualism (Jasinski), change following upon fixity (Barzun), urge rather than restraint (Guérard), strangeness added to beauty (Pater), or cancellation of the classical equilibrium by a process of irrationalistic intensification (Petersen). Despite his strictures on genre and movement definitions, Croce says that romantic literature is a spontaneous and violent effusion of feelings which indulges in vaporous and indeterminate images, half-sentences and powerful, dim outlines, while classicism portrays pacified hearts, sage designs, precise personalities, equilibrium and clarity (representation being to classicism what sentiment is to romanticism).[16] Gundolf, while similarly protesting that Romanticism is no unified "Weltanschauung," let alone a system, but represents a new "Weltgefühl" which has arisen as a primary "Erlebnis" in a few men of genius, nevertheless ventures to compare the contest between "Klassik" and "Romantik" to a struggle between male and female lovers, between the generative and the birth-giving, the plastic and the musical, day and night, dream and intoxication, shape and motion, centripetality and centrifugality,

Apollo and Dionysus. By others, Romanticism is said to incarnate the will to love, self-abandonment, individualism, subjectivity, symbolism, exoticism, bizarreness, mystery, suggestiveness, movement, extremeness, uniqueness, incompleteness, infiniteness, etc., etc., whereas Classicism is said to stand for the will to power, self-control, social organization, objectivity, stability, finiteness, the typical, etc., etc. Differences in presentation are in the foreground of Saintsbury's statement that Classicism introduces an idea directly, whereas Romanticism leaves it to the imagination of the reader, and of Barrère's remark that the Romantic *élan* of feeling and imagination carries words along and away with it, whereas Classicism imposes the measure of words on the emotions.

These contrasting definitions tend to be aphoristic and subjective. We are not left in the dark about the preferences, on the one side, of Goethe (the classical is the sane, the romantic the in-sane) and of Irving Babbitt or Frank Lucas whose somewhat more cautious characterizations echo Goethe's, or, on the other side, of A. W. Schlegel (the romantic is organic and picturesque, the classical is mechanical and plastic), of Stendhal (Romanticism is the literature which pleases people today, Classicism is the literature which pleased their great-grandfathers) or Berchet (the contrast between classical and romantic poetry amounts to the difference between the poetry of the dead and of the living).[17]

More recently, the attempt has been made to clarify the meaning of Romanticism by comparing it to the Renaissance or to the Baroque. Granting certain instructive parallelisms, not much, as Barrère suggests, seems gained by shouldering the additional burden of defining terms which are just about as controversial as Romanticism.

A transitional kind of definition attempts to dwell on, more or less, one central denominator broad enough to support the claim that it covers the entire movement. We think of Friedrich Schlegel's description of Romanticism as "progressive universal poetry," of Guérard who calls it a reaffirmation of life, of Poulet to whom it means a more acute consciousness of the enigma of the self and of the world, of Herford and Barrère who see in it an extraordinary development of imaginative sensibility, or of Hankiss who after despairing of ever reconciling the apparently disparate phenomena of the Romantic movement finally arrived at its "key": intensity.

Sometimes this common denominator appears as a fusion or polarity of two forces. Bowra (one of many critics who follow their insistence that Romanticism defies formulation by still another definition), speaking of English Romantic poets, calls the Romantic movement a prodigious attempt to discover the world of spirit through the unaided efforts of the solitary soul, and Fairchild, also with English Romanticism in mind, refers to the illusioned view of the universe and of human life, produced by an imaginative fusion of the finite and the infinite. Legouis and Cazamian stress the Romantic interplay of emotion and imagination. For Jansen, Romanticism is marked by the cleavage between dream and reality, past and present, the faraway and the nearby.

We are now well on the way toward a second type of definition which honestly tries to be all-inclusive and arrives at what its deviser considers an irreducible minimum of about three Romantic features. These may be considered essentially heterogeneous or coexistent (Lovejoy),[18] or viewed as successive steps on a Romantic ladder (Peckham). Some of them may be listed as follows:

FAIRCHILD: *1]* Naturalism,[19] *2]* Medievalism, *3]* Transcendentalism.

GUNDOLF (interpreting Friedrich Schlegel and Schleiermacher): *1]* Infiniteness ("Unendlichkeit"), *2]* Individuality ("Individualität"), 3] Companionship ("Geselligkeit").

CARLYLE: 1] Dynamism, 2] Unconscious Mind.

LOVEJOY: 1] Organicism, 2] Dynamism, 3] Diversitarianism.

WELLEK:[20] 1] Creative Imagination (for the view of poetry as knowledge of the deepest reality), 2] Organic Nature (for the view of the world), 3] Symbol and Myth (as primary determinants of poetic style).

PECKHAM: 1] Dynamic Organicism (reaction against eighteenth-century static mechanism—"the watch"), 2] Negative Romanticism (rejection of static mechanism but no—or not yet—acquiescence in dynamic-organic universe), 3] Positive Romanticism (acceptance of dynamic-organic universe—the "tree").

Among these ultracompressed statements there still are differences in catholicity. Fairchild's definition seems to contain more specific and limited elements (medievalism, transcendentalism), probably due to his preoccupation with England and personal inclinations. On the other hand, Peckham is trying to force Carlyle's, Lovejoy's, and Wellek's interpretations into a supergeneral, all-embracing formula—a definition to end definitions. But we must keep in mind that this ultrarefinement may be, at least in part, of a linguistic nature, for "dynamic organicism," e.g., is not too meaningful until it is spelled out by Peckham: change, imperfection, growth, diversity, the creative imagination, the unconscious.

Despite Peckham's matchmaking optimism that he may have presided over an effective marriage of hitherto recalcitrant molecules, the prognosis for a lasting union is unfavorable.[21] It is more than likely that we are facing a permanent dilemma in the production of definitions: they are either too narrow or too general. General definitions will be attacked as lacking in precision and being surcharged with subjectiveness, as being so elastic that they are no longer very expressive. Reservations, exceptions, and specifications will be tagged on. The resulting definition will then become so complicated and cumbersome that demands for greater simplification and generalization will be heard. Definitions are subject to a constant process of inflation and deflation, of expansion and contraction. Such tugs of war, let us add, are not only inevitable but healthy in the field of literary history.

Joining the battle of grand definitions is, however, not necessarily the only way of contributing to a solution of the problem we face. As a matter of fact, it is difficult not to become somewhat suspicious about the genesis of these "keys" to Romanticism. We have a feeling that they came about in the following manner: The scholar in question, in reading several Romantic works or authors, develops a hunch that past definitions are not satisfactory; he pounces on one or two or three elements, or combinations of elements, which, to his mind, have been overlooked or improperly evaluated; he goes through the Romantic literature of (we trust) more than one country hoping, of course, to "discover" that his hunch is justified, that the elements he is looking for are really "there," that his theory is "right." Even the most detached student and scholar engaged in such an adventure will find it hard to resist the temptation—of which he may not be conscious, or only semiconscious—to "adjust" or minimize evidence pointing in a direction opposite to his pet theory. The impression persists that the evidence did not come first and the conclusion second, but that the evidence is selected to buttress conclusions.[22] This subtle lure is particularly potent in discussions about Romanticism, a subject capable of involving scholars emotionally as well as mentally, and all the more so since, as we have seen, theories about Romanticism are apt to be keystones of even wider controversial systems.[23]

Another approach more likely to avoid these pitfalls (to the extent that it is humanly possible to escape them) offers itself to the student of comparative literature, an avenue more tedious but, perhaps, more reliable in the long run. Shutting out any fixed preconceived notions about the unity or lack of such of West European Romanticism, we should set about to make a list of alleged representative Romantic characteristics and try to ascertain, for each single one, whether and to what extent it exists in five key literatures of Western Europe. From the tabulated results, conclusions can be drawn as to the national or international character of Romanticism. This is precisely the procedure repeatedly urged by scholars who have written on Romanticism as a supranational phenomenon and are aware of the conjectural tentativeness of their efforts.[24]

We have attempted to draw up such a table, with the distinct understanding that it cannot expect to be more than a rudimentary model, an illustration of a method of procedure. A completely authentic coverage of this vast problem would almost have to be a cooperative undertaking. Again a codification seems, offhand, like a far too mechanical and certainly most unromantic procedure to be applied to Romanticism. But the appearance of complete objectivity is deceptive. The very selection of the items in the table must, in the last analysis, be subjective, and every single entry under every single country is a generalization and therefore open to doubt and debate.[25] This is unavoidable and requires no apology.

The key words had to be extensive enough to be significant for more than one country, but sufficiently distinct to satisfy us that the extent of the occurrence of the mood or attitude covered by it could actually be measured in each country. No claim is made that these key terms have equal qualitative values; there is not and never will be agreement on that score. It can only be hoped that the final balance will be so lopsided as to eliminate inevitable disagreements about the respective weighing of each item as a determinative factor. There is nothing sacrosanct about the arrangement, but a different one could not alter the final outcome much.

For the sake of more reliable results it has seemed preferable to be conservative and to eliminate consideration of pre-Romanticism (with very few exceptions) in the "Elements" table. In the influence table we could afford to be more generous and included not only pre-Romantic influences on the Romantic generations but also a few "semi-" or "post-Romantics" like Landor and the Brownings.

In order to arrive at an affirmative decision on the existence of a Romantic feature in Western European literature, it had to be located in at least three out of the five literatures examined. Germany, France, and England counted, however, somewhat more heavily than Italy and Spain. For a "yes" answer to the question whether a Romantic trait existed in a given literature, a great density or preponderance of this characteristic in the literature within a limited period was not required; what mattered was a significant increase or change as compared to the preceding period(s). The fact that a feature may appear in two or more countries within the chronological boundaries we have set does not, of course, imply that the concepts in question were identical for each country concerned. "Medievalism," e.g., did not mean the same to

Hugo as it did to Novalis. Nevertheless there is a minimum basis of medievalism shared by both which is significant. Nor do we take it for granted that in such cases an influence has been operating. It does seem to us, however, that in borderline cases the burden of the proof should be on those *denying* a common causal bond; during the Romantic period, isolation was less normal than kinship.[26]

Although the question whether these common factors are due to direct influence, similar *ambiance*, or coincidence may give rise to interesting explorations, it is not of primary importance to the argument. The fact that within approximately the same period certain tendencies or, to use Wellek's coinage, "sets of norms" different from preceding and following ones, either as such or in their evolutions, combinations, and accentuations, manage to assert themselves in several countries, points to a supranational literary condition regardless of the causes involved. It needs perhaps to be said that the labeling of certain authors, works, or tendencies as "romantic," or the absence of such designations, by contemporaries of Romanticism or later observers cannot be primary determinants in our own conclusions about the existence or nonexistence of Romantic trends in the countries concerned.

Granting that some decisions in the "Elements" table could seem too close for comfort to other observers and may be subject to reversal, still the evidence pointing to the existence in Western Europe of a widespread, distinct and fairly simultaneous pattern of thoughts, attitudes, and beliefs associated with the connotation "Romanticism" is overwhelming. We believe that an extension of the investigation to Scandinavia and Slavic countries would support this conclusion.[27]

The tally contains some surprises. If it is at all reliable, certain clichés may have to be abandoned: that Romanticism as a whole is "vague" and "unrealistic," that it is opposed to classicism and to the eighteenth century, that it has a set body of metaphysics, and that it is politically liberal (or, for that matter, "reactionary").[28] We see that West European Romanticism possesses a reasonable cohesiveness and shares in certain attitudes toward the past, but with notable qualifications; and that there is sweeping agreement in general attitudes and in specific artistic tendencies.[29]

A number of general observations may now be made with regard to supranational influences during the Romantic period: *1]* Contemporary Romantic authors exerted relatively little influence abroad during the Romantic period. Among those that did—very moderately, in some cases—are A. W. Schlegel, Jean Paul, the Grimm brothers, Schelling, and E. T. A. Hoffmann; Chateaubriand, Madame de Staël, Hugo, Lamartine, and Dumas père; Scott (the most influential of all) and Byron; Manzoni and Leopardi. (None from Spain.) *2]* Far stronger was the influence of older (sometimes considerably older) authors on the Romantic movements in other countries: Böhme, Herder, Bürger, Goethe, Schiller, Kant; Rousseau; Shakespeare, Milton, and eighteenth-century pre-Romantics in England (Richardson, "Ossian," Percy, Young, Gray, etc.); Dante, Vico; Cervantes and Calderón. *3]* The strongest influences on West European Romanticism were German, English, and those of Rousseau. *4]* Germany's tendencies are more extreme than those of any other country. *5]* England's literature appears to be best balanced during the Romantic period; undoubtedly her vigorous eighteenth-century pre-Romanticism (or sentimentalism) and her political steadiness acted as stabilizing factors. *6]* France is the intermediary par excellence between Germanic and Romanic countries, in all directions. Ironically, the Romantic movement came to the Romance countries after it had gained a strong foothold in Germany and England. French Romanticism is more pronounced and prolonged than that of any other Romance country. *7]* Italy and Spain form a Romantic "bloc" apart, exhibiting many similarities despite the dearth of interplay between them: a patriotic, political, practical romanticism; powers of tradition and of a set way of life acting as buffers against striking changes; a long tradition of coexistence between classical and romantic elements in their national character and literature makes for restraint and precludes spectacular developments; this explains probably the considerable vogue in Italy and Spain of the well-balanced Scott. *8]* Italy and Spain (and, to a lesser extent, Germany) influenced other countries chiefly as romantic locales. *9]* The same author may have exerted a very different type of influence in different countries. Rousseau's influence in Germany was primarily of a literary and pedagogical nature, whereas his influence in Italy and Spain was mainly political and social.

Although we hold, with Wellek, that the concept of movements (or at least currents) is vital to literary history as a discipline, let us not forget that it *is* a relativistic concept. Recent research is moving away from the idea that the succession of literary periods corresponds to a predestined, violent swing of the pendulum; it is shying away from brilliant theories of dialectic historical contrasts championed not long ago by German scholarship (Strich, Korff). Instead, it has emphasized the gradual transition between periods, the overlapping and the simultaneousness of contrasting literary phenomena (e.g., Naturalism, Impressionism, and Symbolism in the 1890's). As linguistics has followed philology, so the descriptive method has succeeded (though not supplanted) the causal-historical approach in literary scholarship. With regard to Romanticism, we are more keenly aware now that there was a strong "pre-Romantic" element in what we like to call the

Age of Reason, but we also know that there is a pervasive rationalistic element in, or running concurrent with Romanticism; that there are vigorous Realistic elements in Romanticism as well as Romantic ingredients in Realism; we even admit that Classicism may have romantic connotations, and that the survival of the classical tradition in Romanticism is greater than we had suspected previously.

The way from Rationalism and Sentimentalism via Romanticism to Realism, Naturalism, and Symbolism can perhaps best be described by Miss Nitchie's image of a zigzagging road along which the view on either side differs from that on the other, but only by degrees. We might add, however, that these gradual differences accumulate as the journey proceeds, and that the landscape at the end of the trip is bound to vary considerably from the scenery at the beginning of the literary expedition.

In January 1971, apart from minor adjustments, the preceding essay, the charts, and the bibliography remain essentially as they were when first published. I have endeavored to record and analyze developments since 1961 in my essay, "Trends of Recent Research on West European Romanticism," in *Romantic* (ed. Hans Eichner), University of Toronto Press, Toronto, 1971, to which I refer the reader. That contribution includes an extensive supplementary bibliography. A direct extension of the 1961 essay may be found in my "A Key to West European Romanticism?" *Colloquia Germanica* (1968), nos. 1–2, pp. 37–46, a slightly modified version of which ("Ein Schlüssel zur Westeuropäischen Romantik?") has appeared in volume 150 of *Wege der Forschung, Begriffsbestimmung der Romantik* (ed. Helmut Prang), Darmstadt, 1968, pp. 427–41.

ELEMENTS OF WEST

ELEMENT	GERMANY	FRANCE
Cohesiveness		
Chronology (approximate)	1790's–1830	[1800 Chateaubriand] 1813 (Staël) 1843 (*Burgraves*)
Self-consciousness as a movement or group	Yes	Yes
Coherent body of similar metaphysics, theory, criticism	Primary in beginning, secondary later	Criticism, definitions: yes; metaphysics: little
Pervasiveness of the Romantic movement	Strongest influence on German culture in last 150 years	Yes, but not as strong as in Germany (Berlioz, Delacroix, Michelet, Cousin)
Attitude Toward the Past		
Interest in nonclassical mythology (esp. Nordic)	Yes	Yes, but less than Germany
Interest in folklore, primitivism, cult of "childhood"	Very strong	In primitivism, but little in folklore
Medievalism	Very strong	Yes, but not widely stressed
Antineoclassicism	Yes (aspects of French classicism), no (German classicism)	Yes, though classicism remains strong in France

EUROPEAN ROMANTICISM

ENGLAND	ITALY	SPAIN	WESTERN EUROPE
Cohesiveness			
[1780's] 1798–1830	1816–1850's	1830–1845	Yes
Relatively little	Yes	Yes	Yes
Less than Germany and France, despite Coleridge, Shelley	No	Little	Ques.*
Much more limited (but Carlyle)	Romanticism restricted to literature and politics (but greater picturesqueness of language)		Ques.
Attitude Toward the Past			
Yes, but less than Germany	No	No	Yes
18th-century interest sustained and intensified	Little	Much interest in ballads and folklore	Yes
Yes	Yes	Yes	Yes
Little	No	No	No

ELEMENT	GERMANY	FRANCE
Against prescribed unities of time and place	Yes	Yes
Anti-18th century	Strong rational strain	Only to extent it was dominated by classicism
General Attitudes		
Imaginativeness	Yes	Yes
Cult of strong emotions, sensualism	Stressed emotions but very intellectual at first; sensual current	Fairly restrained
Restlessness, boundlessness	Strong	Less strong, but Staël, Musset
Individualism, subjectivism, introversion, cult of originality	Yes, but loneliness and politics led to collectivism	Yes
Interest in nature beyond "belle nature"	Great surge	Increased understanding
Greater positive emphasis on Religion	Yes, Catholic trends	Yes, within limits
"Mysticism" †	Interest in all phases	A marked fashion, but did not last
Weltschmerz, Mal du siècle, etc.	Yes, but not primary	Yes, but notable exceptions (Hugo)

ENGLAND	ITALY	SPAIN	WESTERN EUROPE
Yes	Yes, except at beginning	Yes	Yes ‡
Derived much from 18th century	No	Yes, for political reasons	No
General Attitudes			
Yes	Yes, relatively	Yes, relatively	Yes
Wordsworth vs. Byron, Shelley	Emotionalism accentuated but rarely overflowing, forms set, themes not very passionate or sensual, desire for clarity		Yes (?)
Less strong, but Shelley, Byron	Less strong	Less strong, but Espronceda, Larra, others	Yes
More restrained than in Germany, but Byron	More restrained	Relatively little	Yes (?)
Increased understanding	Little	Little	Yes
Restrained, no Catholic trends	Traditional place of religion not affected either way		Yes (?)
Limited interest	Not much interest	Little	Yes (?)
Yes, but not primary	Yes, but not primary	Relatively little	Yes

ELEMENT	GERMANY	FRANCE
Liberalism	Sporadic, generally weak	Constantly increasing after conservative start
Cosmopolitanism	Yes, but seeking *Volksseele* abroad	Yes, but seeking *couleur locale* abroad
Nationalism	Strong	Restrained
Works		
Supremacy of lyrical moods and forms	Yes	Yes
Reawakening of national epic	Yes, within limits	No
Historical drama and novel	Yes	Yes
Greater flexibility of form	Yes	Yes, but less than Germany
"Vagueness"	Pronounced, but seldom extreme	Not strong because of persistent classical influence
Symbolism	Yes, especially in early R.	Yes
Rhetoric §	Yes, but moderate	Yes
"Romantic Irony" ‖	Yes	Relatively little (Musset)

ENGLAND	ITALY	SPAIN	WESTERN EUROPE
Contradictory picture #	Yes, but with strong patriotic connotations		Ques.
Yes, but well in hand; characteristic of later Romantics	Moderate	Little	Yes
Self-assured but restrained, regionalism; characteristic of earlier Romantics	Very strong	Very strong	Yes (?)
Works			
Yes	Ques.	Ques.	Yes
Yes	Yes	Yes, within limits	Yes
Yes	Yes	Yes, mostly drama	Yes
Yes, but controlled **	Little	No	Yes
Generally, no	No	No	No
Yes	No	No	Yes
Yes	Yes	Yes	Yes
Little (except Byron)	Little (Leopardi ?)	Very little	No

ELEMENT	GERMANY	FRANCE
Exoticism	Yes, but not central	Yes
Realism (incl. regionalism, local color), more precise differentiation	Yes, increasingly	Yes

Note: A "yes" entry indicates that the element was present. A "yes (?)" entry indicates that the element was present but not overwhelmingly so. "No" indicates that the element was not present, and "Ques." (questionable) that its presence has not been conclusively settled. The number of "no" entries could, of course, have been increased at will if we had included in our chart a greater number of supposedly Romantic features known or strongly suspected to be restricted to one country or at most two, or highly controversial "romantic" traits. We can only plead that we acted in good faith in considering only those concepts which have been regarded as unifying factors of European Romanticism. It is the quantity and intensity of affirmative rather than negative items which is significant.

* Professor Orsini has called my attention to the possibility that the "verdict" in this column might be interpreted as doing less than justice to the tremendous interest and advance in literary criticism shown in German, French, English, and Italian Romanticism. This is not my intention; rather my present qualification is, perhaps wrongly, directed at the assumption, from a European vantage point, of a *coherent body of reasonably similar* criticism.

† Includes interest in the un-, semi-, or subconscious, dreams, divinations, hallucinations, phantasmagory, hypnosis, the occult, cult of death, the "marvelous," etc.

‡ It might be held that there is a contradiction between the "yes" in this column and the "no" in the preceding one. Not necessarily. There is more to neoclassicism than the unity of time and place, and opposition to the *prescribed* use of these unities does not preclude Romantic writers from adhering to them in practice, *grosso modo*, more often than one might suspect. Hellenism is widespread among the Romantics, though it is not identical with the neoclassical kind.

§ By "rhetoric" I mean the conscious stylized manipulation of language to achieve unordinary, oratorical effects.

ENGLAND	ITALY	SPAIN	WESTERN EUROPE
Yes, but far from universal	No	Yes (Mahometan influence)	Yes
Yes	Yes	Yes	Yes

|| For a concise description see Blankenagel in "Romanticism: A Symposium," p. 7; for a full and long overdue treatment see Morton L. Gurewitch's subtle "European Romantic Irony," Ph.D. diss., Columbia University, 1957.

Early liberalism gives way to conservatism—Wordsworth, Coleridge, Southey—but on the other hand we have Byron, Shelley, and Hazlitt.

** It must be remembered that the classic tradition was weaker in England and Spain than in France and Italy; hence in the first two countries there was no violent reaction against classic rigidity of form. In Germany, the first Romantic wave followed immediately (or accompanied) the climax of neoclassicism.

	ROMANTIC	
INFLUENCE of → *on* ↓	GERMANY (*also as locale*)	FRANCE
ENGLAND	*By* Böhme, Goethe, Herder, Schiller, Kant, Fichte, A. W. Schlegel, J. Paul, Schelling. *On* Blake, Wordsworth, Coleridge, Crabb Robinson, Carlyle, De Quincey. Bürger, Goethe, A. W. Schlegel→ Scott. Goethe→ Byron, Shelley. Tieck, Novalis→ Carlyle	Limited influence of Rousseau
ITALY	Not much. *By* Goethe (→ Manzoni), A. W. Schlegel. Bürger→ Berchet, Schiller→ Manzoni. (Staël)	Rousseau, Chateaubriand (→Leopardi) and Staël had certain impact
SPAIN	*By* Herder, A. W. Schlegel, Grimm bros.→ Böhl de Faber. Goethe (*Faust*)→ Espronceda (*El diablo mundo*)? Schiller discussed in *El Europeo*	Limited by Rousseau (political and social ideas), Chateaubriand, Staël, Béranger, Delavigne, Hugo, Lamartine, Dumas père. Spaniards in Fr. incl. Larra, Rivas, Espronceda, Martínez de la Rosa

INFLUENCES		
ENGLAND (*also as locale*)	ITALY (*chiefly as locale*)	SPAIN (*chiefly as locale*)
	On Byron, Shelley (S. Rogers, Hazlitt, Hunt). Dante→ Byron, Shelley, Hunt. Eng. travelers in It. include Coleridge, Keats, Beckford, Landor, R. & E. Browning	*On* Southey, Byron, Beckford. Calderón→ Shelley. Intermediaries: Blanco-White, translations by Lockhart
Limited *by* Shakespeare, Milton & Eng. pre-R (Richardson, Young, Sterne, Gray, "Ossian") & by Scott, Byron, Shelley. *On* It. pre-R (Baretti, Foscolo). Scott→ Manzoni		*On* Berchet, Monti
Limited *by* Shakespeare, Young, "Ossian," Scott, Byron	*On* Martínez de la Rosa. Theses of *Il Conciliatore* briefly known (*El Europeo*). Monteggia in Spain	

INFLUENCE of → *on* ↓	GERMANY (*also as locale*)	(*chiefly as locale*) FRANCE
GERMANY		Pervasive *by* Rousseau, restricted by Diderot. *On* German pre-R (*Sturm und Drang*)
FRANCE	*By* Goethe (*Werther*→ *René, Faust, W. Meister*, lyrics), Klopstock (→ Vigny), Bürger, Schiller's dramas, A. W. Schlegel, Novalis (→ Sénancour), J. Paul (→ Musset, Vigny, Hugo), E. T. A. Hoffmann, national character (idyllic, medieval, etc.). *On* Staël, Constant, Stendhal, esp. 2nd Fr. R wave: Hugo, Quinet (←Herder, Nodier, Nerval, Cousin, Ampère, Michelet, etc.	

ENGLAND (*also as locale*)	ITALY (*chiefly as locale*)	SPAIN (*chiefly as locale*)
By Milton and very strong *by* Shakespeare and 18th-c. pre-R (Richardson, Young, "Ossian," Percy, etc.). *On* German pre-R & R. Richardson, Sterne, Fielding, Smollett→ J. Paul. Scott→ Hauff. Byron	*On* Goethe (←Manzoni), Heinse, Tieck, F. Schlegel, Chamisso (←Corsica), Eichendorff, Werner, Waiblinger, Heine. Dante→ A. W. Schlegel	*By* Cervantes, Calderón, ballads, esp. *On* (Herder), Tieck, A. W. Schlegel, Schelling, Eichendorff, Heine. (Lope→ Grillparzer.) Locale → F. Schlegel
By Milton, Shakespeare, "Ossian," Young, Gray, Byron (→ Lamartine, Musset), Scott. *On* Chateaubriand, Stendhal, Hugo, Vigny, etc. Wordsworth→ Sainte-Beuve. Th. Moore in Paris	*On* Staël, Stendhal, Musset, Deschamps, Barbier, Quinet, Hugo, Mérimée, Delavigne. *By* Sismondi. Dante (little). Some by Vico (→ Quinet, Michelet) and Manzoni. Leopardi→ Musset, Vigny. Fr. travelers in It. incl. Chateaubriand, Lamartine, G. Sand	*By* Sp. drama. *On* Sismondi, V. Hugo, A. Hugo (←ballads), Mérimée, Musset, Gautier, Dumas père. G. Sand in Mallorca. Maury's & Ochoa's anthologies of Sp. lit. published in Fr.

SELECTED CRITICAL BIBLIOGRAPHY

1 *Introductory Articles*

BORGESE, G. A. "Romanticism," in *Encyclopedia of the Social Sciences*, 13 (1942), 426–34. Remarkable, packed international survey of the historical roots and (especially ideological) aspects of the Romantic movement. Bibliography.

MARCH, HAROLD M. "Romanticism," in Joseph T. Shipley (ed.), *Dictionary of World Literature*. New York, 1959, pp. 492–95. Informative, sensible introduction to the word, the movement and its implications from a comparative point of view, with good selective bibliography.

SAMUEL, R. H. "Romanticism," in S. H. Steinberg (ed.), Cassell's *Encyclopedia of World Literature*. New York, 1954, pp. 478–80. Brief sketch of European Romanticism followed by a number of bibliographical references (General, National, Theory).

2 *General Surveys*

VAN TIEGHEM, PAUL. *Le Mouvement romantique*. Paris, 1923. Collection of basic comments on Romanticism by its outstanding representatives in England, Germany, Italy, and France, carefully excerpted, translated, introduced, annotated, and connected. Summary bibliographies. Thoroughgoing revision of first edition (1912).

FARINELLI, ARTURO. *Il Romanticismo nel mondo latino*. 3 vols. Turin, 1927. Traces chief features of Romanticism (individualism, primitivism, medievalism, etc., etc.), to which author devotes separate chapters, through Italy, Spain, and France (primarily), and Catalonia, Portugal, Romania, and Latin America (secondarily). Incidental consideration also given to Germany and England. Forceful, alternately lyrical and dramatic, highly personal but richly informative treatment hostile to theoretical attempts of compressing Romanticism into formulas. Volume 3 entirely devoted to bibliographical notes, organized by countries, and to an extremely detailed table of contents amounting to a summary of each chapter (almost sixty pages). No index.

STRICH, FRITZ. "Europa und die deutsche Klassik and Romantik," in *Deutsche Klassik und Romantik*. Bern, 1949, pp. 339–63. Sweeping survey of the European antecedents and effects of German Romanticism. Strich's dialectic generalizations on the basis of national characteristics are in need of much pruning. This essay was first published in 1928.

"Romanticism: A Symposium," *PMLA*, 55 (March 1940), 1–60. Objective but interesting surveys of Romanticism in England (Fairchild, Nitchie), France (Havens), Germany (Blankenagel), Italy (McKenzie), and Spain (Tarr), with ample documentation and selected, annotated bibliographies. Represents excellent introduction to Romanticism as a European phenomenon for the nonspecialized student of comparative literature.

BARZUN, JACQUES. *Romanticism and the Modern Ego*. Boston, 1943. Revised, expanded version entitled *Classic, Romantic and Modern* available in Anchor paperback edition, 1961. Self-assured, animated, highly readable lectures, amazing in their breadth but already somewhat dated, in defense and explanation of Romanticism (and romanticism) as pan-European phenomena. Note particularly "Romanticism—Dead or Alive" (pp. 3–26), "The Classic Objection" (pp. 52–80), "Romantic Art" ("romanticism is realism," pp. 81–108), "The Four Phases of Romanticism" (i.e., Romanticism, Realism, Symbolism, and Naturalism, pp. 134–60), and "'Romantic'—a Sampling of Modern Usage" (pp. 213–30). Notes, references, and index.

VAN TIEGHEM, PAUL. *Le Romantisme dans la littérature européenne*. Paris, 1948. Best factual survey of European Romanticism, including Pre-romanticism and the transition to Realism. Describes and compares various national Romanticisms as units, then traces certain ideas, sentiments and forms through the major as well as less well-known (Dutch, Scandinavian, Slavic, Hungarian, Portuguese, Brazilian, etc.) literatures. Written without exceptional finesse, but with integrity.

Clearly organized and readable. Suggestive of many topics for papers and theses. International bibliography (books and periodical articles) and index of names.

BERNBAUM, ERNEST. "The Romantic Movement," in *The English Romantic Poets: A Review of Research*. New York, 1950, pp. 1–37. Despite the apparent limitation to England, Bernbaum's pithy and cutting survey of critical literature on Romanticism is relevant to the entire European movement. No index. Reprinted unchanged in second edition, 1956.

ABRAMS, M. H. *The Mirror and the Lamp: Romantic Theory and the Critical Tradition*. New York, 1953. Also available in W. W. Norton paperback edition, 1958. While primarily concerned with the English theory of poetry during the first four decades of the nineteenth century, considers also relations of English critical theory to foreign, especially German thought. Its thesis (that Romanticism brought about a basic shift of stress from the audience to the poet himself, from the mirror to the lamp) is relevant to European Romanticism as a whole. Copious notes, detailed index.

FRIEDERICH, WERNER P., and MALONE, DAVID H. "Pre-Romanticism" and "Romanticism," in *Outline of Comparative Literature*. Chapel Hill, 1954, pp. 199–331. General observations, followed by a wealth of references to supranational influences in European and American literature. Suggestive of many topics for papers and theses. Index, but no bibliography.

WELLEK, RENÉ. *A History of Modern Criticism: 1750–1950*. New Haven, 1955. *Volume 2, The Romantic Age*. Sees the rejection of neoclassicism and the establishment of a dialectical and symbolistic view of poetry as the unifying factors in Romantic criticism. Thorough treatment of German, English, French, and Italian criticism, and of relevant aspects of German philosophy. Complete scholarly apparatus (bibliographies, notes, chronological tables, index of names, topics, and terms). Written in a clipped, incisive, and admirably lucid style. Promises to be standard work on criticism in the Romantic age for decades to come.

MARCAZZAN, MARIO. "Romanticismo italiano e romanticismo europeo," *Humanitas* (Brescia) 11 (1956), 33–50. Upholds the basic cultural unity exemplified by European Romanticism which admits, of course, of many ethnic, political, historic, etc., variations in countries (such as Italy) and groups of countries.

OPPEL, HORST. "Englische und deutsche Romantik," *Die Neueren Sprachen*, no. 10 (1956), 457–75. Without minimizing national differences (as those between English and German Romanticism), Oppel defends the usefulness of the concept of a European Romanticism provided it is interpreted historically and sociologically.

PICON, GAËTAN. "Le Romantisme," in *Encyclopédie de la Pléiade, Histoire des Littératures, II, Littératures Occidentales*, Paris, 1956, pp. 140–61. Superb introduction to the main features of European Romanticism. Brief bibliography.

FOGLE, RICHARD H. "The Romantic Movement," in *Contemporary Literary Scholarship*. Ed. L. Leary. New York, 1958, pp. 109–38. Although concerned with trends of contemporary scholarship on English Romanticism only in the last thirty years, this rich and sprightly "bibliographie raisonnée" provides a valuable frame of reference for students of European Romanticism, particularly on pp. 109–18.

MASON, EUDO C. *Deutsche und englische Romantik*. Göttingen, 1959. Lively, readable, and critical confrontation of English and German Romanticism.

3 Definitions

CROCE, BENEDETTO. "Le Definizioni del romanticismo," *La Critica*, 4 (1906), 241–45. (Reprinted in *Problemi di Estetica* [Bari, 1910], pp. 287–94). Croce distinguishes between three types of romanticism: moral, artistic, and philosophical. Political romanticism, being a consequence of philosophical romanticism, is rejected as a fourth category. Writers and works should be studied as to which of these types—singly, in combination with each other, or with nonromantic elements—they exhibit.

BABBITT, IRVING. "The Terms Classic and Romantic," in *Rousseau and Romanticism*. Boston, 1919, pp. 1–31. Also available in a Meridian paperback edition, 1957. Biased but not unreasonable confrontation of these terms, without distinguishing between Romanticism as a period and an ever-recurrent romantic attitude, temper, or mood, by a scholar frankly concerned about state of the world and, in particular, about the naturalistic fallacy. Favors a classicism based on experience vivified by imagination, as against a romantic indiscriminate apotheosis of imagination. See also the introduction and the last chapter, "The Present Outlook." Extensive bibliography and index.

GRIERSON, HERBERT J. C. "Classical and Romantic: A Point of View," in *The Background of English Literature and Other Collected Essays and Addresses.* London, 1925, pp. 256–90. Example for an urbane discussion of the classical and romantic systoles and diastoles in ancient, medieval, and modern literature. First published in 1923.

LOVEJOY, ARTHUR O. "On the Discrimination of Romanticisms," in *Essays in the History of Ideas.* Baltimore, 1948, pp. 228–53. Spirited plea for the abandonment of the categories used in classifying "movements" and substitution of simpler, more distinguishable, diversely combinable components. First published in *PMLA,* 39 (1924), 229–53. The reprint contains a few additional characterizations of Romanticism proposed subsequent to 1923.

ROBERTSON, JOHN G. *The Reconciliation of Classic and Romantic.* Cambridge, England, 1925. Dissatisfied with the obscurities and contradictions in current definitions of Romanticism, Robertson finds that initial contrasts between the Classical and the Romantic diminish progressively until the advent of their common adversary, Realism, reveals that their differences were far less important than had been thought previously.

AYNARD, JOSEPH. "Comment définir le Romantisme?" *Revue de littérature comparée,* 5 (1925), 614–58. Sees in European Romanticism a revolution marked by sensibility, anxiety, and nostalgia, but without a common program or common principles. Interesting pages on the far-reaching differences between Romantic literature and (first-class) art in France, the latter being more realistic and sincere.

KAUFMAN, PAUL. "Defining Romanticism: A Survey and a Program," *Modern Language Notes,* 40 (1925), 193–204. Urges cooperative effort in compiling definitions, assembling a critical bibliography, analyzing the existing chaos of definitions with particular attention to the relationship between "romance" and "romanticism," to the distinctions between romanticism as form, content, or temper, and as an aesthetic, psychological, philosophical, political, or merely human phenomenon. Also advocates finer discrimination of diverse elements in writers labeled "romantic."

PRAZ, MARIO. "*Romantic*; An Approximate Term," in *The Romantic Agony*. New York, 1951, pp. 1–16 (notes: 17–21). Also available in a Meridian paperback edition, 1956. Defense of "romantic" as an approximate but necessary definition of a peculiar kind of sensibility in a fixed historical period, from which it should not be detached. Sensible argument, impaired by restlessness and lack of firmness in its organization. First published in 1933. Translated from the Italian.

LUCAS, FRANK L. *The Decline and Fall of the Romantic Ideal*. New York, 1936. Spirited, intensely personal essays on the nature, past, and future of romanticism with many illustrations from European literatures. Second edition (1948) unchanged except for omission of an essay on Iceland. 3rd ed. 1963.

LOVEJOY, ARTHUR O. "Romanticism and the Principle of Plenitude," in *The Great Chain of Being*. Cambridge, Massachusetts, 1936, pp. 228–314. Shift from uniformitarianism to diversitarianism, prepared (especially in theory) during the Enlightenment, as the most distinctive single feature of the Romantic revolution, See especially pp. 292–99.

LOVEJOY, ARTHUR O. "The Meaning of Romanticism for the Historian of Ideas," *Journal of the History of Ideas*, 2 (June 1941), 257–78. While asserting that the proffered interpretations of Romanticism have been so incongruous and opposed as to make it useless as a verbal symbol, Lovejoy admits the existence of a "Romantic period" and singles out three important "Romantic" ideas which were destined to gain far-reaching political significance: holism or organicism (*Das Ganze*), voluntarism or dynamism (*Streben*), and diversitarianism (*Eigentümlichkeit*).

WELLEK, RENÉ, and WARREN, AUSTIN. "Literary History," in *Theory of Literature*. New York, 1948, pp. 262–82 in particular 274–82, 343–45 (notes, in particular 345) and 380–83 (bibliography, in particular 381–82). A moderately revised second edition appeared in 1956; also available in Harvest paperback edition, 1956. "Romanticism" used as one of the illustrations of the crucial periodization problem faced by literary history. Succinct bibliographies on other period terms: Renaissance, Classicism, Baroque, Realism, and Symbolism.

WELLEK, RENÉ. "The Concept of 'Romanticism' in Literary History," *Comparative Literature*, 1 (1949), 1–23, 147–72. Impressive defense of the essential unity of the Romantic movement in Europe, based on numerous, specific examples taken primarily from English, French, and German, incidentally from Italian, Spanish, Scandinavian, and Slavic literatures and criticism. Valuable references. Some questionable evaluation of detail does not affect general soundness of thesis. Reprinted in Wellek, *Concepts of Criticism* (1963).

PECKHAM, MORSE. "Toward a Theory of Romanticism," *PMLA*, 66 (March 1951), 5–23. By adding his concepts of negative and positive Romanticism to the notion of dynamic organicism derived from Lovejoy, Peckham hopes to have found the keys to a valid theory of Romanticism. While his argument is limited to English literature, it is potentially applicable to other European literatures. Written with an unabashed, refreshing gusto. Bibliographical equipment is uneven.

LEVAILLANT, MAURICE. "Problèmes ou Problème du Romantisme?" *Revue des sciences humaines*, 62–63 (Apr.–Sept. 1951), 89–92. Witty account of the attempts to streamline French Romanticism so as to squeeze it into neat jackets of periodization. Proposes to substitute the notion "current" for those of "movement" and "school."

BARRÈRE, JEAN-BERTRAND. "Sur quelques définitions du Romantisme," *Revue des sciences humaines*, 62–63 (Apr.–Sept. 1951), 93–110. Although chiefly concerned with French Romanticism, this article presents a vivid picture of the innumerable combinations, reservations, exclusions, and additions involved in the maddening process of arriving at a definition of Romanticism. Attributes many difficulties to confusion arising from viewing Romanticism as a historical phenomenon ("fait de guerre") and/or an artistic-aesthetic term ("fait d'âme").

PECKHAM, MORSE. "Toward a Theory of Romanticism: II. A Reconsideration," *Studies in Romanticism*, 1 (1961), 1–8. Amends his earlier theory by acknowledging that organicism and the values derived from it are products of the Enlightenment, but these values are constitutive to late Enlightenment, instrumental to Romanticism.

4 *Bibliographies*

BALDENSPERGER, FERNAND, and FRIEDERICH, WERNER P. *Bibliography of Comparative Literature*. Chapel Hill, 1950. "Romanticism," pp. 353–56. Supplementary bibliographies in issues of *YCGL*, 2 (1953) ff. See also annual bibliographies in *PMLA*.

DERBY, J. RAYMOND, and NURMI, MARTIN K. "The Romantic Movement: A Selective and Critical Bibliography." This immensely valuable bibliography which appeared in *English Literary History* beginning in 1937 (for 1936), was published annually in the April issue of Philological Quarterly from 1950 (for 1949) until 1964 (for 1963). Covers "movement" rather than period. The English section is limited to 1800–1837, but the other sections are not. While, unfortunately, it does not have a comparative section, its subdivisions by languages—English, French, German, Danish (1953–58), Spanish, Portuguese, Italian (since 1954)—list comparative studies along with many others. Inclusion of Slavic and Scandinavian sections would be highly desirable. Some entries are followed by (sometimes extensive) descriptive and/or critical remarks. Lists many reviews. From 1965 (for 1964) on, in *English Language Notes*.

5 *Periodicals*

Studies in Romanticism, 1961–. Quarterly. Specialized and interdisciplinary articles on all aspects of Romanticism: literature, history of art and music, education, religion, science, politics, etc.

12

LITERATURES OF ASIA

ARTHUR E. KUNST

ASIA CONTAINS three great literary traditions, each as rich before modern times as the Western tradition. One of the three, the Middle Eastern tradition, is closely bound by history, geography, and religion to the European, beginning with the epic of Gilgamesh and continuing until Rostam of the *Shāhnāmeh* becomes Pushkin's Ruslan. The co-inheritor of Graeco-Semitic culture, the Middle Eastern tradition lies outside the view of this study.

Asia's two other cultural traditions are of similar complexity and antiquity. One, the South Asian, centers on the creative homeland of India and extends itself across the Bay of Bengal to Burma, Thailand, Laos, Cambodia, Malaysia, and Indonesia, southward to Ceylon and northward to Nepal, Tibet, and Central Asia. The second is cradled in the valleys of Northern China and has spread to Japan, Korea, Mongolia, Turkestan, and Vietnam. The continuity and range of international influences are such that no comparatist can hope to grasp all the essential relationships *within* South Asian or East Asian tradition before modern times or *between* them and Western tradition since the nineteenth century. This essay will try only to give a broad survey of the perplexing problems and fortunate advantages that offer themselves to the comparatist who takes an interest in South Asian or East Asian literatures.

Some of the questions which arise are familiar to the student of comparative literature: those of influence, reception, intermediaries, translation, and historical affinity. Other questions present themselves as bonuses of the necessity for comparing independent literary traditions, questions about the universal validity of our European-Oriental notions of the form, purpose, and evolutionary development of literature itself.

The classical positions of Chinese and of Sanskrit in East Asian and South Asian traditions (respectively) give a unity and tightness to the story of international exchange in Asia. Even Latin and Greek cannot occupy the dominant, regal place that Chinese occupied in its Far Eastern sphere of influence. Influence means the influence of writers of Chinese upon writers of Japanese or Vietnamese, never the reverse. Indeed relations between the other literatures, even between Korean and Japanese, can scarcely be said to figure in history. Chinese, like Latin in Renaissance Europe, is the medium for the communication of educated men. If Chinese is central to an understanding of every other East Asian literature, it is partly because by Chinese literature we mean 2500 years of evolution. Chinese literary history is continuous because of the extraordinary unity of the classical language during those 2500 years. The emergence of the national literatures around China is marked by their effort to get out from under Chinese as the mode of written expression and their adaptation of the classical Chinese writing system to the divergent needs of the national tongue. Certainly the independent existence of Korean and Vietnamese literatures is due to their intransigeance in the face of the evident glories of Chinese, a resistance which fortifies itself by giving written form to the native folk art. A Korean or a Vietnamese, as a gentleman, will write in Chinese; as a man he may find an outlet for his feelings only in the language of his people. Again and again Chinese modes of seeing the world creep into Korean verse, and again and the closeness to popular song and popular life revives the Koreanness of the form: *changga, sijŏ*, formally and inevitably national. The history of Japan's relation to China is different: Japanese culture since the sixth century has been characterized by an eagerness to learn what is new, fashionable, and useful. Equally, Japan, across the sea, resisted all attempts at conquest. Japan deliberately seeks out and absorbs Chinese influences, and the Japanese gentleman can be equally dignified in Chinese and in Japanese.

On the general similarity of Korean and Vietnamese romances (*Cloud Dream of the Nine, Kim Van Kien*) to Chinese romances there is no doubt; the only question remains to specify which Chinese romances. On the indebtedness of the Japanese short *tanka* poems, however, the research problem is more indefinite. To what extent can we attribute a taste for landscape, for self-revelation, for brevity, and for wit to the reading of Tang Dynasty *jue-ju* (*chüeh-chü*) and *lüshi* (*lü-shih*) lyrics? Do not the oldest recorded Japanese lyrics also show a psychological point of view and a tendency to break down into the smallest units? If so, then the comparatist must pose his question not in terms of these general affinities but in terms of details—of allusions, of discrete images, of techniques of construction.

If we cast our eyes over the history of Japanese literature, we are not infrequently struck by the insufficiency of the Chinese example to account for the vitality of its presumed Japanese development. Where in Chinese Buddhism is the ancestor of the sophisticated Nō play? Where in Chinese biography and anecdote did Lady Murasaki find the models for the intensely human profundity of the *Tale of Genji*? How was it that Akinari found inspiration for his sardonic and moving *Ugetsu* tales in some mildly edifying Chinese fables?

If anything, the reception of Chinese literature in Korea and Vietnam was better than in China itself. In Japan, the reception seems to have been in spurts of enthusiasm separated by long periods of assimilation and sublimation. Although the Chinese did occasionally prize a Korean celadon or a Japanese sword, the arrogance of the Chinese toward the "barbarian" literatures was unceasing, protected as it was by necessary ignorance. Here once more, the direction is one way: China gives, others receive. Nevertheless, some of the best scholarship on Chinese literature was done outside China; more than that, we owe to the careful Japanese instinct for preservation of the past several of our most precious Chinese literary texts, especially in the genre of the novel. For the Chinese novel was of dubious propriety in China, not to be considered "literature" at all, while the undeniable authenticity of genius in Japanese fiction perhaps allowed Japanese connoisseurs to savor the delights of Chinese fiction with less embarrassment.

One might not be too far wrong if he considered the Indian subcontinent as parallel to the European subcontinent in its linguistic development and diversity. The great modern languages of the North, Hindi-Urdu, Bengali, Marathi, Gujurati, Oriya, trace their literary development back to the Middle Ages, when a combination of foreign invasions and religious revival called attention to their expressive potential. Before that, Sanskrit, the language of Hindu scriptural truth, the language of the courts, the language of education, had constituted the fundamental mode of literary expression. Except in the South. Whereas in Europe the Germanic languages had a literate flourishing despite the presence of Latinate culture in the church, so in India the Dravidian languages, Kannada, Telugu, and especially Tamil, developed styles and conventions of their own, despite the impinging prestige of Sanskrit religious culture from the North.

Sanskrit was a "classical" language, dead to change and fixed in its perfect grammar by the school of Pānini, before the earliest surviving literary movements took their final shape. It was, however, presumably a living language for the first reciters of the Vedas, and perhaps was also for the earliest recitations of the Indian epics. But the Sanskrit epics of the *Mahābhārata* and the *Rāmāyana* as we have them are vast conglomerations of literate and preliterate story, primitive and learned opinion, moral instruction, and exuberant adventure. No one seems sure just when or how they were composed (the miserable undatability of events in Indian tradition is notorious). We are certain, though, that these vast anthologies of tales within tales (the *Mahābhārata* is ten times as long as the *Iliad* and *Odyssey* put together) contain within their limits the majority of the fictional material for all South Asia. At what must have been a later stage, Sanskrit literature turned to new forms of the epic, to a new theatre, but these and what came subsequently were content to retell the old stories. Nothing could be simpler for the comparatist than to identify Kamban's source in the *Rāmāyana* or the predecessor of Kālidāsa's *Śakuntalā* in the *Mahābhārata*—but the illuminating exercise is not to rest with that trivial acknowledgment but to discover the meaning of the differences. Why are the characters of the Kannada Rama story so much more humanized? Why does the medieval Javanese poet transfer the great battle of the Bharatas into his own native milieu, and with what effect?

Aside from the obvious provenience of stories and situations, there remains the muddled issue of the origination of novel techniques and styles. So cloudy are the transitions from one era to another of Indian literature, so sporadic the survival of texts and the proper attribution of others, this more interesting side of South Asian literary history may always remain the playground for learned speculation, as it is today. In some ways, one is better advised to ignore chronological precedence in favor of selecting certain figures, like Kālidāsa or Amaru or Dandin, from whom other works may be gauged as deviations. It is doubtful whether the origin of the masked drama or the puppet stage will ever be found; that sad fact ought not to prevent us from showing the varied affinities of dance-drama in parts of South Asia.

There are some notable relations *among* the various literatures of South Asia, the source of the Thai Einao stories from the Malay-Indonesian Panji cycle, for example, or the operation of bilingual poets and translators in South India. The fact that Buddhism of South Asia is associated with Pali, not Sanskrit, is one reason for this greater interchange. The late arrival of certain peoples on the South Asian scene—the Burmese, the Thais and Laos—and the service of others—the Mons, the Khmers—as intermediaries is another reason. And just as Buddhism presents an alternative network of relationships not incompatible with the Sanskrit tradition, so in the later centuries Islamic evangelism adds an overlay of Middle Eastern cultural patterns in several countries.

Much story material and patterns of argument must have gone overland with Buddhism from South to East Asia. Distinctly literary, as separate from those philosophical-religious imports that expand the imagination, literary influences from India to China and beyond are elusive. First of all, there are few scholars capable of reading the wide variety of materials in the several languages which would presumably have been involved. Second, much of the intervening Central Asian portion of the evidence has been lost or still awaits excavation. Finally, a superficial acquaintance with the literatures of India and China shows that they have relatively little decisively in common; few literary prejudgments could be more absurd than the assumption of Europeans that an "Oriental" mode of literature exists.

Before modern times, South Asian and East Asian literature have no more relation to each other than they do to Middle Eastern or to European literature. The extraordinary thing about these Asian literatures in the twentieth century is that although they have very much in common in their modern phase, there has been almost no contact between them. The single outstanding fact of modern Asian literature is that European influence is all-pervasive. To put the question of Western influence on a modern Asian writer is like asking to know what is the European influence behind Anton Chekhov or Jorge Luis Borges or Sherwood Anderson. Such questions must be put biographically, and in countries with a long modern educational history like Japan or India, one must be ready to include the influence of willingly Westernized Japanese or Indians of an earlier generation.

Curiously, while the European influence on modern Asian literatures is strong and growing stronger, most studies of influence and reception have turned their gaze in the opposite direction. To be frank, there has hardly been *any* influence of Asian literature on European. What influence there is has been on insignificant authors, as in Lafcadio Hearn's use of Japanese literature, or has been insignificant in the career of a major author, such as the place of the Nō in the career of W. B. Yeats. Or we may have the post-facto justification of a preexisting impulse, as when Eisenstein analyzes the presence of montage, cutting, and separable tracks in Kabuki to corroborate his previous use of such techniques in his films. Asian literature has been often translated and well received in Europe and America in the last few decades, yet there is a paucity of definite literary results. We have been fortunate in the sons of missionaries and others who have brought Asian literatures to our attention. Yet the fact remains that the use of European literature by Asian writers (and readers) is of far greater importance. Why then is it not so often studied? Is it that greatness among Asians in the modern manner is not clearly distinguishable (the Nobel Prize to Kawabata should disprove that)? Or is it that it is more pleasing to Asians to write about the influences from Asia rather than upon Asia?

There is nothing especially comparative about travel records of Europeans in Asia (Loti, Claudel, Wenceslau de Morães) nor about the travel records of Asians outside Asia (Kafū) or elsewhere in Asia (Tagore). Nor are Voltaire's Chinese usefully different, for our purposes, from his inhabitants of Eldorado. We must shamefacedly admit that much of what passes for "East-West Literary Relations" is neither literary nor relevant.

But the very *lack* of significant interchange between traditional South Asia, East Asia, and the West is the most redeeming feature of the comparative study of the literatures of Asia. We thereby have two nearly independent evolutions of sophisticated, imaginative literature. Such a stroke of good fortune is not offered to Eurasian biologists! Whatever may be our theories of history, we now have the opportunity to put those theories not once but twice to an elegant test. And having corrected the parochialism of our European-oriented view, we have the inductive base necessary to formulate a more satisfactory theory of literature as well.

Wherever we turn in Western literary theory, we find conclusions extrapolated from a single line of evidence, the progression of works from Greek and Latin to modern

Europe and America. The continuing presence of Greek models (in education, in translation, inherent in subsequent works) has probably tended to confirm our prejudices, even when we are in revolt against them. Greek theory, too, tends to guide our expectations of what literature can and may do, with its Aristotelian emphasis on physical action, philosophical import, and formal unity.

If one looks at the stunning impact that Western ideas of the appropriate spheres of literature have had on Asian traditions, one wishes that there were some equally devastating way (short of colonialism) by which a deadly, objective scrutiny could be turned on our own tradition. We unshackled fiction and drama in the South Asian tradition from a bondage to verse: who would have thought so much could be done with prose? We forced the Chinese to celebrate their own masterpieces in the art of the theatre and of the novel. What then is the beam in our own eye?

Even the old, dignified genres of China have had to be rethought. Satisfied for millennia with a criticism compounded of learned glosses and polite impressionism, the Chinese critic today has the happy duty of being the first real "critic" (in the modern sense) of his nation's oldest works. How exciting to be in the generation of C. T. Hsia, James J. Y. Liu, and Joseph S. M. Lau! Likewise when Makoto Ueda looks at Japanese aesthetics with the taste of a new critic, when Brower and Miner know what is good about Japanese court poetry because they know what to do with a metaphysical poet from England, when Ingalls analyzes Sanskrit literary aesthetic in terms of European post-Renaissance philosophy and when Ramanujan and Krishnamurthi creatively translate because they are trained to sensitive analysis. Where then are the critics who, having read both in East and West, can suggest something as yet untried?

I would like to suggest a series of questions, some of which have already been raised (explicitly or obliquely) by others. First, what can we make of the presence of formulaic elements in the Sanskrit epics, the *Mahābhārata* and the *Rāmāyana*? What bearing does the Lord and Parry theory of oral transmission have on our assumption that they have accreted materials throughout their history? Has the practice of rote memorization destroyed the purely formulaic structure or is it possible to indicate which passages are from the period of memorization by the absence of true formulaic structure in them? As with *Beowulf*, we do have an excellent body of relevant evidence by which to test and expand our understanding of the nature of the oral epic.

Second, given our assumptions about the probable ancestry of prose fiction in the verse narrative and about the associations of epic technique with celebrations of the deaths and wanderings of heroes—why is it then that the earliest narratives of length in China, imaginatively reconstructing heroic and historical adventures, are not associated with poetic form but with prose? Are these works, *The Men of the Marshes* cycle or *The History of the Three Kingdoms*, novels? Prose epics? Or, more profoundly, do they reveal structural connections that nevertheless place them with other, early popular narrative? Is it just to put them in the same genre with the *Jin Ping Mei* (*Chin P'ing Mei*)?

Third, would it not be useful, when we are attempting to understand what ancient Greeks meant about their theatre, to look closely at a living performance tradition of theatre which combines action, spectacle, and song—such as the Nō? And after we have finished clearing away the debris of centuries of decadent Indian eclecticism, hadn't we better place the Aristotelian dictum that plotted action, scenes of suffering, pity and fear produce catharsis next to Bhārata's theory that drama is a sequence of evolving situations, unified by a dominant emotion, varied by subordinate ones and attractive by its capacity to enact the universally human? Especially if Bhārata's basic emotions (humor, awe, disgust, sorrow, terror, bravery, and eroticism) seem to include Aristotle's and yet account for plays unsampled by Aristotle?

Fourth, despite Croce, we still yearn to divide college courses and bookseller's lists by the old genres: what are we to make of the (presumed) neat line between drama and narrative, when (as in Nō) the actor may speak his lines or narrate his actions, may have his lines spoken for him by the chorus? Or of the *bunraku* puppet theatre, where the narrator in full view speaks both the lines and describes what we see.

Fifth, can we suppose that the novel had to evolve the way it did in Europe? Did Faulkner and Proust have to come after decades, centuries of the invention of techniques of expressing the complexities of mind, after (as Watt suggests in the *Rise of the Novel*) centuries of giving increasingly slowed pace to the narrative? Why then is the *Tale of Genji* at the start, not the finish of Japanese literary history? If technical reasons are to be put forward, what was it about the Japanese language that European languages had to wait nine centuries to attain? If sociological, what resemblance is there between the sickly Jewish homosexual and the willful Heian bluestocking? Are psychological novels a taste of a leisure class? A dying class?

As we have learned from studies of Saikaku and the revival of the novel after the Japanese Medieval age, there seems to be a connection between the growth of a self-assertive, prosperous town-life and the appearance of a kind of novel—picaresque, plotted on the getting and missing of steady incomes, competitively erotic. Is there really an affinity between Boccaccio and Saikaku? If so, does the resemblance exist beneath the natural resemblances of subject matter?

Sixth, and last in this rapid list of the kind of projects offering themselves to the comparatist, does not the overwhelming evidence about lyric poetry from East Asian and from South Asian literatures (and Middle Eastern, too) suggest that lyric poetry without music is unthinkable or at least perverse? Doesn't this fact of the universal past marriage of verse to song have something to do with the fact that the only widely-loved modern poetry is that of the Beatles and the other pop writers?

Asian works should be used as correctives upon our parochial assumptions. However, the ultimate object of a comparative study of Asian and European literatures should be the creation of a truly comprehensive theory of literature, based not on a knowledge of mutually reinforcing works from English, French, Spanish, German, and a few other languages, but on a knowledge of independently evolved imaginative traditions. This should be sufficient, at least, to give literary theory validity at the descriptive level. If we are so fortunate as to discover new techniques and new kinds of experience in Asian literature, then we might even hope, as comparatists, to help in generating kinds of literature unknown yet in either European or Asian literature.

BIBLIOGRAPHICAL NOTE

Scholars new to the comparative study of Asian literatures should be warned that coverage of materials in such presumably serious works as standard encyclopedias of literature, bibliographies of comparative literature, *PMLA* bibliographies, and theories of literature is quite unreliable up to 1965, and that even the annual bibliography of scholarship in the *Journal of Asian Studies* does not include publications by scholars who prefer to write in an Asian language. The scandalous vestige of the colonial period is not likely to cease in the near future. The first general compendium of literary knowledge to give a fair share of space to the literatures of Asia was the *Encyclopedia of Poetry and Poetics*, ed. Alex Preminger (Princeton, 1965). Coverage in other general works is unbalanced, superficial, or inexplicably biased. Theorists still issue general "rhetorics of fiction" or "ideas of the theatre" but readers will look in vain for references to Asian literature and literary theory, let alone Czech or Russian. Notable exceptions to this rule are found in the allied fields of folklore (cf. the series directed by Stith Thompson) and linguistics (cf. J. Lotz, "Metric Typology," in Sebeok, *Style in Language* [Bloomington, Ind., 1960]).

Studies of influence, reception, intermediaries, translation, and sources have been a part of Japanese and other Asian scholarly traditions from early times: they concentrated, of course, on the affinities of their native literature with some neighboring or classical literature. Their work is now incorporated in standard texts and commentaries. Studies of the concrete historical relations between Asian and European literatures, contrary to the above remarks on general scholarship, are both reliable and, insofar as they are composed in a non-Asian language, well indexed. A model historical survey is Earl Miner, *The Japanese Tradition in British and American Literature* (Princeton, 1958).

Recent works employing modern Western critical techniques for the elucidation of an Asian tradition are James J. Y. Liu, *The Art of Chinese Poetry* (Chicago, 1962); Robert R. H. Brower and Earl Miner, *Japanese Court Poetry* (Stanford, Calif., 1961); C. T. Hsia, *The*

Classic Chinese Novel: A Critical Introduction (New York, 1968); Makoto Ueda, *Zeami, Bashō, Yeats, Pound: A Study in Japanese and English Poetics* (The Hague, 1965); Daniel H. H. Ingalls, introductory remarks to Vidyākara, *An Anthology of Sanskrit Court Poetry* (Cambridge, Mass., 1965); and A. K. Ramanujan, *The Interior Landscape: Love Poems from a Classical Tamil Anthology* (Bloomington, Ind., 1967). Tentative motions toward extending the theory of oral epic could be found as early as Jan de Vries, *Heroic Song and Heroic Legend* (Utrecht, 1959; Oxford, 1963); recent investigations along this line include K. Kailaspathy, *Tamil Heroic Poetry* (Oxford, 1968) and a doctoral dissertation by C. H. Wang on the *Shi Jing* and formulaic theory (Berkeley, 1970). To my knowledge, no significant developments in literary theory have as yet come from the exchange of knowledge with Asian literary traditions, but already one finds elegant suggestions like those about diaries, fictions, and plots in Earl Miner's *Japanese Poetic Diaries* (Berkeley, 1969).

NOTES / INDEX

NOTES

1 Definition and Function

1. The approach deliberately chosen in this essay is descriptive and synchronic, not historical and genetic. A combination of both approaches would have gone beyond the intent and proportions of this volume, but remains an ultimate desideratum. Nor are this study or the bibliography concerned with the status of comparative-literature research and programs in particular universities and countries except to the extent that they bear directly on the basic question of definition.

2. Represented by such leading scholars as the late Fernand Baldensperger, Jean-Marie Carré, Paul Hazard, Paul Van Tieghem, Henri Roddier, as well as Marcel Bataillon, Charles Dédéyan, Basil Munteano, M.-F. Guyard, Jacques Voisine, Claude Pichois, Simon Jeune, and others. Although care has been taken to concentrate in this essay on problems not covered in my *Yearbook* 1960 contribution (see Bibliography), there is occasional slight overlapping with it in those portions which contrast American with European trends.

3. In weighing the possibility of coincidence against the possibility of influence, the comparatist could learn a great deal from the techniques of the folklorist who has long had to face this problem in his examination of motifs. Many folklore studies are comparative par excellence.

4. A few sentences in this paragraph have been taken from my review of Fritz Neubert, *Studien zur vergleichenden Literaturgeschichte*, in *Modern Language Forum*, 39 (1954), 154–55.

5. Even in theory, we find some signs of wavering. Late in his survey (see Bibliography), Guyard reports that recently there has been a movement toward a more aesthetic appreciation of literature (p. 121). He also concedes that influence studies

and vast syntheses, though perilous, are necessary (pp. 77, 108–9), and even sees a place for "coincidence" studies (p. 24). Van Tieghem, while excluding "coincidental" comparisons from Comparative Literature, somewhat arbitrarily welcomes them to "General Literature" (p. 174). Certain French scholars (Bémol, Etiemble, etc.) challenged the traditional goals of French comparatism in writing or as early as in the debates of the First French Congress of Comparative Literature (Bordeaux, 1956) and of the Second International Comparative Literature Congress (Chapel Hill, 1958). Moreover, such prominent French spokesmen at the latter meeting as Frappier, Roddier, Munteano, Escarpit, etc., while defending the basic soundness of the French comparative tradition, were already cognizant of its past and potential abuses and were suggesting new applications of their methods. Etiemble's *Comparaison n'est pas raison* as well as the manuals of Claude Pichois-A.-M. Rousseau and of Simon Jeune, while not breaking with the "French" tradition of comparative literature, have constructively incorporated in their guidelines ideas current in American theory and practice.

6. In America, too, theory and practice are not identical. It seems safe to say that the majority of American scholars, including those in comparative literature, do their actual research along more or less traditional historical lines regardless of their theoretical adherence or nonadherence to Criticism.

7. At the First French Congress of Comparative Literature held in Bordeaux in March of 1956, Basil Munteano assigned the relationship between literature and the other arts to "general literature" (*Littérature générale et Histoire des idées*, 1957, p. 25). Simon Jeune has followed suit (1968).

8. The Italian and English concepts of comparative literature follow French ideas quite closely. English comparative scholarship, which has little *Gestalt*, seems, however, somewhat less restrictive than French in its greater attention to the literature of the Middle Ages, although the original French position which excluded antiquity and the Middle Ages from comparative literature has undergone a revision in the last fifteen or twenty years (see Jean Frappier, "Littératures médiévales et littérature comparée: problèmes de recherche et de méthode," in the *Proceedings* of the Second Congress of the International Comparative Literature Association, Chapel Hill, 1959, 1:25–

35). Italian comparatists, no doubt due to the influence of Croce, do not hesitate to emphasize the aesthetic side of literature despite their general adherence to French models. The trend in Germany, as in the United States, was very decidedly in the direction of literary criticism, of intrinsic work analysis, until the mid-1960's. The interest in literary criticism and especially in twentieth-century literature as well as in the "contemporary" features of earlier literature continues, with a strong admixture of current social and political preoccupations. On the other hand, the orientation of the main body of comparative scholarship in both countries remains historical, and the scholarly organ of German comparatists, *Arcadia,* has a strong historical drift. Japan, long beholden to the French tradition, is veering in the American direction. For details on the situation of Comparative Literature in various countries, see the *Yearbook of Comparative and General Literature,* the *Forschungsprobleme der Vergleichenden Literaturgeschichte* 1 and 2, the *Revue de littérature comparée,* and the Congress *Proceedings.*

9. To the American comparatist, such a "lack of logical coherence" would be more apparent than real, for he would see a fundamental connection between the inclusion of "literature and the arts," "literature and music," etc., in Comparative Literature, and the "analogy *inside* literature" approach recognized by American practicioners: in both cases, comparison (whether "pure" or causally connected) brings out inherent or potential characteristics of literature.

10. The quarterly bibliographies of the *Revue de littérature comparée* contributed to the same confusion. What are such titles as *Erzählformen in den Werken Gerhart Hauptmanns* or *Zur erlebten Rede im englischen Roman des 20. Jahrhunderts* doing in a comparative bibliography (33 [January–March 1959], 148–49)?

11. The terms "international literature" and "universal literature" are more or less synonymous with world literature, but have not been able to establish themselves. The Dutch scholar J. C. Brandt Corstius gives, in his *De Muze in het Morgenlicht,* (Zeist, 1957), pp. 149–70, an excellent account, both descriptive and critical, of the evolution of the term "world literature" from the threshold of history via Herder and Goethe to the twentieth century. Lately, Marxist scholarship

in Eastern Europe has shown a certain partiality for "World Literature" as a preferred approximation to "Comparative Literature."

12. August Wilhelm von Schlegel's pioneering *Lectures on Dramatic Art and Literature* (1808) may serve as an illustration. They belong to comparative literature not because he covers the literatures of Greece and Rome in the first, and the literatures of Italy, France, England, Spain, and Germany in the second volume, although, were they restricted to independent discussions of these literatures, his essays would still provide a rich nutrient for comparative literature. They *are* comparative literature because, e.g., in his first lecture, he compares not only Greek with Latin drama but the classical with the romantic drama, and brings in the Spanish, Portuguese, and German drama; because he constantly refers back to the classical literatures when he treats, e.g., Italian and French literature; because he avails himself of every opportunity to draw general comparisons (between the dramatic literatures of England and Spain, of Spain and Portugal, of France and Germany, etc.); because he consistently keeps the general polarities of the drama in mind (tragic-comic, poetical-theatrical, "Ernst und Scherz," etc.); because, wherever possible, he directs attention to the fine arts. It is the combination of these factors which makes this work clearly comparative. But not every one of his chapters would (or need) qualify for the overall label "comparative": e.g., his eleventh lecture is completely limited to France, his thirteenth to England.

13. Julius Petersen makes the interesting point that *any* treatment of a foreign literature is, in a way, comparative, inasmuch as it utilizes, consciously or unconsciously, criteria derived from the writer's own national environment. (*Die Wissenschaft von der Dichtung*, Berlin, 1939, 1: 7). This is a valid observation, but it is clear that the comparative angle of a literary study must be explicit rather than implicit if we are going to have standards at all.

14. Sometimes Van Tieghem uses the alternate term "Synthetic Literature."

15. This definition was suggested by Professor Craig La Drière in addressing the Comparative Literature section of the Modern Language Association of America, New York, December 1950, and elaborated on by him in the *Proceedings* of the

Second Congress of the International Comparative Literature Association, 1:160–75.

16. Equally unacceptable, because artificial, is Werner P. Friederich's compromise suggestion that comparative-literature scholars might well restrict themselves to the "French system" in teaching but could indulge in the "American point of view" in their researches ("Zur Vergleichenden Literaturgeschichte in den Vereinigten Staaten" in *Forschungsprobleme der Vergleichenden Literaturgeschichte,* 2 [ed. Ernst and Wais]. Tübingen, 1958, p. 186.)

2 On Defining Terms

1. Among others Meyer H. Abrams, *A Glossary of Literary Terms* (New York, 1966), based on earlier edition by Daniel S. Norton and P. Rushton (New York, 1953); Sylvan Barnet, *A Dictionary of Literary Terms* (Boston, 1962); Raymond W. Barry, *Literary Terms: Definitions, Explanations, Examples* (San Francisco, 1966); Karl E. Beckson and Arthur Ganz, *A Reader's Guide to Literary Terms: A Dictionary* (New York, 1961); William R. Benét, *The Reader's Encyclopedia,* 2nd ed. (New York, 1965); *Cassell's Encyclopædia of Literature* (London, 1953); *Columbia Dictionary of Modern European Literature* (New York, 1947); Charles Duffy and Henry J. Pettit, *A Dictionary of Literary Terms,* rev. ed. (New York, 1952); Henry W. Fowler, *A Dictionary of Modern English Usage,* 2nd ed. (Oxford, 1965); Cardinal Georges Grente et al., *Dictionnaire des lettres françaises* (Paris, 1951–64); Heinz Kindermann and Margarete Dietrich, *Lexikon der Weltliteratur* (Wien, 1950); M. M. Liberman and Edward E. Foster, *A Modern Lexicon of Literary Terms* (Glenview, Ill., 1968); Laurie Magnus, *A Dictionary of European Literature* (New York, 1927); Paul Merker and Wolfgang Stammler, *Reallexikon der deutschen Literaturgeschichte* (Berlin, 1925–31); *The Oxford Companion to English Literature,* 4th ed. (Oxford, 1967); Mario Pei and Frank Gaynor, *Liberal Arts Dictionary in English, French, German, Spanish* (New York, 1952); Federico Carlos Sainz de Robles, *Ensayo de un diccionario de la literatura,* 3rd ed. (Madrid, 1964–65); Arthur F. Scott, *Current Literary Terms: A Concise Dictionary of their Origin and Use* (London and New York, 1965); Joseph T. Shipley, *Dictionary of World Literary Terms* (London, 1955), and *Dictionary of World Literature,* rev. ed. (New York, 1959);

William F. Thrall and Addison Hibbard, *A Handbook to Literature*, rev. ed. C. H. Holman (New York, 1962); Hedley L. Yelland et al., *A Handbook of Literary Terms* (New York, 1966).

2. *Works* (London, 1764), 2:136.

3. Section *Beaux-Arts* (Paris and Liége, 1788), 1:338.

4. Cf. Émile Deschanel, *Le Romantisme des classiques* (Paris, 1885–98); Ferdinand Brunetière, "Classiques et romantiques," in *Etudes critiques sur l'histoire de la littérature française*, 3ᵉ série (Paris, 1898), pp. 291–326; Pierre Moreau, *Le Classicisme des romantiques* (Paris, 1932).

5. Thus we find, in France, the earliest use of *pittoresque*, in the Romantic sense of that quality "which speaks to the soul and inspires melancholy ideas," in Letourneur's preface to his translation of Shakespeare (1776), the year before Rousseau applied the term to landscape in *Les Rêveries du promeneur solitaire* ("Cinquième Promenade").

6. Part 1, sec. 1, member 3, subsection 4.

7. *L'Amour médecin* (1666), 3:viii; *Le Malade imaginaire* (1673), 2:ix.

8. *Portraits contemporains*, new ed. (Paris, 1891), 1:174.

9. E.g., by Philarète Chasles, cited in Joachim Merlant, *Sénancour* (Paris, 1907), p. 303. Merlant credits the *Night Thoughts* with Sénancour's taste for "l'expression lugubre" (p. 100), and suggests that some of his pessimism and stoicism was derived from Voltaire, Rousseau, and Hindu literature.

10. André Monglond, *Vies préromantiques* (Paris, 1925), pp. 153–54.

11. *Impressions et souvenirs*, 3rd ed. (Paris, 1873), p. 39.

12. Cf. *Lettres d'un voyageur*, new ed. (Paris, 1869), p. 138; also her letter to Musset, June 26, 1834: "Ce sont de ces choses-là qui me donnent le spleen et qui réveillent mon idée de suicide, la triste compagne cramponnée après moi"; another to the same, May 12, 1834; to Duleil, Feb. 15, 1831; to Mme D'Agoult, July 10, 1836, etc.

13. Edmond Estève, *Byron et le romantisme français* (Paris, n.d.), p. 164.

14. Cf. Théophile Gautier's lines describing his own youth, in *Poésies complètes* (Paris, 1882–84), 1:103:

J'étais sombre et farouche;
Mon sourcil se tordait sur mon front soucieux

Ainsi qu'une vipère en fureur, et mes yeux
Dardaient entre mes cils un regard fauve et louche.
Un sourire infernal crispait ma pâle bouche.

15. *Le Préromantisme français* (Grenoble, 1930), 1:18, 245.

16. *Mémoires pour servir à l'histoire des mœurs et usages des Français . . .* (Paris, 1827), 3:360.

17. For example, Henry Seidel Canby, *Definitions* (New York, 1922; 2nd series, 1924); Stuart Chase, *The Tyranny of Words* (New York, 1938); Louis Grudin, *A Primer of Aesthetics* (New York, 1930); Martin Kallich, *The Association of Ideas and Critical Theory in Eighteenth-Century England* (Baltimore, 1945), also in *ELH*, 12 (1945), 290–315; Abraham Kaplan, "Definition and Specification of Meaning," *Jl. of Philosophy*, 40 (1946), 281–88; H. N. Lee, "The Use and Abuse of Words," *Jl. of Philosophy*, 39 (1942), 625–30; I[vor] A. Richards, *Principles of Literary Criticism* (New York, 1965); Wilbur Marshall Urban, *Language and Reality. The Philosophy of Language and the Principles of Symbolism* (New York, 1939). For additional titles, see annual *PMLA* bibliographies, section "Aesthetics, Literary Criticism, and Literary Theory."

3 Literary Indebtedness

1. For example, Dmitry Čiževsky attacks the "genetic method" as it has been used in the study of Slavic literatures (*Outline of Comparative Slavic Literatures* [Boston, 1952] p. 134), and states that "after decades of raptures over the search for 'borrowings' and 'influences,' historians of literature have, fortunately, lost interest in investigations of this kind" ("A Comparativist Looks at Mickiewicz," *Adam Mickiewicz: Księga w stulecie zgonu* [London, n.d.] p. 481). Harry Levin states that good examples of source study are rare, "et des signes de plus en plus nombreux indiquent que la chasse aux sources et aux influences ne rapporte plus grand'chose. En ce moment les traditions et les mouvements attirent de plus et plus l'interet" ("La Littérature Comparée: Point de vue d'Outre Atlantique," in *Revue de Littérature comparée*, 27 [1953] 25). Henri Peyre, though not denying the validity of influence studies, suggests that "studies of countries and relations between two or more writers would be well advised to give up in most cases the search for causes or in-

fluences, and to engage in the exploration of families of minds and of fortuitous analogies linking authors who had no awareness of one another" (*YCGL*, 1 [1952] 7).

2. See, for example, David H. Malone, "The 'Comparative' in Comparative Literature," *YCGL*, 3 (1954), 13–20, and especially p. 17. Also see Čiževsky's articles cited above in note 1.

3. See R. M. Samarin, "Sovremennoe sostojanie sravnitel'nogo literaturovedenija v nekotoryx zarubežnyx stranax," *Izvestija Akademii nauk SSSR: Otdelenie literatury i jazyka*, 18 (1959), 334–47.

4. Boris Ejxenbaum, *Lermontov* (Leningrad, 1924), pp. 28–34. On this basis he denies any meaningful influence of Byron on Lermontov's verse tales, in that Pushkin had already naturalized the genre in Russia, and hence Lermontov is acting within the "needs" of the new Russian genre. Viktor Žirmunskij, *Bajron i Puškin* (Leningrad, 1924), does not deny influence in international literary relationships, but argues that it is demonstrable only in the influence of literary works upon literary works; he shows how Pushkin took the genre of the romantic or Byronic verse tale from Byron and what he did with it.

5. Ihab H. Hassan, "The Problem of Influence in Literary History: Notes Toward a Definition," *Journal of Aesthetics and Art Criticism*, 14 (1955), 66–76.

6. For example, see the annual *PMLA* bibliographies, or F. Baldensperger and W. Friederich, *Bibliography of Comparative Literature* (Chapel Hill, 1950), and annual supplements in *YCGL*.

7. Haskell M. Block points this out in an able apologia for "The Concept of Influence in Comparative Literature," *YCGL*, 7 (1958), 30–37.

8. For example, see Paul Van Tieghem, *La Littérature comparée* (3rd ed., Paris, 1946), and such handbooks as André Morize, *Problems and Methods of Literary History* (Boston, c. 1922), and Gustave Rudler, *Les Techniques de la critique et de l'histoire littéraires en littérature française moderne* (Oxford, 1923). All these works discuss reception, though often using different phraseology, and all discuss influence, though often, as in Morize, there is confusion between reception and influence.

9. Renato Poggioli, "The Added Artificer," in *On Translation*, ed. Reuben A. Brower (Cambridge, Mass., 1959), p. 141. Two articles in this stimulating book discuss how translations

differ with various ages and reflect them: Reuben A. Brower, "Seven Agamemnons" (pp. 173–95), and Douglas Knight, "Translation: The Augustan Mode" (pp. 196–204).

10. Pushkin wrote these words in 1836, the year before he died, and of a young author who had echoed the "farewell" lines from Byron's *Childe Harold,* Canto 1. Pushkin was no doubt remembering that he himself had echoed the same lines in a poem ("Pogaslo dnevnoe svetilo") fifteen years earlier and was thinking how far he had developed since that time. The discussion is from Pushkin's review, "Frakijskie èligii: Stixotvorenija Viktora Tepljakova, 1836," in *Polnoe sobranie sočinenij* (16 vols. in 20, Ak. nauk, SSSR, 1937–49), 12:82.

11. Žirmunskij, *Bajron i Puškin.*

12. N. Otzoupe, "Vigny's *Éloa* and Lermontov's *Demon,*" *Slavonic and East European Review,* 34 (1956), 311–37. That Lermontov knew of Vigny's *Éloa* in 1841, the date of the last version of the *Demon,* is shown by his rejecting an "improvement" suggested for his poem, as "smacking" too much of Vigny. See A. P. Šan-Girej, "M. Ju. Lermontov," in E. K. Xvostova (Ekaterina Suškova), *Zapiski: 1812–41,* ed. Ju. G. Oksman (Leningrad, 1926), p. 361. For discussion see my "Lermontov's *Demon* and the Byronic Verse Tale," *Indiana Slavic Studies,* 2 (1958), 178.

13. See Block, paper cited, *YCGL,* 7:35–36.

14. See my paper cited above in note 12, and my "Byron, the Byronic Tradition of the Romantic Verse Tale in Russian, and Lermontov's *Mtsyri,*" *Indiana Slavic Studies,* 1 (1956), 165–90.

15. See N. I. Konrad, "Problemy sovremennogo sravnitel'nogo literaturovedenija," *Izvestija Akademii nauk SSSR: Otdelenie literatury i jazyka,* 18 (1959), 315–33.

16. Edmond Estève, *Byron et le romantisme français* (Paris, 1907).

4 The Art of Translation

1. *The British Academy Third Annual Shakespeare Lecture* (London, 1913), p. 11.

2. See Friedrich Gundolf's preface to his edition of *Shakespeare in deutscher Sprache* (Berlin, 1920), 1:5–7.

3. *Faust II* (Boston and New York, 1871), p. vi.

4. *Faust* (New York, n.d.), p. 4.

5. W. H. van der Smissen, *Goethe's Faust: Done into English Verse in the Original Metres with Commentary and Notes* (London, 1926), p. xviii.

6. Ibid., p. xiii.

7. *Faust* (New York, 1941), p. iv.

8. *Faust: Part I,* Rinehart Editions no. 75 (New York, 1955), p. xxxv.

9. Alfred McKinley Terhune, *The Life of Edward FitzGerald* (New Haven, 1947), p. 223.

10. *North American Review,* 109 (Oct. 1869), 575–76. John D. Yohannan, in his review of the *Rubaiyyat* as translated by Robert Graves and Omar Ali-Shah, reaffirms the value of FitzGerald's version when he asserts that "despite its occasional dictional felicities, it [the new translation] fails, like the others, to match even the time-worn colors of that superb Victorian re-creation of Khayaam." (*The New York Times Book Review,* July 28, 1968, p. 10.)

11. Terhune, *Life of FitzGerald,* p. 222.

12. George Sampson, *The Concise Cambridge History of English Literature* (Cambridge, England, 1941), p. 724.

13. Theodore Savory, *The Art of Translation* (London, 1957), p. 39. See also F. O. Matthiessen, *Translation, an Elizabethan Art* (Cambridge, Mass., 1931).

14. Savory, *Art of Translation,* p. 101.

15. Edmond Cary, *La Traduction dans le monde moderne* (Geneva, 1956), p. 185.

16. Ibid., p. 165.

17. Ibid., p. 62. The Jugoslav Nobel Prize winner, Ivo Andrič, in an address to an international assembly of translators, made the following remark printed in *Babel,* 9 (1963), 175: "Qu'est-ce que traduire, en somme? C'est l'art et l'aptitude de prendre le lecteur par la main, de le conduire à travers des régions et des espaces où seul il n'aurait jamais pénétré, de lui faire découvrir des objets et des phénomenes qu'il n'aurait jamais vus autrement."

18. Samuel Putnam, *The Portable Rabelais* (New York, 1946), p. 5.

19. Ibid., pp. 6–41.

20. Cf. Pauline Steiner and Horst Frenz, "Anderson and Stallings' *What Price Glory?* and Carl Zuckmayer's *Rivalen.*" *German Quarterly,* 20 (Nov. 1947), 239–51.

21. Cf. Putnam, *Portable Rabelais,* p. 10, note.

22. Hermann Sudermann, *The Joy of Living* (New York, 1902), p. 56. Cf. the note on the bowdlerization of the first (1890) American translation of Giovanni Verga's *The House by the Medlar Tree* by the recent translator, Raymond Rosenthal, in Signet Classic C225 (New York, 1964), p. viii: "The extensive cuts in this first translation [by Mary A. Craig, with an introduction by William Dean Howells], which amount to more than fifty pages, seem to have been dictated by Victorian prudery and caution. Thus, all overt or even covert references to sex, all especially savage or ironical overtones, not to mention all expressions of anticlerical or antigovernmental feeling, were carefully excised. Strangely enough, the second translation into English, by Eric Mosbacher, which was published in 1953 . . . followed these cuts."

23. See my article on "Eugene O'Neill in Russia," *Poet Lore,* 49 (Autumn 1943), 242–47.

24. Cf. Douglas Bub's review in *YCGL,* 3 (1954), 99–101. In an article in *Harper's,* 232 (April 1966), 94–102, called "The Hazardous Art of Mistranslation," Andrew R. MacAndrew gives numerous examples of distortion in the works of such authors as Celine, Tolstoy, and Dostoevsky. For instance, after comparing passages from *Notes from the Underground* in translations by Constance Garnett and David Magarshack, the writer concludes that "both translators convey the impression that Dostoevsky is not much of a writer" (p. 100).

25. *New York Times Book Review,* Nov. 19, 1950, p. 45.

26. *Flowers of Evil* (New York, 1936), p. vii. Cf. Jackson Matthews' opinion on this point in *On Translation,* ed. R. A. Brower (Cambridge, Mass., 1959), p. 68.

27. *Dante. The Divine Comedy. I: Hell,* Penguin Classics L6 (Harmondsworth, Middlesex, 1954), p. 56.

28. *Dante. Inferno,* Mentor Book MD113 (New York, 1959), translator's note.

29. *The Aeneid of Virgil* (New York, 1951), p. xii. John Cairncross, in the foreword to his translation of Racine's plays, reflects his dilemma with the particularly terse and calculated lines of seventeenth-century French when he says that he finds it necessary to adopt the "blank verse of ten syllables as the medium for the English version, while the French poet has twelve (the Alexandrine). The translator has therefore to con-

dense Racine by a sixth and to strip his version of every syllable that is not utterly essential, or else abandon literal transposition and devise a concise formula which gives the gist of Racine's line." (*Phaedre and Other Plays*, Penguin Books L122 [Baltimore, 1963], p. 7.)

30. *Aeneid*, Anchor Book A20 (New York, 1952), p. 8.

31. *The Theban Plays* (New York, 1956), p. xvi.

32. *Euripides. Alcestis and Other Plays*, Penguin Classics L31 (Harmondsworth, Middlesex, 1953), pp. 24–25.

33. *The Antigone of Sophocles* (New York, 1951), p. vii.

34. *Oedipus Cycle of Sophocles*, Harvest Books HB8 (New York, 1949), pp. 239–40.

35. *The Aeneid of Virgil*, p. xii.

36. *The Song of God: Bhagavad-Gita*, Mentor Book M103 (New York, 1951), pp. 10–11.

37. *Flowers of Evil*, p. vii. Cf. George Steiner's passage on the inadequacy of prose translation in the introduction to his edition of *The Penguin Book of Modern Prose Translations*: "The point is simply this: though always imperfect, a verse translation, in that it re-presents, re-enacts that selection of language, that stylization or innovation of syntax inseparable from the nature of poetic composition, is more responsible to the intent, to the movement of spirit in the original than a downward transfer into prose can ever be." (Penguin Poets D94 [Baltimore, 1966], p. 27.)

38. *Homer. The Odyssey*, Mentor Classics M21 (New York, 1949), pp. vii and 278 respectively.

39. Ibid., p. vii.

40. Lawrence, *The Odyssey of Homer* (London, 1955), p. 440.

41. *Homer. The Odyssey*, Penguin Books No. 613 (New York, 1946), p. ix.

42. *Virgil. The Pastoral Poems*, Penguin Classics L8 (Harmondsworth, Middlesex, 1949), p. 16.

43. *Dante. The Divine Comedy*, Rinehart Editions No. 72 (New York, 1954), p. xiii.

44. *Goethe. Faust I*, The Library of Liberal Arts LLA33 (New York, 1954), p. viii. See also B. Q. Morgan's comments on translating Goethe's *Faust II* in *YCGL*, 10 (1961), 33–38.

45. *The Autobiography of Benvenuto Cellini*, Penguin Classics L49 (Harmondsworth, Middlesex, 1956), p. 13.

46. *Thucydides. The Peloponnesian War,* Penguin Classics L39 (Harmondsworth, Middlesex, 1954), p. 9.

47. *Plato. The Republic,* Penguin Classics L48 (Harmondsworth, Middlesex, 1955), p. 48.

48. Samuel Putnam (trans.), *The Ingenious Gentleman Don Quixote de la Mancha by Cervantes* (New York, 1949), pp. xvi, xviii.

49. *Voltaire. Candide,* Penguin Classics L4 (Harmondsworth, Middlesex, 1951), pp. 13–14. Cf. Vladimir Nabokov's reference to Butt's translation as an "execrable English version of *Candide*" in *On Translation,* p. 110.

50. *Honoré de Balzac. Old Goriot,* Penguin Classics L17 (Harmondsworth, Middlesex, 1951), p. 23.

51. *Cervantes. Don Quixote,* Penguin Classics L10 (Harmondsworth, Middlesex, 1950), p. 11.

52. Mentor Book MD113, translator's note.

53. *Inferno,* Croft's Classics (New York, 1948), p. xii.

54. Penguin Books No. 613, pp. vii and xiv respectively.

55. *Tacitus on Imperial Rome,* Penguin Classics L60 (Harmondsworth, Middlesex, 1956), pp. 23–24.

56. *Henrik Ibsen. Three Plays,* Penguin Classics L16 (Harmondsworth, Middlesex, 1950), p. 22.

57. *Émile Zola. Germinal,* Penguin Classics L45 (Harmondsworth, Middlesex, 1954), p. 14.

58. The fact that J. M. Cohen's pamphlet *English Translators and Translations* (London, 1962) was included in the "Writers and Their Work" series of the British Book Council, shows that a history of translation now deserves a place in a series devoted to major authors. Other volumes might be mentioned, such as *Teoria e storia della traduzione* by Georges Mounin (Turin, 1965) and *Uebersetzen: Vorträge und Beiträge vom Internationalen Kongress literarischer Uebersetzer,* ed. Rolf Italiaander (Frankfurt am Main, 1965).

59. See Reuben A Brower, ed., *On Translation* (Cambridge, Mass., 1959), pp. 141, 173–95, 196–204.

60. "Il est assez remarquable que la théorie de la traduction . . . fleurisse en Union Soviétique." (Cary, *La Traduction,* p. 73, note.)

61. The term has been suggested by Kurt Heinrich Hansen, translator of William Faulkner's *A Fable* and other American works into German.

62. This is a paraphrase of a definition by Ludwig Fulda, "Die Kunst des Uebrsetzens," *Aus der Werkstatt* (Stuttgart and Berlin, 1904), p. 162.

63. André Gide, *Divers* (Paris, 1931), p. 189.

6 Ideas and Literature

1. R. G. Collingwood, *Outlines of a Philosophy of Art* (London, 1925), pp. 98–99.

2. R. G. Collingwood, *The Idea of History* (London, 1948), p. 252.

3. The student will find a theory of unit-ideas ably set forth by such writers as A. O. Lovejoy and George Boas. See especially Lovejoy's *The Great Chain of Being* (Cambridge, Mass., 1936), pp. 3–24. Although I cannot accept their theory, I am ready to admit that their practice is often unaffected by its shortcomings. The term "unit-idea" is, however, a dangerous one that can often mislead the student by its unfortunate connotation. Nonetheless, Lovejoy's *The Great Chain of Being* is a classic in its field and should be read in its entirety by anyone interested in the history of ideas and in the relations of philosophy and literature. This study might well be supplemented by readings in some of the less technical histories of philosophy. For descriptive bibliography including such books see N. P. Stallknecht and R. S. Brumbaugh, *The Spirit of Western Philosophy* (New York, 1964), pp. 511–30; also Wellek and Warren, *Theory of Literature*, chap. 10. The beginning student will do well to examine Etienne Gilson, ed., *History of Philosophy* 4 vols. (New York, 1962–63), and current editions of Crane Brinton, *Men and Ideas*, and John Herman Randall, *The Making of the Modern Mind.*

4. In recent years there have been many excellent studies of the way in which scientific hypotheses newly accepted in a given period have been reflected in its literature. Professor Marjorie H. Nicolson's studies of the influence of the new astronomy and physics of the seventeenth century are among the most distinguished of these investigations. She has made very vivid the new sense of spatial orientation, of distance and of scale, that followed upon the theoretical revolution in astronomy and upon the use of telescope and microscope. This new orientation is gradually recognized and makes itself felt in diverse ways in the work of many authors, as for instance in Milton, Donne, Swift, and Pope among major British writers. In each case, however, it

is not newly discovered facts or newly established hypotheses that by themselves capture the literary imagination and "command the muse." It is rather the relation of certain discoveries or points of view to an inclusive *Weltanschauung* of philosophical, even of mythological, origin. Professor Nicolson has done much to make this apparent (see especially her *Science and Imagination,* Ithaca, N. Y., 1956). In so far as scientific ideas influence the self-consciousness of the individual by reshaping his orientation in the world and his sense of his own destiny, they will appeal to the imagination of the serious writer. Otherwise their significance lies primarily in their amusement value as curiosities and approaches that in run-of-the-mill science fiction. Indeed thoughtful science fiction might better be called "philosophical fiction," as would seem to be true in the case of Aldous Huxley's *Brave New World.* Furthermore, in our age when scientific investigation assumes great importance and enjoys an increasing prestige, the personal and professional problems of the scientist, considered as a human individual, may well appeal to the novelist. Consider Sinclair Lewis' *Arrowsmith* and the recent novels of C. P. Snow. But here it is clear that the situations described and the problems faced are moral rather than strictly scientific in nature.

5. See Plato *Phaedrus* 264, and Aristotle *Poetics* 7. 1450^b.

6. Simone de Beauvoir, *Le Sang des Autres* (Paris, 1945); translation taken, with minor changes in the last sentences, from English version by Roger Senhouse and Yvonne Moyse (New York, 1948), p. 83.

7. The application of this notion to the theory of tragedy is interesting. Consider from this point of view Sartre's play *Les Mouches,* an existentialist adaptation of the Electra story. Here we find the classical standards of value boldly inverted. *Hybris* or extreme independence on the part of the individual becomes a virtue. See Albert W. Levi, *Philosophy and the Modern World* (Bloomington, Ind., 1959), chap. 10, "The Drama of Choice: Karl Jaspers and Jean Paul Sartre."

8. Henri Bergson, *The Two Sources of Morality and Religion,* trans. R. A. Audra and C. Brereton (New York, 1935), chap. 2.

9. D. A. Traversi, *An Approach to Shakespeare* (Garden City, N. Y., 1956), pp. 10–11.

7 Literature and the Arts

1. See, for example, John Crowe Ransom's *The World's Body* (London and New York, 1938) and Francis Fergusson's *The Idea of a Theater* (Princeton, N. J., 1949). Others associated with the new criticism as well as other critics have been sensitive to this problem of communication and analysis. Such works as I. A. Richards' *The Meaning of Meaning* (London and New York, 1923), William Empson's *Seven Types of Ambiguity* (London, 1930), and Cleanth Brooks' and Robert Penn Warren's *Understanding Poetry* (New York, 1938) and *Understanding Fiction* (New York, 1943) illustrate this awareness of the need for clarification of the use of language in criticism.

2. The subjects or art forms which lend themselves to this category are obviously the opera and the ballet, depending as they must upon the combined efforts of writers, musicians, choreographers, set and costume designers, etc. No such studies will be discussed in this paper, but the reader is referred to Calvin Brown, "The Dilemma of Opera," in *Music and Literature* (Athens, Ga., 1948), pp. 87–99, and Joseph Yasser, "The Variation Form and Synthesis of Arts," *JAAC*, 14 (1956), 318–23, as two examples which deal with these art forms.

3. New York, 1949.

4. *The Aeneid*, trans. J. W. MacKail (New York, 1934), bk. 2.

5. *Laocoön, Nathan the Wise, Minna von Barnhelm*, tr. William A. Steel (London, 1930), p. 11.

6. "Spatial Form in Literature," *Sewanee Review*, 53 (1945), 225. Mr. Frank states that his intention in his essay is "to apply Lessing's method to modern literature."

7. One third of Mr. Frank's essay is a detailed analysis of this novel as it illustrates the principle of reflexive reference.

8. *Selected Prose*, ed. John Hayward (Harmondsworth, Middlesex: Penguin, 1953), pp. 66–67.

9. *The Art of T. S. Eliot* (London, 1949), pp. 37–48.

10. *Selected Prose*, p. 60.

11. For a wholly different analysis of Eliot's *Four Quartets* in terms specifically keyed to Beethoven's *Quartet in A Minor*, Opus 132, see Howard Howarth, "Eliot, Beethoven and J. W. N. Sullivan," *Comparative Literature*, 9 (1957), 322–32. Mr. Howarth is convinced that Eliot was drawn to this particular quartet

as a "holy thanksgiving to Godhead for recovery" and tries to show Eliot's varying degrees of success in a formal reproduction of Beethoven's pattern in the respective poems comprising the *Four Quartets*. He then proceeds to show also how ideas, even exact phrases from Sullivan's biography of Beethoven crop up in the poems. In contrast to Helen Gardner's point that Eliot conceived the *Four Quartets* at the outset as a unity, Howarth sees them as gradually evolving along the five-movement pattern of the Beethoven *Quartet* over a period of several years. Howarth's study is provocative for the influences he contends operated upon Eliot, but it is based too much upon "supposition," "perhaps," "probably," "speculation," and "if" to be wholly dependable.

12. Herbert Read, *The Philosophy of Modern Art* (New York, 1955), pp. 143–48.

13. Helmut Hatzfeld, *Literature Through Art* (New York, 1952), pp. v, 211–23.

14. *Music and Literature: A Comparison of the Arts* (Athens, Ga., 1948).

15. *Wechselseitige Erhellung der Künste* (Berlin, 1917).

16. *Deutsche Klassik und Romantik, oder Vollendung und Unendlichkeit* (Munich, 1922).

17. *Four Stages of Renaissance Style: Transformations in Art and Literature, 1400–1700* (New York, 1955).

18. R. Wellek and A. Warren, *Theory of Literature* (New York, 1956).

19. H. Hungerland, "The Aesthetic Response Reconsidered," *JAAC*, 16 (1957), 32, 43.

20. K. Aschenbrenner, B. C. Herl, in *JAAC*, 18 (1960), 108, 393.

21. *A Bibliography on the Relations of Literature and the Other Arts, 1952–1967* (New York, 1968).

9 Two Types of Classical Tragedy

1. The first section is a slightly revised version of what appeared in the original edition of this book. The second is a modification of "From Oedipus to Lear," *Classical Journal*, 61 (1965), 49–57.

2. Francis Fergusson, *The Idea of a Theater*, Anchor Books A4, pp. 38–39, 31.

3. The following five quotations are from David Grene's translation (D. Grene and R. Lattimore, *The Complete Greek*

Tragedies 3 (Chicago, 1959), pp. 219, 216, 208, 215, 179–80.

4. H. D. F. Kitto, *Greek Tragedy: A Literary Study*, Anchor Books A38, p. 217. I am indebted to Professor Kitto's ideas about the *Hippolytus*.

5. Norman T. Pratt, "The Stoic Base of Senecan Drama," *Transactions of the American Philological Association*, 79 (1948), 1–11.

6. Seneca, *On Anger*, trans. J. W. Basore in *Seneca, Moral Essays* 1 (Loeb Classical Library; London, 1928), p. 107.

7. Seneca, *Hippolytus*, trans. F. J. Miller in *Seneca's Tragedies* 1 (Loeb Classical Library; London, 1917), p. 333.

8. Ibid., pp. 357–61.

9. Ibid., pp. 333–35.

10. See Robert B. Heilman, *This Great Stage: Image and Structure in "King Lear"* (Baton Rouge, La., 1948), pp. 22–23.

11. Bernard M. W. Knox, *Oedipus at Thebes* (New Haven, 1957), pp. 195–96.

12. Knox, pp. 116–38, collects the language expressing the search for truth.

13. Heilman, pp. 115–16.

14. G. Wilson Knight, *The Wheel of Fire*, 4th ed., rev. and enl. (London, 1949), p. 177.

15. Heilman, pp. 10–11, 26, 204; John F. Danby, *Shakespeare's Doctrine of Nature: A Study of "King Lear"* (London, 1949), p. 124; Hiram Haydn, *The Counter-Renaissance* (New York, 1950), pp. 637, 648.

16. Danby, especially pp. 20–21, 33–34.

17. Danby, p. 125.

18. Haydn, pp. 648, 651.

19. Harold C. Goddard, *The Meaning of Shakespeare* (Chicago, 1951), pp. 529–30, 533–34.

20. Kenneth Muir, *King Lear* (Arden ed., 1952), p. lvii.

21. Oscar J. Campbell, "The Salvation of Lear," *ELH* 15 (1948), 93–109.

22. Lily B. Campbell, *Shakespeare's Tragic Heroes: Slaves of Passion* (New York, 1952), p. vi.

23. Norman T. Pratt, "Major Systems of Figurative Language in Senecan Melodrama," *Transactions of the American Philological Association*, 94 (1963), 199–234.

24. Miller (see note 7), pp. 397–99, slightly modified.

10 Study of Literary Genres

1. In order to avoid terminological confusion, *kind* will be used in the sense of *major kind* (drama, epic, fiction, lyric poetry) and *genre, form,* or *type* to designate all other classes of literary phenomena.

2. The appropriate quotations are found in Irene Behrens, *Die Lehre von der Einteilung der Dichtkunst, vornehmlich vom 16. bis 19. Jahrhundert* (Halle, 1940). A summary of that author's findings and conclusions is given by Irwin Ehrenpreis in his book *The "Types" Approach to Literature* (New York, 1945), pp. 9–16.

3. Lines 23 and 92 respectively.

4. Letter of December 29, 1797.

5. See the opening lecture of Brunetière's course *L'Evolution des genres dans l'histoire de la littérature* (Paris, 1890), where reference is made to the way in which "un genre naît, grandit, atteint sa perfection, décline, et enfin meurt" (p. 13).

6. The Proceedings of this congress were published in *Helicon, Revue internationale des problèmes généraux de la littérature,* 2 (1940), 113–226.

7. Germaine Brée, "The Ambiguous Voyage: Mode or Genre"; Eliseo Vivas, "Literary Classes: Some Problems"; and Sheldon Sacks, "The Psychological Implications of Generic Distinctions" in *Genre,* 1 (1968), 87–123.

8. The term *mode,* popularized by Northrop Frye in his *Anatomy of Criticism* (Princeton, N. J., 1957), ought to be discarded since it is not primarily a generic category but a synonym for technique (point of view) with strong thematological overtones.

9. The evidence is found in Croce's *Estetica* as well as his *Nuovi saggi di estetica.* The whole question is dealt with by Gian N. Orsini, *Benedetto Croce: Philosopher of Art and Literary Critic* (Carbondale, Ill., 1961). Joel Spingarn, one of the editors of the short-lived American *Journal of Comparative Literature,* shared Croce's views on this matter.

10. *Revue de Synthèse historique,* 31 (1921), 16.

11. Anglosaxon readers can now be directed to René Wellek's essay "Genre Theory, the Lyric and *Erlebnis,*" *Festschrift für Richard Alewyn,* ed. H. Singer and B. von Wiese (Cologne and Graz, 1967).

12. Ed. Alex Preminger et al. (Princeton, N. J., 1965).

13. See Behrens, pp. 22, 35. Whether *tota nostra* implies originality or perfection is not entirely certain. The point has, once again, been raised by E. N. Tigerstedt in his contribution to *The Disciplines of Criticism: Essays in Literary Theory, Interpretation and History,* ed. P. Demetz et al. (New Haven, 1968), pp. 593–613.

14. Paget Toynbee's translation, as found in his edition of the letters, *Dantis Alagherii Epistolae,* 2nd ed. (Oxford, 1966), p. 201.

15. *Theory of Literature* (New York, 1949), p. 242.

16. *La Littérature comparée,* 3rd ed. (Paris, 1961), p. 18 f.

17. "The pages which follow first advance a critical proposition, that satire is a distinct genre with a number of marked characteristics, and then make use of this proposition to describe the complex and seemingly disparate mass of prose, poetry and drama which is English satire of the late Renaissance" (*The Cankered Muse: Satire of the English Renaissance* [New Haven, 1959], p. 7). Germaine Brée seems to embrace this view in her contribution to the MLA forum referred to above.

18. See my essay "Parody, Travesty, and Burlesque: Imitations with a Vengeance" in *Proceedings of the IV. Congress of the ICLA,* ed. François Jost (The Hague, 1966), 2, 803.

19. *Comparaison n'est pas raison: La Crise de la littérature comparée* (Paris, 1963), p. 97 f.

20. "On the Methods and Aims of Literary History as a Science," trans. Harry Weber, *YCGL,* 16 (1967), 39.

21. *Poetics* 26. 1462[a], in S. H. Butcher's translation.

22. This is the title of a book by Ralph Freedman (Princeton, N. J., 1963).

23. *Poetics* 1. 1447[b].

24. See Roy Pascal, *Design and Truth in Autobiography* (London, 1960); Leon Edel, *Literary Biography* (Toronto, 1957); Franz H. Mautner, "Maxim(e)s, Sentences, *Fragmente, Aphorismen*" in *Proceedings of the IV. Congress of the ICLA,* 2, 812–19.

25. See the author's essay "The Libretto as Literature," *Books Abroad,* 35 (1961), 15–22, and his anthology *The Essence of Opera* (New York, 1964), as well as Karl-Ludwig Selig's bibliographical survey "Emblem Literature: Directions in Recent Scholarship," *YCGL,* 12 (1963), 36–41. Most of the

recent book-length studies of the essay and the radio play come from Germany.

26. *Poetics* 1. 1447[a].

27. See Hardison's perceptive analysis "*Poetics*, Chapter I: The Way of Nature," *YCGL*, 16 (1967), 5–15.

28. See Douglas Feaver, "Words and Music in Ancient Greek Drama," *The Essence of Opera*, pp. 10–17. This is an adaptation of the more scholarly article "The Musical Setting of Euripides' *Orestes*" in the *American Journal of Philology*, 81 (1960), 1–15.

29. *Lexikon der alten Welt* (Zurich, 1965), col. 1798.

30. *Sämmtliche Werke*, ed. B. Suphan, 32 (Berlin, 1883), 80.

31. Second edition (Berlin, 1944), p. 144 ff.

32. *Grundbegriffe der Poetik* (Zurich, 1946), p. 10.

33. Ibid., p. 7. The view expressed in the next-to-last sentence of the quotation is a critique, in anticipation of an opinion voiced by René Etiemble on p. 99 of *Comparaison n'est pas raison*, whereas the last sentence finds an echo in T. S. Eliot's notions regarding the relationship between tradition and the individual talent.

34. Second edition (Berne, 1954), p. 334.

35. A third edition of Jolles' book was recently (1963) published by Niemeyer in Tübingen.

36. This formulation stems from Wolfgang Mohr's discussion of Jolles' theory in the *Reallexikon der deutschen Literaturgeschichte*, 1, 2nd ed. (Berlin, 1962), p. 321.

37. The order *is* alphabetical in the original German.

38. *Das sprachliche Kunstwerk*, p. 330.

39. The quotations from Goethe are taken from Ernst Beutler's edition of the *Werke und Briefe* 3 (Zurich, 1948), 480 f.

40. Column 1797.

41. The quotations are taken from G. Fricke's edition of Schiller's works (Munich, 1962), 5: 694, 710.

42. Aristotle's arguments to the contrary, as presented in *Poetics* 14. 1453[b], are not entirely convincing; for few plots are so constructed that "even without the aid of the eye, any one who is told the incidents, will thrill with horror and pity at the turn of events."

43. Norfolk, Conn., 1963, p. 212.

44. *A Portrait of the Artist as a Young Man,* Signet Books 664 (New York, 1948), p. 163.

45. B. Jowett's translation, with slight emendations.

46. See Melvin Friedman, *Stream of Consciousness: A Study in Literary Method* (New Haven, 1955); Robert Humphrey, *Stream of Consciousness in the Modern Novel* (Berkeley, Calif., 1955); Shiv Kumar, *Bergson and the Stream of Consciousness Novel* (New York, 1963); Dorrit Cohn, "Narrated Monologue: Definition of a Fictional Style," *Comparative Literature,* 18 (1966), 97–112.

47. *Theory of Literature,* p. 241.

48. Lines 73 and 83 f.

49. *Theory of Literature,* p. 241.

50. Irving Howe wrote a book entitled *Politics and the Novel* (New York, 1957) but wisely states that he has "no ambition of setting up still another rigid category" and is solely "concerned with perspectives of observation" (p. 16).

51. From the rich literature on this genre we mention only Claudio Guillén's contribution to the Utrecht meeting of the ICLA (*Proceedings,* pp. 252–66) and W. M. Frohock's essay in the *YCGL,* 16 (1967), 43–52.

52. Georg Lukács. *The Historical Novel,* trans. H. and S. Mitchell (Boston, 1963); Lion Feuchtwanger, *The House of Desdemona,* trans. H. Basilius (Detroit, 1963).

53. *Theory of Literature,* p. 242.

54. The essay is found in *The Creative Vision: Modern European Writers on their Art,* ed. H. M. Block and H. Salinger (New York, 1960), pp. 29–39. See also Herman Meyer's extremely subtle essay "On the Spirit of Verse" in *The Disciplines of Criticism,* pp. 331–48.

11 Romanticism

1. We could find no generally accepted guide regarding the capitalization or noncapitalization of "Romantic" and "Romanticism." We decided to use upper case whenever speaking of the (supposed) period movement, but lower case when alluding to the psychological inclination. Other similar terms were treated in the same manner.

Authors and titles not identified in the notes or described and evaluated in the critical bibliography at the end of the essay can be found in the bibliographies and indices of the larger works listed.

2. *PMLA,* 66 (March 1951), 5–23. Although Peckham states (p. 5) that "such a theory . . . must show that Wordsworth and Byron, Goethe and Chateaubriand, were all part of a general European literary movement," his article contains practically no reference to German or French Romanticism; cursory mentions of Kant, Leibniz, Beethoven, Mozart, Haydn, Eduard von Hartmann, and Picasso can hardly compensate for this omission.

3. Italo Siciliano, *Il romanticismo francese* (Venice, 1955). Mario Marcazzan, "Decadenza romantica e decadentismo," *Humanitas* (Brescia), 11 (1956), 543–57. Ladislao Mittner, *Ambivalenze romantiche* (Messina, 1954).

4. For the whole question of literary periodization (including Romanticism), the reader may still consult with profit the papers and recorded discussions of the second International Congress of Literary History (Amsterdam, 1935) devoted to this problem (*Bulletin* of the International Committee of Historical Sciences, 9, no. 36, September 1937, pp. 255–408).

5. These critics include F. J. Billeskov Jansen in Denmark, J. G. Robertson, L. P. Smith, and Tymms in England, Bremond, Carré, Desprès, Dubois (*Globe*), Mercier, Moreau, Roddier, Van Tieghem, and Valéry in France, Nicolai Hartmann, Hatzfeld, Klemperer, Milch, Nadler, Petersen, Franz Schultz, and Wais in Germany, Teesing in Holland, Croce, Farinelli and Gioberti in Italy, Eckhoff in Norway, Folkierski in Poland, and Bernbaum, Chew, Lovejoy, Nitchie, Peyre, Wimsatt, and Brooks in the United States. The positions taken by these and other scholars must be reduced to their barest common denominators for the sake of our argument. Such a procedure obviously cannot do justice to the subtlety and differentiation of their dialectics. Nor do we aim at anything even remotely approaching completeness in reporting the multitude of attitudes taken on this hotly contested question. All we can hope to do is to outline a few representative views.

6. See, e.g., Arturo Farinelli, *Il Romanticismo nel mondo latino* (Turin, 1927), 1: 4 ff., and John E. Smith, "Rousseau, Romanticism and the Philosophy of Existence," *Yale French Studies,* no. 13 (Spring–Summer 1954), p. 52.

7. In this last article, while continuing to insist that it is futile to seek to define "romanticism," Lovejoy does, however, pick "out of the many new [German] ideas of the 1780's and 1790's" (p. 272), which he holds to be "in large part hetero-

geneous" (p. 261), three notions: organicism, dynamism, and diversitarianism—terms on which Peckham will pounce in order to save the positive Lovejoy from the negative Lovejoy.

8. *Essays in the History of Ideas* (Baltimore, 1948), p. xvi.

9. In his paper, "The Originality of French Romanticism," *Symposium* (Fall–Winter 1969), pp. 333–45. Speaking about Spanish Romanticism, Tarr has made a parallel assertion: The real Spanish Romantic school in the nineteenth century is, he suggests, not represented by the generation of Espronceda and Larra (about 1830–40), but by the "Generation of 1898": Unamuno, Baroja, Azorín, etc. "Romanticism: A Symposium," *PMLA*, 55 (March 1940), 1–60.

10. In his "Romantic Poetry and Rhetoric," *Yale French Studies*, no. 13 (Spring–Summer, 1954), pp. 39–40, Peyre underscores the gap between French Romanticism, on the one hand, and German and English Romanticism, on the other, and breaks up the French phenomenon into several waves or ripples, beginning with preromanticism (1760–75) and ending with Symbolism.

11. While this radical simplification of Croce's views gives, we hope, a rough idea of the direction of his impact on modern criticism, it must not convey the impression that Croce's interests were restricted. He was far from neglecting the fields of history, biography, politics, etc.; in fact, he is the most encyclopedic European intellectual of the first half of the twentieth century.

12. Professor Orsini, who has read this essay in manuscript, takes strong exception to the picture of Croce presented here. He states that Croce built up a masterly synthesis of Romanticism in his *History of Europe in the 19th Century* (1932), was by no means averse to grouping authors and works according to place and time in his works on the Italian Renaissance (1951), the Italian Baroque (1929), and Italian literature from 1870 to 1900 (1915), and arrived, in his work on poetry (*La Poesia*, 1936), at "a complete methodology for the definition of an artist's aesthetic personality, as evidenced by *the whole* of his work."

I intend in no way to give a just and balanced appreciation of the totality of Croce's thought. Rather, I tried to pinpoint one particular aspect of his incredibly vast and versatile output that seems to have had the most obvious impact on contemporary criticism outside of Italy. The meaning attributed to his theory by these readers may have been a gross simplification or even falsification, but this is not relevant in *this* context; what counts is the nature of the influence. Rousseau suffered a similar fate.

13. Italian Romanticism has likewise been held to be non-existing; see Gina Martegiani's *Il Romanticismo italiano non esiste* (Florence, 1908).

14. Werner P. Friederich and David H. Malone, *Outline of Comparative Literature* (Chapel Hill, 1954), p. 256. Irving Babbitt suggests that those telling us that the terms "classic" and "romantic" cannot and need not be defined are themselves romantic, representing just another facet of the movement from Rousseau to Bergson attempting to discredit the analytic intellect (*Rousseau and Romanticism*, Boston, 1919, p. 1). See also John G. Robertson, *The Reconciliation of Classic and Romantic* (Cambridge, England, 1925).

15. Ernest Bernbaum lists twenty-eight well-known definitions (*Guide Through the Romantic Movement*, New York, 1948, p. 301). See also Lovejoy, *Essays in the History of Ideas*, pp. 228–31; and Jacques Barzun, *Romanticism and the Modern Ego* (Boston, 1943), pp. 16, 19, 20, 213–30.

16. Croce is quick to add, however, that the great artists and the great works (or rather the strong parts of these works) are classical as well as romantic, representational as well as sentimental. Lucas and Guérard agree with this position. It is quite clear that Croce's and Farinelli's ideas on classicism and romanticism are deeply colored by what they consider the admirable fusion of both elements in their compatriot, Manzoni.

17. Many definitions and often critical characterizations of romanticism, especially but not only in France, have political, social, religious and ethical tinges and biases, e.g., those of Barrès, Léon Daudet, Faguet, Lasserre, Maurras, Louis Reynaud, and Seillière.

18. Note also Croce's tripartite division of Romanticism into three distinct categories: moral, artistic, and philosophical.

19. Not in the sense of Zola, of course, but as a new penetration and cult of nature.

20. Wellek's theory has undoubtedly found much support (e.g., R. H. Samuel, "Romanticism," Cassell's *Encyclopedia of World Literature*), though not everywhere (e.g., Ronald

S. Crane in *Philological Quarterly*, 29, 1950, 257–59). Wellek's more general approach to literature, of which his concept of Romanticism is an important part, has subsequently been endorsed by Mario Praz ("Literary History," *Comparative Literature*, 2, Spring 1950, 97–106) and Manfred Kridl ("The Integral Method of Literary Scholarship: Theses for Discussion," *Comparative Literature*, 3, Winter 1951, 18–31), among others. His physical and ideological proximity to such "new critics" as Brooks and Wimsatt may well have something to do with his emphasis of symbol and myth as cardinal features of European Romanticism.

21. Friederich (*Outline of Comparative Literature*, p. 257), e.g., has been chipping away at "organicism," which, he says, does not chime in with the Romantic fondness for Catholicism or Neoplatonism with its insistence on absolute values and forms. Be it noted that in the sequel to his first article on Romanticism Peckham qualifies his former antithesis between Enlightenment and Romanticism.

22. Sometimes phraseology will give the scholar away, as Wellek's constantly repeated, gleeful assertion that this or that author "fits [ties] into our scheme [pattern]." "The Concept of 'Romanticism' in Literary History," *Comparative Literature*, 1 (1949), 149, 154, 155, 157, 158, 170.

23. We have already examined the nature of the involvement of Lovejoy, Peyre, Croce, and Wellek. As to other definers: Carlyle was certainly far from being objective; in Fairchild one senses a certain insularism and religious proclivities which might have had a bearing on his attitude toward Romanticism; and Peckham, in a forthright confession at the end of his first article, avows that he, himself, is a "positive romanticist."

24. The desirability, necessity, or difficulties of such an undertaking have been referred to or dwelled on by Kaufmann, Lovejoy, Nitchie, and Wellek. A good beginning has been made by Farinelli and Van Tieghem. But Farinelli takes in Latin countries only (particularly France, Italy, and Spain), and in the forty years since the appearance of his work a tremendous amount of scholarship on the subject has been added. Since the publication of Van Tieghem's synthesis in 1948, important suggestions have been made. Neither Farinelli's three volumes nor Van Tieghem's 560 pages lend themselves to the graphic survey which we have prepared for this essay.

25. Each "verdict" was arrived at after careful consideration of evidence which, by necessity, had to be largely secondhand. It is impossible, in a summary of this kind, to retrace the steps leading up to each of the decisions.

26. "Au temps du romantisme, les idées littéraires circulaient avec une force et une rapidité inconnues jusque-là. Les nations européennes échangeaient sans cesse leurs thèmes et leurs formes littéraires." (F. J. Billeskov Jansen, *L'Age d'Or*, Copenhagen, 1953, pp. 36–37.)

27. Van Tieghem and Wellek have initiated coverage of these literatures as part of the European picture.

28. The political ambiguity of Romanticism, as we have found it, bears out Peckham's note of caution on the subject (paper cited, *PMLA*, 66:5). Wellek, too, is aware of it ("The Concept of 'Romanticism,'" p. 171), but feels that political criteria are not paramount.

29. To prevent any misunderstanding, we should like to state that after the clarification of the more specific components of Romanticism, after the analytical and "additive" spade work has been done, the justification of and need for a "key" approach still exists, but this key may be a different one in the light of the preceding analysis.

INDEX OF NAMES

Abrams, M. H., 306, 333
Addison, Joseph, 74
Adler, Alfred, 7, 139, 140
Aeschylus, 223, 257
Aiken, Conrad, 194, 195
Akinari, 314
Albérès, R.-M., 47
Alcaeus, 261
Alcman, 261
Aldridge, A. Owen, 31, 45
Alexander, Franz, 124
Alexander, Samuel, 151
Ali-Shah, Omar, 338
Amaru, 317
Ampère, 302
Anacreon, 261
Anderson, George, 55
Anderson, Maxwell, 106, 338
Anderson, Sherwood, 318
Andrič, Ivo, 338
Apuleius, 216
Aquinas, Thomas, 93
Armato, Rosario P., 45
Aristotle, x, 56, 93, 122, 257, 259, 260, 267, 271, 273, 322, 343, 349
Arnold, Matthew, 147
Aronson, A., 82
Arrowsmith, William, 117, 118
Aschenbrenner, K., 345
Auden, W. H., 143, 185, 254
Audra, R. A., 343
Auerbach, Erich, ix, 32, 159
Augustine, Saint, 150
Aynard, Joseph, 308
Azorín, 3, 12, 352

Babbitt, Irving, 180, 277, 282, 307, 353
Babcock, R. W., 73, 74, 75
Bacchylides, 261
Bachelard, Gaston, 125, 134
Bacon, Francis, 178
Balakian, Anna, 40, 42
Baldensperger, Fernand, 4, 5, 24, 25, 38, 49, 51, 259, 277, 311, 329, 336
Balzac, Honoré de, 3, 7, 33, 59, 62, 63, 69, 104, 115, 123, 137, 279, 341
Banks, Theodore H., 110, 111
Barasch, Frances K., 75
Barbier, Henri A., 303
Baretti, Giuseppe, 301
Barnes, Djuna, 188, 189
Barnet, Sylvan, 333
Baroja, Pío, 3, 12, 352
Barrère, Jean-Bertrand, 277, 282, 283, 310
Barrès, Maurice, 353
Barry, Raymond W., 333
Barzun, Jacques, 281, 305, 353
Bashō, 325
Basile, Giambattista, 216
Basilius, H., 350
Basler, Roy P., 144
Basore, J. W., 346
Bataillon, Marcel, 329
Bate, W. Jackson, 74, 75
Bateson, F. W., 72
Baudelaire, Charles, 10, 33, 69, 109, 200, 278
Baudissin, Count von, 98
Baudouin, Charles, 125, 143
Baur, Frank, 35, 36
Beauvoir, Simone de, 343
Becker, George J., 79
Beckford, William, 301
Beckson, Karl E., 333

Beethoven, Ludwig van, 183, 344, 345, 351
Behrens, Irene, 347, 348
Bémol, Maurice, 35, 36, 330
Benét, William R., 333
Benham, Allen R., 54
Benson, Adolph B., 54
Béranger, Jean-Pierre de, 300
Berchet, Giovanni, 282, 300, 301
Bergel, L., 42
Bergin, Thomas G., 116
Bergson, Henri, 126, 169, 343, 350, 353
Berlioz, Hector, 279, 292
Bernbaum, Ernest, 306, 351, 353
Berr, 277
Beutler, Ernst, 349
Beyerle, Dieter, 43
Bhārata, 322
Billeskov Jansen, F. J., 283, 351, 355
Blair, Robert, 59
Blake, R. E., 57
Blake, William, 11, 122, 166, 300
Blanco-White, José, 301
Blankenagel, John C., 299, 305
Block, Haskell M., 37, 56, 336, 337, 350
Boas, George, 342
Boase, A. M., 76
Boccaccio, 85, 90, 241, 258, 323
Bodkin, Maud, 133
Boethius, 164
Böhl de Faber, 300
Böhme, Jakob, 167, 289, 300
Boileau, Nicolas, 253, 267
Bompiani, Valentino Silvio, 49, 53
Bonaparte, Marie, 136
Bond, Donald F., 75
Borges, Jorge Luis, 318
Borgese, G. A., 304
Bourdaloue, Louis, 62
Bowling, L. E., 81
Bowra, C. M., 283
Brady, F., 80
Brahmer, M., 76
Brandl, Alois, 99
Brandt Corstius, Jan, 30, 45, 331
Brecht, Bertolt, 45, 256, 258
Brée, Germaine, 250, 347, 348
Bremond, 351
Brereton, C., 343
Breton, André, 125
Brett-James, Antony, 49
Breughel, Pieter, 185
Brinton, Crane, 342
Bronson, Bertrand, 29
Brooks, Cleanth, 47, 344, 351, 354
Brooks, Van Wyck, 125
Brower, Reuben A., 117, 118, 336, 337, 339, 341
Brower, Robert R. H., 320, 324
Brown, Calvin S., 28, 194, 195, 344
Browne, William, 163
Browning, Elizabeth Barrett, 287, 301
Browning, Robert, 137, 166, 287, 301
Brumbaugh, R. S., 342
Brunetière, Ferdinand, 249, 257, 334, 347
Bub, Douglas, 339
Büchner, Georg, 11, 33
Buck, Philo, 54
Bull, George, 114
Bullitt, John, 74, 75
Bundy, Murray W., 74, 75, 76
Bunyan, John, 150
Bürger, Gottfried August, 289, 300, 302
Burke, Kenneth, 72, 125
Burns, Robert, 147
Burton, Robert, 64, 67
Bury, J. B., 79
Butcher, S. H., 348
Butt, John, 115, 341
Byron, George Gordon, Lord, xiv, 85, 87, 89, 90, 93, 94, 96, 289, 295, 297, 299, 300, 301, 303, 334, 336, 337, 351

Caillot, Antoine, 69
Cairncross, John, 339
Calderón de la Barca, 289, 301, 303
Calverley, Edwin E., 54
Campbell, Joseph, 143
Campbell, Lily B., 241, 346
Campbell, Oscar J., 238, 239, 346
Campion, Charles-Michel xiv
Camus, Albert, 11

Canby, Henry Seidel, 335
Capote, Truman, 93
Capua, A. G. de, 72, 76
Carapetyan, Armen, 75
Cargill, Oscar, 77, 79
Carlyle, Thomas, 284, 293, 300, 354
Carr, C. T., 72, 80
Carré, Jean-Marie, 2, 3, 4, 27, 34, 40, 329, 351
Cary, Edmond, 117, 338
Casanova, 137
Cathea, Willa, 12
Caylus, 66
Cazamian, Louis, 125, 143, 283
Céline, Louis-Ferdinand, 339
Cellini, Benvenuto, 114, 340
Cervantes, 115, 116, 162, 289, 303, 341
Chamisso, Adalbert von, 303
Champigny, Robert, 81
Chapman, George, 102
Chase, Stuart, 335
Chasles, Philarète, 334
Chateaubriand, François René de, 3, 67, 68, 194, 289, 292, 300, 303, 351
Chaucer, Geoffrey, 145, 170, 241
Chekhov, Anton, 318
Chew, Samuel C., 351
Chrapcenko, 44
Ciardi, John, 110, 116
Cicero, 238, 248
Cimabue, Giovanni, 145
Cioranescu, Alejandro, 28
Čiževsky, Dmitry, 335, 336
Clark, Kenneth, 74
Claudel, Paul, 255, 256, 319
Cohen, J. M., 116, 341
Cohn, Dorrit, 350
Coleridge, Samuel Taylor, 122, 123, 151, 293, 299, 300, 301
Colie, Rosalie, 29
Collingwood, R. G., ix, 145, 149, 160, 161, 342
Constant de Rebecque, Benjamin, 67, 302
Cooper, James Fenimore, 104
Corneille, Pierre, 8
Corrigan, Robert W., 118
Courbet, Gustave, 194
Cousin, Victor, 292, 302
Craig, Mary A., 339
Crane, Ronald S., 354
Crawford, Marion Ayton, 115
Creanga, Ioan, 12
Crews, Frederick C., 29, 125, 144
Croce, A., 48
Croce, Benedetto, 40, 250, 262, 277, 279, 280, 281, 307, 322, 330, 347, 351, 352, 353, 354
Cromwell, Oliver, 153
Curtius, Ernst Robert, 14, 32, 41

D'Agoult, Madame, 334
Danby, John F., 236, 237, 346
Dandin, 317
Dante Alighieri, 32, 46, 109, 110, 113, 171, 254, 258, 289, 301, 303, 339, 340, 348
Darío, Rubén, 9
Daudet, Léon, 353
David, Jacques Louis, 194
De Armond, Anna, 79
De Deugd, Cornelis, 40
Dédéyan, Charles, 329
Deffand, Madame du, 69
Delacroix, Eugène, 279, 292
Delaroche, 194
Delavigne, Jean F. C., 300, 303
Del Noce, A., 81
Demetz, Peter, 44, 79, 348
Dennes, William R., 77
Denny, William, Sir, 65
De Quincey, Thomas, 300
Derby, J. Raymond, 311
Descartes, René, 178
Deschamps, Émile, 303
Deschanel, Émile, 334
Desprès, 351
Deutschbein, 281
Dickens, Charles, 3, 91, 104, 137
Diderot, Denis, 3, 11, 66, 302
Dietrich, Margarete, 333
Dillon, George, 109
Dima, Alexandru, 31
Dimaras, 46
Dinesen, Isak, 12
Dionysius Thrax, 261
Döblin, Alfred, 33, 129
Dolanski, 46
Donne, John, 11, 342

Dostoevsky, Feodor, 87, 93, 104, 123, 124, 131, 137, 339
Douglas, Wallace W., 77
Droste-Hülshoff, Annette, 3
Dryden, John, 102, 119, 253
Dubois, 351
Duffy, Charles, 333
Du Fresnoy, 82
Dujardin, Edouard, 127
Duleil, 334
Dumas, Alexandre (*fils*), 11
Dumas, Alexandre (*père*), 11, 289, 300, 303
Dumesnil, René, 77, 79
Durisin, 44, 46
Dyserinck, Hugo, 39

Eckhoff, 351
Eddy, Mary Baker, 137
Edel, Leon, 29, 125, 143, 144, 348
Ehrenpreis, Irwin, 347
Eichendorff, Joseph von, 303
Eichner, Hans, 291
Eisenstein, Sergei, 318
Ejxenbaum, Boris, 336
Eliot, George, xv, 251
Eliot, T. S., 9, 140, 171, 172, 180, 187, 190, 191, 200, 254, 344, 345, 349
Elliott, R. C., 80
Ellis-Fermer, Una, 116
Elton, O., 73, 80
Elton, William, 71
Eminescu, 12
Empedocles, 151, 258, 259
Empson, William, 131, 344
Epictetus, 238
Eppelsheimer, Hanns W., 52
Erikson, Erik, 124, 136
Ermatinger, Emil, 26
Ernst, Fritz, 36, 37, 333
Escarpit, Robert, 330
Espronceda, José de, 12, 295, 300, 352
Estève, Edmond, 96, 334, 337
Etiemble, René, 4, 10, 36, 41, 256, 330, 349
Euripides, 111, 218, 220, 223, 224, 226, 228, 231, 260, 340, 349
Faguet, Émile, 353
Fairchild, Hoxie, 280, 283, 284, 305, 354
Farinelli, Arturo, 14, 304, 305, 351, 353, 354
Faulkner, William, 11, 128, 129, 322, 341
Feaver, Douglas, 349
Fergusson, Francis, 183, 219, 344, 345
Feuchtwanger, Lion, 273, 350
Fichte, T. G., 300
Fielding, Henry, 85, 303
Fisher, John H., 50
Fitts, Dudley, 111
FitzGerald, Edward, 102, 103, 338
Fitzgerald, F. Scott, 12
Fitzgerald, Robert, 111, 118
Flaubert, Gustave, 43, 67, 188, 194, 269
Fleischmann, Wolfgang B., 43, 55, 56
Fogle, Richard H., 307
Folejewski, Z., 74
Folkierski, Wladyslaw, 82, 351
Fontane, Theodor, 12, 43
Fontenelle, Bernard le Bovier de, 62
Foscolo, Ugo, 301
Foster, Edward E., 333
Fowler, Henry W., 333
Fraiberg, Louis, 143
France, Anatole, 3
Frank, Joseph, 187, 188, 189, 344
Frankl, P., 74
Frappier, Jean, 330
Frazer, James, Sir, 134
Freedman, Ralph, 348
Frenz, Horst, 55, 338
Frenzel, Elisabeth, 55
Freud, Sigmund, ix, 7, 93, 122, 123, 124, 125, 130, 132, 136, 137, 140, 141, 143
Fricke, G., 349
Friederich, Werner P., 5, 14, 15, 25, 34, 36, 46, 49, 51, 259, 280, 306, 311, 333, 336, 353, 354
Friedman, Melvin, 350
Frisch, Max, xv
Fröding, 12
Frohock, W. M., 350

Fromm, Erich, 124, 140
Frye, Northrop, 29, 125, 133, 144, 274, 347
Fulda, Ludwig, 342
Furetière, Antoine, 62

Galsworthy, John, 11
Gandhi, Mahatma, 136
Ganz, Arthur, 333
García Lorca, 183
Gardner, Helen, 190, 191, 192, 345
Garnett, Constance, 339
Gauguin, Paul, 194
Gautier, Théophile, 303, 334
Gaynor, Frank, 54, 333
Gérard, 194
Gérard, Abbé, 67
Gershman, H. S., 74, 81
Gessner, Salomon, 11
Gibian, George, 56
Gicovate, Bernardo, 40
Gide, André, 3, 120, 141, 342
Gifford, Henry, 30
Gillet, J., 36
Gillies, Alexander, 33
Gilson, Étienne, 342
Gioberti, 351
Giono, Jean, 3
Girodet-Tricson, 194
Glycon, 163
Gobbers, W., 35
Goddard, Harold C., 237, 346
Godwin, William, 151
Goethe, Johann Wolfgang von, 8, 10, 15, 68, 93, 99, 100, 101, 113, 122, 127, 158, 249, 258, 262, 263, 265, 266, 282, 289, 300, 302, 303, 331, 338, 340, 349, 351
Gogh, Vincent van, 183, 194
Gogol, Nikolai, 91, 130
Gotthelf, Jeremias, 251
Grant, Douglas, 78
Grant, Michael, 116
Graves, Robert, 125, 338
Gray, Thomas, 271, 289, 301, 303
Greenacre, Phyllis, 124, 136
Greenwood, E. B., 79, 80
Grene, David, 345
Grente, Georges, Cardinal, 333
Grierson, Herbert J. C., 277, 308
Grillparzer, Franz, 303
Grimm, Jakob and Wilhelm, 216, 289, 300
Grudin, Louis, 335
Guérard, Albert, 27, 37, 281, 283, 353
Guillén, Caludio, 39, 40, 56, 79, 350
Gummere, Francis B., 217
Gundolf, Friedrich, 281, 283, 337
Gurewitch, Marton L., 299
Guyard, Marius-François, 2, 3, 4, 27, 28, 29, 34, 251, 254, 269, 329

Hagstrum, Jean H., 56, 82
Haight, Elizabeth H., 82
Hamm, V. M., 75
Hamsun, Knut, 3, 104
Hankiss, J., 32, 37, 38, 283
Hansen, Kurt H., 341
Hardison, O. B., Jr., 260, 349
Hardy, Thomas, 3
Hartmann, Eduard von, 351
Hartmann, Nicolai, 351
Hassan, Ihab H., 76, 336
Hatzfeld, Helmut, 43, 72, 192, 193, 194, 195, 196, 345, 351
Hauff, Wilhelm, 303
Hauptmann, Gerhart, xiii, 3, 331
Hauser, Arnold, 76
Havens, George R., 77, 305
Havens, Raymond D., 82
Hawthorne, Nathaniel, 3, 7, 12, 123
Haydn, Franz Joseph, 351
Haydn, Hiram, 237, 346
Hayward, John, 344
Hazard, Paul, 4, 15, 16, 329
Hazlitt, William, 299, 301
Hearn, Lafcadio, xiv, 318
Hebbel, Friedrich, 12
Hedge, 281
Hegel, G. W. F., 93, 151, 153, 160
Heidegger, Martin, 118
Heilman, Robert B., 235, 237, 346
Heine, Heinrich, 3, 104, 303
Heinse, Johann J. W., 303
Helmont, J. B. van, 63
Hempel, W., 78, 82

Henley, William E., 148
Herbert, George, 177
Herder, Johann Gottfried, 3, 12, 33, 57, 262, 289, 300, 302, 303, 331
Herford, C. H., 283
Herl, B. C., 345
Hermand, Jost, 56
Hesse, Hermann, 11, 107
Hewlett, Maurice, 110
Heyl, Bernard C., 72, 80
Hibbard, Addison, 334
Highet, Gilbert, 80, 108
Hill, D. M., 72
Hitler, Adolf, 136
Hobbes, Thomas, 74, 236, 237
Hoffmann, E. T. A., 289, 302
Hoffmann, Frederick J., 143
Hofmannsthal, Hugo von, 9, 12
Holbrook, William C., 74
Hölderlin, Friedrich, 11, 137
Holinshed, Raphael, 85, 90
Holland, Norman, 144
Höllerer, Walter, 32, 33, 36
Holman, C. H., 334
Homer, 112, 113, 118, 138, 187, 208, 213, 215, 217, 220, 221, 257, 259, 340
Hooker, Edward N., 82
Hooker, Richard, 236, 237
Hopkins, Gerard Manley, 147
Horace, 82, 198, 248, 253, 261, 267, 270, 274
Horney, Karen, 140
Howarth, Howard, 344, 345
Howe, Irving, 350
Howells, William Dean, 339
Hsia, C. T., 320, 324
Huet, 62
Hugo, A., 303
Hugo, Victor, 279, 281, 287, 289, 294, 300, 302, 303
Humphrey, Robert, 350
Humphries, Rolfe, 110, 112
Hungerland, H., 198, 199, 345
Hunt, Leigh, 301
Huse, H. R., 54, 113
Hussey, Christopher, 79
Huxley, Aldous, 343

Iancu, Victor, 31
Ibsen, Henrik, 104, 116, 123, 341
Ibycus, 261
Immerwahr, 281
Ingalls, Daniel H. H., 320, 325
Isherwood, Christopher, 112
Isidore of Seville, 253
Italiaander, Rolf, 341

Jacobsen, Jens Peter, 12, 104
James, Henry, xiii, 7, 123, 127, 132, 137, 138, 269
James, William, 126
Jasinski, 281
Jaspers, Karl, 343
Jean Paul, 123, 289, 300, 302, 303
Jefferson, Thomas, 150
Jensen, Johannes V., 12
Jensen, Wilhelm, 123
Jerome, Saint, 108
Jeune, Simon, 4, 30, 45, 251, 329, 330
Johnson, Samuel, 63, 77
Jolles, André, 264, 265, 349
Jones, Ernest, 124, 131, 137, 143
Jones, Iva G., 78
Jost, François, 42, 45, 78, 348
Jowett, B., 350
Joyaux, George S., 41
Joyce, James, 128, 129, 187, 188, 268, 269
Jung, Carl G., ix, 7, 47, 124, 132, 133, 143
Jurji, Edward J., 54
Juvenal, 253

Kafka, Franz, 9, 130
Kafū, Nagai, 319
Kailaspathy, K., 325
Kālidāsa, 316, 317
Kallich, Martin, 74, 76, 83, 335
Kamban, 316
Kang, Younghill, 54
Kant, Immanuel, 289, 300, 351
Kaplan, Abraham, 335
Karamzin, 90, 91
Kaufman, Paul, 74, 308, 354
Kawabata, 319
Kayser, Wolfgang, xv, 75, 264, 265, 266, 271, 272
Keats, John, 177, 301

Keller, Gottfried, 9, 12
Ker, William P., 281
Kerman, Joseph, 118
Kernan, Alvin, 255
Khayyam, Omar, 103, 338
Kiell, Norman, 144
Kierkegaard, Søren, 11
Killigrew, 65
Kimball, Sidney F., 80
Kindermann, Heinz, 333
Kitching, Laurence, xi
Kitto, H. D. F., 224, 346
Klee, Paul, 184, 185
Kleist, Heinrich von, 137
Klemperer, Viktor, 351
Kliger, Samuel, 75
Klopstock, Friedrich Gottlieb, 302
Kluckhohn, Paul, 277
Knight, Douglas, 337
Knight, G. Wilson, 346
Knox, Bernard, 233, 346
Kohlschmidt, Werner, 48
Konrad, N. I., 337
Korff, Hermann August, 290
Korzybski, Alfred, 138
Kotzebue, August von, 11
Kozlov, Ivan I., 94
Krapp, Robert M., 81, 83
Krauss, Werner, 44, 45
Kretzer, Max, 11
Kridl, Manfred, 354
Kris, Ernst, 124, 135, 143
Krishnamurthi, 320
Kruse, Margot, 43
Krutch, Joseph Wood, 125
Kumar, Shiv, 350
Kunisch, H., 76

La Drière, Craig, 38, 332
Laffont, Robert Raoul, 53
Lagerlöf, Selma, 104
Laird, Charlton, 28, 54
Lamartine, Alphonse de, 69, 279, 289, 300, 303
Lamb, Charles, 135
Landor, Walter S., 287, 301
Lancaster, H. C., 81
Langland, William, 170
Lanson, 281
Lao-Tsu, 153
Larra, Mariano José de, 12, 295, 300, 352
Lasserre, 353
Lattimore, R., 345
Lau, Joseph, 320
Laurentius, 65
Lautréamont, 278
Lawrence, T. E., 112, 113, 340
Leach, Maria, 53
Leary, Lewis, 28, 307
Leblanc, Abbé, 66
Lee, A. van der, 36
Lee, H. D. P., 114
Lee, H. N., 335
Lee, Shao Chang, 54
Legouis, Émile, 283
Leibniz, Gottfried Wilhelm von, 351
Leonardo da Vinci, 124
Leopardi, Giacomo, 289, 297, 300, 303
Lermontov, Mikhail, 91, 94, 336, 337
Lesser, Simon O., 144
Lessing, Gotthold Ephraim, ix, 185, 186, 187, 200, 344
Letourneur, 334
Levaillant, Maurice, 310
Levi, Albert W., 343
Levin, Harry, 33, 43, 45, 56, 79, 335
Lévy-Bruhl, Lucien, 169
Lewis, C. Day, 110
Lewis, Matthew, 59
Lewis, Sinclair, 43, 343
Lewisohn, Ludwig, 125
Liberman, M. M., 333
Lillo, George, 11
Lincoln, Abraham, 195
Linden, Walther, 77
Liu, James J. Y., 320, 324
Locke, John, 74
Lockhart, J. G., 301
Long, Richard A., 78
Longueil, Alfred E., 75
Lope de Vega, 303
Lord, Albert, 213, 321
Lorrain, Claude, 193
Loti, Pierre, 319
Lotz, J., 324
Louis XV, 80

Lourié, Arthur, 71
Lovejoy, A. O., ix, 34, 77, 152, 278, 279, 283, 284, 308, 309, 310, 342, 351, 352, 353, 354
Lowenthal, Leo, 29
Lucas, Frank, 277, 281, 282, 309, 353
Lucretius, 151, 155, 164, 258
Lukács, Georg, 273, 350
Luther, Martin, 108, 118, 136
Lydgate, John, 241

MacAndrew, Andrew R., 339
Macaulay, Thomas, 161, 162
McCutchion, David, 42
Mackail, J. W., 344
Mackenzie, A. S., 217
McKenzie, Kenneth, 305
McRae, Robert, 75
Maeterlinck, Maurice, 9
Magarshack, David, 339
Magnus, Laurie, 333
Mahomet, 153
Malinowski, Bronislaw, 206, 217
Mallarmé, Stéphane, 93
Malone, David H., 14, 15, 34, 36, 45, 46, 306, 336, 353
Man, Paul de, 42
Mann, Heinrich, xv
Mann, Thomas, 3, 9, 11, 130
Manzoni, Alessandro, 289, 300, 301, 303, 353
Marcazzan, Mario, 277, 306, 351
March, Harold M., 304
Marcus Aurelius, 148, 238
Marcuse, Herbert, 143
Maritain, Jacques, 71
Markiewicz, 46
Marmor, Judd, 144
Martegiani, Gina, 353
Martínez de la Rosa, Francisco, 300, 301
Marx, Karl, 93
Mason, Eudo C., 307
Matlaw, Ralph E., 41
Matthews, Jackson, 339
Matthiessen, F. O., 338
Mattingly, Alethea Smith, 77
Maupassant, Guy de, 12
Maurras, Charles, 353
Maury y Benítez, Juan María, 303
Mautner, Franz H., 348
Mayo, Robert S., 57
Meeüs, Xavier de, 277
Melville, Herman, 7, 11
Mencken, H. L., 9
Mercier, 351
Meredith, George, 151, 179
Mérimée, Prosper, 303
Merker, Paul, 333
Merlant, Joachim, 334
Mesmer, Franz, 137
Meyer, Conrad Ferdinand, 9
Meyer, Herman, 350
Michéa, R., 80
Michelet, Jules, 279, 292, 302, 303
Mickiewicz, Adam, 335
Milch, Werner, 281, 351
Millay, Edna St. Vincent, 109, 112
Miller, Betty, 137
Miller, F. J., 346
Miller, J. Hillis, 29
Milton, John, 148, 174, 289, 301, 303, 342
Miner, Earl, 320, 324, 325
Mischel, Theodore, 82
Mitchell, H., 350
Mitchell, Margaret, 11
Mitchell, S., 350
Mittner, Ladislao, 73, 277, 351
Modern, R. E., 73
Mohr, Wolfgang, 48, 349
Molière, 66
Momigliano, Attilio, 48
Monglond, André, 69, 334
Monk, S. H., 81
Montaigne, Michel de, 151, 159, 175, 176
Monteggia, 301
Monti, 301
Moore, Thomas, 87, 303
Morães, Wenceslau de, 319
Moravia, Alberto, 11
Moreau, Pierre, 72, 334, 351
Morgan, Bayard Quincy, 54, 113, 118, 340
Morize, André, 336
Morrison, John, 54
Mosbacher, Eric, 339
Moses, 208
Motte-Fouqué, Friedrich de la, 11
Motteux, Peter, 106

Mounin, Georges, 341
Moyse, Yvonne, 343
Mozart, Wolfgang Amadeus, 351
Muir, Kenneth, 237, 346
Munro, Thomas, 77
Munteano, Basil, 34, 35, 38, 43, 329, 330
Murasaki, Lady, 314
Muschg, W., 143
Musset, Alfred de, 3, 67, 279, 294, 296, 302, 303, 334

Nabokov, Vladimir, 341
Nadler, 351
Nelson, Lord, 161
Nerval, Gérard de, 11, 279, 302
Nethercot, Arthur H., 77
Neubert, Fritz, 329
Neumann, Erich, 144
Neupokoeva, I. G., 41, 44, 46
Newton, Isaac, Sir, 78
Nichols, Madaline W., 54
Nichols, Stephen G., 29, 30, 45, 56
Nicolson, Marjorie H., 342, 343
Nietzsche, Friedrich, 33, 137, 167, 180
Nitchie, Elizabeth, 280, 291, 305, 351, 354
Nodier, Charles, 302
Norton, Charles Eliot, 102
Norton, Daniel S., 333
Norton, W. W., 306
Novalis, 3, 184, 185, 262, 287, 300, 302
Novicov, Mihai, 31
Nurmi, Martin K., 311

Obstfelder, Sigbjørn, 12
O'Casey, Sean, 9
Ochoa, Eugenio de, 303
Ogden, C. K., 138
Oksman, J. G., 337
O'Neill, Eugene, xiii, 46, 107, 129, 130, 339
Oppel, Horst, 307
Orsini, G. N. G., 48, 298, 347, 352
Ortega y Gasset, José, 118
Ossian, 289, 301, 303
Otzoupe, N., 337
Ovid, 208, 271
Owen, Wilfrid, 162
Oxenhandler, Neal, 56

Parmenides, 164
Parry, 321
Pascal, Blaise, 59, 164
Pascal, Roy, 348
Passmore, J. A., 71
Pater, Walter, 182, 281
Paul, Saint, 71
Peckham, Morse, 275, 277, 278, 280, 283, 284, 310, 311, 351, 352, 354, 355
Pei, Mario A., 54, 333
Pellegrini, Carlo, 39, 48
Percy, Thomas, 289, 303
Pérez Galdós, 12
Pericles, 163
Perrault, Charles, 216
Persius, 253
Peter the Great, 89
Petersen, Julius, 26, 263, 281, 332, 351
Petöfi, Sándor, 12
Petriconi, Hellmuth, 43
Pettit, Henry J., 333
Peyre, Henri, 33, 39, 72, 277, 278, 279, 335, 351, 352, 354
Pfister, Oskar, 124
Picasso, Pablo, 351
Pichois, Claude, 2, 3, 4, 29, 251, 273, 329, 330
Pico, della Mirandola, 181
Picón, Gaëtan, 281, 307
Pindar, 257, 261
Pinero, Arthur Wing, Sir, 11
Plato, 93, 114, 151, 155, 157, 158, 161, 170, 269, 341, 343
Plekhanov, Georgi V., 35
Plon, Eugène, 114
Plotinus, 153
Plutarch, 151, 238
Poe, Edgar Allan, 10, 104, 130, 136
Poggioli, Renato, 27, 88, 336
Pope, Alexander, 59, 102, 342
Porta, Antonio, 28
Posin, J. A., 54
Posnett, H. M., 257
Posso, Gianni M., 77
Potter, G. R., 73
Poulet, Georges, 283

Pound, Ezra, 119, 162, 187, 325
Prabhavananda, Swami, 112
Prang, Helmut, 291
Pratt, Norman T., 346
Praz, Mario, 48, 143, 277, 278, 309, 354
Preminger, Alex, 324, 348
Prescott, Frederick C., 144
Prévost, Abbé, 69
Prezzolini, Giuseppe, 54
Priest, George Madison, 101
Priestley, F. E. L., 78
Proust, Marcel, 128, 138, 141, 187, 188, 322
Pushkin, Alexander, xiv, 89, 90, 91, 93, 94, 312, 336, 337
Putnam, Samuel, 105, 114, 338, 339, 341
Pythagoras, 153

Quinet, Edgar, 302, 303
Quintilian, 163, 248, 253

Rabelais, François, 59, 105, 106, 115, 338, 339
Racine, Jean, 8, 193, 339, 340
Radcliffe, Ann, 59
Radin, Paul, 54
Ramanujan, A. K., 320, 325
Randall, John H., 342
Rank, Otto, 124, 139, 143
Ransom, John Crowe, 73, 183, 344
Raphael, Alice, 101
Read, Herbert, Sir, 192, 345
Remak, Henry H. H., 39
Remarque, Erich Maria, 11
Reynaud, Louis, 353
Richards, I. A., 71, 131, 138, 139, 335, 344
Richardson, Dorothy M., 127, 128
Richardson, Samuel, 14, 15, 289, 301, 303
Richelet, Pierre, 62
Rieu, E. V., 112, 113, 116
Rilke, Rainer Maria, 9, 20, 271
Rimbaud, Arthur, 194, 278
Rivas, Duque de, 300
Robertson, John G., 308, 351, 353
Robinson, Henry Crabbe, 300
Roddier, Henri, 34, 35, 37, 47, 329, 330, 351
Rogers, Samuel, 301
Rolleston, Thomas W., xiii
Rosenberg, Ralph P., 50
Rosenthal, Raymond, 339
Rouse, W. H. D., 112, 113
Rousseau, A.-M., 2, 3, 4, 29, 251, 273, 330
Rousseau, Jean-Jacques, 14, 15, 59, 60, 61, 62, 63, 67, 77, 83, 122, 289, 290, 300, 302, 307, 334, 351, 353
Rousset, Jean, 72
Rüdiger, Horst, 40
Rudler, Gustave, 336
Rushton, Peters, 333
Ruttkowski, W. V., 57

Sachs, Hans, 124
Sack, F. L., 143
Sacks, Sheldon, 250, 347
Sadoveanu, Mihail, 12
Saikaku, Ibara, 322, 323
Sainte-Beuve, Charles Augustin, 67, 68, 303
Saint-Péravi, Guérineau de, 66
Saintsbury, George, 282
Sáinz de Robles, F. C., 56, 333
Salinger, H., 350
Samarin, R. M., 336
Sampson, George, 338
Samuel, R. H., 304, 353
Sand, George, 68, 69, 251, 303
Ŝan-Girej, A. P., 337
Sansone, 48
Santayana, George, xv
Santoli, Vittorio, 48
Sappho, 261
Sartre, Jean-Paul, 33, 167, 172, 181, 343
Sassoon, Siegfried, 162
Sastre, A., 79
Savill, Mervyn, 107
Savory, Theodore, 117, 118, 338
Sayers, Dorothy, 109, 110, 112
Scaliger, 167
Schelling, Friedrich W., 151, 262, 289, 300, 303
Schevill, Rudolph, 54
Schiller, Friedrich von, 93, 249, 267, 289, 300, 302, 349
Schinz, Albert, 78, 83

Schlegel, August Wilhelm, 98, 99, 100, 101, 103, 262, 282, 289, 300, 302, 303, 332
Schlegel, Friedrich, 123, 262, 283, 303
Schleiermacher, Friedrich, 283
Schmidt, Erich, 15
Schnitzler, Arthur, 129
Schultz, Franz, 351
Schwarz, Egon, 42
Scott, Arthur F., 333
Scott, Geoffrey, 281
Scott, Walter, Sir, 85, 93, 104, 251, 289, 290, 300, 301, 303
Scribe, Augustin Eugène, 11
Scrivano, R., 76
Seillière, 353
Selig, Karl-Ludwig, 348
Selle, C. M., 73
Sénancour, Étienne de, 67, 68, 302, 334
Seneca, x, xiv, 218, 228, 229, 230, 231, 232, 238, 240, 241, 242, 243, 244, 245, 246, 254, 346
Senhouse, Roger, 343
Shaftesbury, 3d Earl of, 175
Shakespeare, William, 33, 65, 85, 87, 90, 91, 93, 95, 98, 99, 100, 101, 131, 144, 145, 151, 162, 170, 171, 196, 218, 235, 236, 237, 238, 239, 240, 241, 242, 244, 245, 246, 289, 301, 303, 334, 337, 343, 346
Shattuck, Roger, 117, 118
Shaw, George Bernard, 9, 154
Shelley, Percy Bysshe, 148, 151, 154, 156, 157, 158, 159, 167, 293, 295, 299, 300, 301
Shenstone, William, 58
Shipley, Joseph T., 13, 27, 52, 304, 333
Shlonsky, T., 78
Siciliano, Italo, 39, 277, 351
Silberschlag, Eisig, 54
Simón Díaz, 48
Simonides, 261
Singer, H., 347
Sismondi, 261, 303
Smissen, W. H. van der, 101, 338
Smith, F. Kinchen, 111
Smith, Horatio, 52
Smith, John E., 351
Smith, Logan Pearsall, 70, 73, 74, 78, 351
Smollett, Tobias, 303
Snow, C. P., 343
Soame, William, Sir, 253
Socrates, 47, 159, 170, 269
Sommerhalder, H., 76
Sophocles, 110, 169, 232, 233, 234, 235, 236, 240, 246, 340
Sorbelli, 48
Sötér, Istvan, 40, 42, 76
Southey, Robert, 299, 301
Spalek, John M., 45
Spemann, Adolf, 49
Spender, Stephen, 184
Spengler, Oswald, 153
Spielhagen, Friedrich, 11
Spingarn, Joel, 347
Spinoza, Baruch, 177
Spitzer, Leo, 81
Staël, Madame de, 33, 281, 289, 292, 294, 300, 302, 303
Staiger, Emil, 263, 264, 266
Stallings, Laurence, 106, 338
Stallknecht, N. P., 342
Stammler, Wolfgang, 48, 333
Steel, William A., 344
Steinberg, S. H., 54, 304
Steiner, George, 340
Steiner, Pauline, 338
Stekel, Wilhelm, 124, 143
Stendhal, 3, 137, 282, 302, 303
Sterne, Laurence, 68, 301, 303
Stesichorus, 261
Stevens, Wallace, xv
Stifter, Adalbert, 9
Stone, E., 77
Störig, Hans Joachim, 117
Strich, Fritz, 26, 32, 196, 290, 305
Strindberg, August, 104, 123, 130, 258
Struve, Gleb, 34, 39
Sudermann, Hermann, 11, 107, 339
Sullivan, Harry Stack, 140
Sullivan, J. W. N., 344, 345
Supek, O., 42
Suphan, B., 349
Suttie, I. D., 143
Svevo, Italo, 129

Swanwick, Anna, 100, 101
Swift, Jonathan, 136, 342
Sypher, Wylie, 80, 196, 197
Szili, Joseph, 56

Tacitus, 116, 341
Tagore, Rabindranath, 319
Tancock, L. W., 116
Tarr, F. Courtney, 305, 352
Tasso, Torquato, 167
Taylor, Bayard, 100, 101, 102, 103
Teesing, H. P. H. 32, 41, 351
Tennyson, Alfred, Lord, 179
Terhune, Alfred M., 338
Texte, Joseph, 4
Thackeray, William Makepeace, 12
Thompson, Stith, 217, 324
Thorlby, Anthony, 31, 56
Thorpe, James, 29, 144
Thrall, William F., 334
Thucydides, 114, 341
Tieck, Dorothea, 98, 99, 100
Tieck, Ludwig, 98, 99, 100, 300, 303
Tigerstedt, E. N., 348
Titian, 145
Tolstoy, Leo, 87, 104, 131, 137, 339
Toynbee, Arnold, 34
Toynbee, Paget, 348
Trakl, Georg, 12
Traversi, D. A., 170, 171, 343
Trilling, Lionel, 125, 135, 143
Triomphe, Robert, 39
Trousson, Raymond, 41, 42
Turbeville, F. S., 73, 74, 82
Turgenev, Ivan, 12, 87, 104
Tyler, E. B., 217
Tymms, 351

Ueda, Makoto, 320, 325
Unamuno, Miguel de, 352
Undset, Sigrid, 104
Urban, Wilbur M., 335
Urquhart, Thomas, Sir, 105, 106

Valéry, Paul, 93, 274, 351
Van Tieghem, Paul, 2, 4, 14, 15, 16, 27, 29, 30, 35, 38, 46, 49, 73, 250, 251, 275, 277, 280, 304, 305, 329, 330, 332, 336, 351, 354, 355
Vellacott, Philip, 111
Verga, Giovanni, 339
Vergil, 102, 110, 113, 185, 339, 340
Verhaeren, Émile, 9, 194
Veselovsky, Alexander, 35, 256
Vico, Giambattista, 128, 289, 303
Vidyākara, 325
Vigny, Alfred de, 67, 91, 279, 302, 303, 337
Viscardi, Antonio, 48
Vivas, Eliseo, 250, 347
Voigt, E.-M., 266
Voisine, Jacques, 28, 329
Voltaire, 64, 66, 115, 319, 334, 341
Vowles, Richard B., 30, 45, 56
Vries, Jan de, 325

Wagner, Richard, 127
Waiblinger, Wilhelm, 303
Wais, Kurt, 32, 36, 37, 41, 333, 351
Walpole, Horace, 272
Walzel, Oskar, 196, 198
Wang, C. H., 325
Warner, Rex, 114
Warren, Austin, 27, 198, 250, 270, 271, 273, 309, 342, 345
Warren, Robert Penn, 344
Warton, Joseph, 59
Warton, Thomas, 59
Wasserman, Earl R., 73
Watt, Ian, 322
Weber, Harry, 348
Wees, W. C., 83
Wehrli, Max, 28
Weisinger, Herbert, 41, 42
Weisman, Philip, 144
Weisstein, Ulrich, 30, 72, 74, 78, 82, 83
Wellek, René, 9, 21, 23, 27, 29, 30, 34, 38, 40, 41, 42, 43, 47, 56, 71, 73, 79, 80, 198, 250, 270, 271, 273, 278, 279, 280, 284, 288, 290, 306, 309, 310, 342, 345, 347, 353, 354, 355
Wendell, Barrett, 74
Werner, Zacharias, 11, 303
Wharton, Edith, 107
Whitehead, Alfred North, 93, 151

8-3-72
UNIV. PRESS
8.95

Whitman, Walt, xiii, 194, 195
Wiese, Benno von, 347
Will, Frederic, 39
Williams, Tennessee, 9
Wilpert, Gero von, 55
Wilson, Edmund, 125, 143
Wimsatt, W. K., 47, 351, 354
Wölfflin, Heinrich, 195, 196
Wood, Theodore E. B., 81
Woolf, Leonard, xiii
Woolf, Virginia, xiii, 128, 189
Wordsworth, William, xv, 151, 153, 155, 156, 158, 159, 160, 164, 167, 174, 175, 295, 299, 300, 303, 351
Wrenn, Charles L., 29

Xvostova, E. K., 337

Yasser, Joseph, 344
Yeats, William Butler, 256, 318, 325
Yelland, Hedley L., 334
Yohannan, John D., 338
Young, Edward, 59, 67, 68, 289, 301, 303

Zeami, 325
Zhirmunsky (Žirmunskij), Viktor, 35, 44, 46, 90, 336, 337
Zhukovsky, Vasily, 94
Ziegengeist, Gerhard, 41, 44
Ziolkowski, Theodore, 56
Zola, Émile, 104, 341, 353
Zuckmayer, Carl, 106, 108, 338
Zweig, Stefan, 137, 138